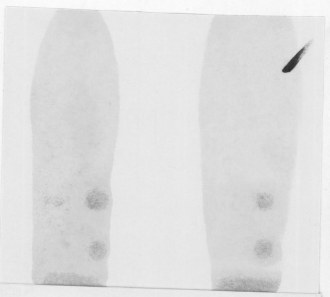

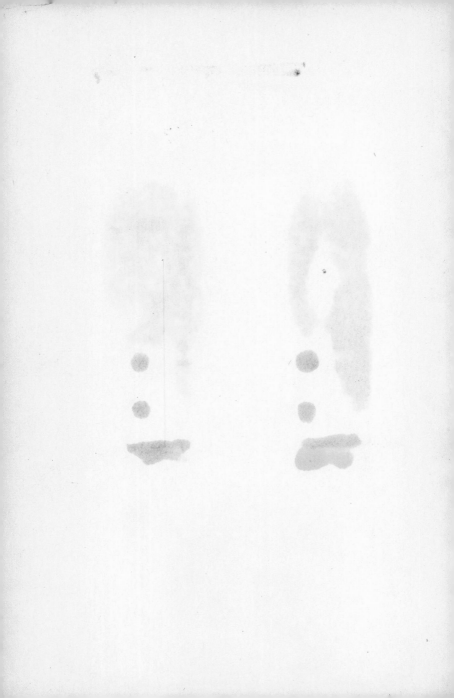

Wild Flowers
of the Pacific Coast

In which is described 332 flowers and shrubs
of Washington, Oregon, Idaho, Central and
Northern California and Alaska
182 full-page illustrations

By Leslie L. Haskin

Photographs by Leslie L. and Lilian G. Haskin

37112

BINFORDS & MORT, PUBLISHERS

PORTLAND, OREGON

PRINTED IN THE UNITED STATES OF AMERICA
BY METROPOLITAN PRESS, PORTLAND, OREGON

CONTENTS

CONTENTS—Continued

INTRODUCTION

THE HUMID COAST REGION of the North Pacific constitutes a domain that in its botanical characteristics is a distinct unit. Sheltered by the Cascade Range from the dry cold of the interior, and open to the warm, moisture ladened winds of the Pacific, a peculiar condition of climate and humidity is created that is especially favorable to plant growth. On the east the line of demarcation is clear and sharp at the summit of the Cascades. On the south it grades less sharply into the typical California flora, while on the north it extends its sway far beyond accustomed latitudes almost to the line of arctic frosts. Of this region the present book treats; a land of mild beauty, and overawing grandeur; a land of quiet, pastoral peace, and of wild, untouched wilderness; a land of high, icy mountains, and of gently smiling valleys; a land of clear, sparkling sunshine, and of soft, trailing mists.

To be the first to write in popular form of the flora of this region, has not been an easy task. In the older section of the country many volumes of this sort have been written treating of the flowers. Their character has been brought out by various writers—has been personified as it were, and visualized to the common mind. The history that has shaped itself about them is known, and their folk-tales and traditions have been published again and again. Here, on the contrary, only books of a technical character, or such as were intended for class-room use, have thus far been published, making it difficult for the layman to name the flowers. Many of them also, have no popular names, and only by a constant study of the plants at first hand, and by delving deep into original sources has it been possible to paint a word characterization of the plant that is true, and which may be plainly read. Such of their history as exists—and there is much and of an intensely interesting character—must be searched for, tirelessly, in old manuscripts, in hidden nooks and corners, and from the lips of surviving pioneers; a search covering a great mass of irrelevant matter from which must be gleaned the occasional grain of floral history. Many of our most interesting plants have, indeed, no Anglo-American history, for our flowers have not yet fully woven themselves into the lives of the people. We must look to an older nation for their true story, and for folk-tales and traditions we must trace out those vague stories that, even yet, though fast passing, are to be found, here and there in the lodges of the Indians. Thus I have given large space to Indian plant uses, and Indian myths.

In recent years the publishing of books in which the flowers are arranged according to their color has been very popular. I have not followed this pattern, because though it is an easy method for the beginner, it leads nowhere, while the grouping of flowers according to their natural relationship lead to a broader understanding of plant families; a most important aid to the student, and one that in the end gives a sure foundation in knowledge.

For the same reason I have not shunned to use some technical terms in my descriptions. A book like this should be a beginning, not an end in itself, and a few unknown terms to stimulate the mind to deeper thought are an advantage rather than otherwise. The meaning of all botanical terms used is given at the end of the book.

Only native flowers have been described. So many volumes already exist which describe the introduced species that it has seemed needless to increase the bulk of this volume by including them here. Other flowers too rare, or of too local distribution to be of general interest, also those of weedy, uninteresting character have been eliminated for the same reason.

I am quite aware that some, even among my well-wishers, will find fault with my choice of nomenclature. My only answer is that in most cases I have humbly followed the lead of the late Charles V. Piper. I have, therefore, no apology to make, since few who would criticise can hope to take precedence over that eminent scientist.

Without the consistent, inspiring help of my wife, Lilian G. Haskin, this book would never have been completed. If I, by courtesy, may be called a botanist, she is that better thing, a flower lover. Not only is she responsible for many of the best pictures, but she has patiently carried heavy floral loads for me up many a steep trail— never down, she insists—her husband being the only person ingenious enough to leave camp in the morning and return in the evening, having gone up hill the whole day, both coming and going! She has, moreover, helped my investigations by cooking for me many a strange and dubious food from the wild, and has also insisted on sharing these dishes with me, even though she suspected many of them of being actually poisonous.

Acknowledgement and thanks are due to the following persons for aid given me, especially in the identification of plant material: Dr. Helen M. Gilkey of the Oregon State College; Professors Albert R. Sweetser, and Louis F. Henderson, of the University of Oregon; Professor Leroy Abrams of Stanford University; and Mr. Paul C. Standley of the Smithsonian Institution, Washington, D. C.

To list all of the published sources from which facts have been gleaned for this work would be impossible, but I have been especially aided by Messrs. Piper and Betttie's *Flora of the Northwest Coast.* With few exceptions the classification used has followed that book. I am also greatly indebted to C. V. Piper's *Flora of the State of Washington;* to Thomas Howell's *Flora of Northwestern America,* to Professor Abrams' *Illustrated Flora of the Pacific Coast,* so far as it has been issued; and to *A Catalogue of the Flora of Vancouver and Queen Charlotte Islands,* published by the Provincial Museum of Natural History, Victoria, B. C. For Indian lore I am much indebted to the published volumes of the Bureau of American Ethnology, dealing with our western tribes and their manner of life.

Brownsville, Oregon.

Wild Flowers of the Pacific Coast

WATER PLANTAIN FAMILY

WAPPATO. ARROWHEAD
Sagittaria latifolia Willd.

White. Tuber, oblong or oval; edible. Leaves, all basal; long petioled; arrow-shaped; the lobes varying from linear to very broad. Scape, angled; one to two feet tall. Flowers, white; in whorls of threes. Petals, three. Stamens and Pistils, occurring in different flowers, often on different plants. Habitat, the borders of streams and ponds. Blooming period, July and August.

This, the first flower of our book, is unalterably linked with first things in the history of the Columbia River Valley, and the old Northwest. Long before the white man visited this coast it was one of the most important plant foods of the natives, especially of the Chinooks of the Lower Columbia, and was an article of well organized commerce between them and the surrounding tribes. The name wappato is of Indian origin, and the plant is woven into their age-old stories as being an article of food in the mythical times "Before the salmon came to the Columbia." The edible part of the plant is the smooth, solid tuber growing in the soft mud at the bottom of the pond. It is not possible to secure these tubers by pulling the plant, as they are borne at the extremity of long, flabby, root-stocks, and are sure to break off and be lost if disturbed. To secure them the squaws entered the water, often nearly shoulder deep, and supporting themselves by clinging to small canoes, rooted them out with their toes. When the bulb was dislodged it immediately rose to the surface, and was then tossed into the canoe. Boiled, they are very good, and resemble Irish potatoes, though with a sweetish flavor suggesting chestnuts. A genuine Indian feast, such as I was recently privileged to enjoy, consisting of wappato and bear's-meat, is not to be despised. From the journals of Lewis and Clark it appears that their principal

WAPPATO   *Sagittaria latifolia*

[4]

diet during their winter in Oregon was elk beef, secured by their hunters, and wappato bulbs purchased from the Indians.

No plant fills a more decorative place in nature than the wappato, raising its arrow-shaped leaves and spikes of waxy-white, curious flowers above the water along the shores of quiet lakes and sluggish streams. The plant loves the shallows, preferring places where the water is from a few inches to several feet deep, but it will also grow in any situation where the soil is permanently muddy.

ARUM FAMILY

SKUNK CABBAGE
Lysichiton camtschatcense (L.) Schott.

Yellow. Rootstocks, large; fleshy; drastic. Leaves, all basal; oblong, very large; rank-scented when crushed. Flowers, green; small; numerous; crowded in a fleshy, club-shaped spadix, and enclosed in a showy yellow spathe. Habitat, swamps. Blooming period, February to May.

There is nothing more typical of this humid western coast in early spring than the big swamps of yellow skunk cabbage. The great spathes begin to appear in February, and from then until May the swales and swamps are bright with the magnificent blooms. Following the blossoms come the great tropical looking leaves in dense clusters, single blades often three or more feet long, and a foot broad. Here is real beauty. Forget the name; disabuse your mind of any connection with the mephitic animal and the plebeian vegetable, and see this swamp for what it really is—a veritable "field of the cloth of gold." Think of what the name Lysichiton means—a loosened mantle (chiton). Think of a cloak of golden weave thrown carelessly over the shoulders of a water-sprite, or of fairy boatmen in coats of gold who have gathered to honor the coming of spring with a water fete. Thus only may you see this glorious plant in its true person.

When the flowers are fresh their scent is very sweet, and although rather sickish, not excessively unpleasant. The older or wilting flowers, or the bruised or crushed stems, however, give some excuse for the common name. The roots are very hot and peppery, but bears and elk are fond of them and plow up whole swamps in their search for this food. Among the North Coast Indians, also, the roots were an

SKUNK CABBAGE
Lysichiton camtschatcense

important article of diet, particularly in early spring when famine was threatening, and this poor, despised plant has saved thousands from starvation. They cooked them in pits together with scrapings of the tender inner bark of hemlock, and when the pits were opened it was said: "It was so savory that the whole village was scented with it!" Cooking destroys much of the acrid, peppery flavor. I myself have tried this food and found it quite passable.

The Kathlamet Indians have an interesting myth concerning the skunk cabbage. In the ancient days, they say, there was no salmon. The Indians had nothing to eat save roots and leaves. Principally among these was the skunk cabbage. Finally the spring salmon came for the first time. As they passed up the river, a person stood upon the shore and shouted: "Here come our relatives whose bodies are full of eggs! If it had not been for me all the people would have starved."

"Who speaks to us?" asked the salmon.

"Your Uncle, Skunk Cabbage," was the reply.

Then the salmon went ashore to see him, and as a reward for having fed the people he was given an elk-skin blanket and a war-club, and was set in the rich, soft soil near the river. There he stands to this day, wrapped in his elk-skin blanket and holding aloft his war-club.

LILY FAMILY

OOKOW

Hookera pulchella Salisb.

Violet-purple. Bulb, deep seated. Leaves, linear; roundish; often drying before the flowers appear. Scape, upright; stiff; wiry; one to five feet tall. Inflorescence, a compact, head-like umbel. Flowers, nearly sessile; violet-purple; accompanied by purple bracts; perianth six-cleft for about half its length, the lobes spreading. Stamens, fertile, three; sterile, three; purple; deeply cleft, petal-like. Habitat, open fields. Blooming period, May and June.

The ookow belongs to an extremely interesting and beautiful group of flowers which, as a whole, have been given the appropriate name of cluster-lilies. The cluster lilies are exclusively plants of western North America, being found nowhere else in the world, but within their range, and especially on the Pacific Slope they are very

OOKOW

Hookera pulchella

abundant and are represented by many species. Throughout western
Oregon and Washington the ookow is perhaps the most plentiful of
all, and in favorable localities whole fields are made purple with its
blooms.

If our florists, who spend untold time and pains in lengthening the
stems of certain flowers, could but learn the secret of the ookow's
growth, their labours would be at an end. To the careless observer
this plant seems nothing but a naked, wiry scape, two, three, or, in
rich soil, even five feet tall, carrying at its summit a close, head-like
cluster of dark purple flowers. Before the blossoms appear the plant
has set out a few narrow, grass-like leaves, but these soon dry up,
and are so inconspicuous as to pass unnoticed. Another feature much
sought by florists, and which this plant, and in fact all species of
Hookera possess to a marked degree, is its long keeping qualities.
After being picked, the flowers, if placed in water, will remain fresh
for several weeks.

The plant's name is of Indian origin, and its starchy bulbs were
among the many known and consumed for food by the natives of the
Pacific Coast.

HARVEST CLUSTER-LILY. HARVEST BRODIAEA
Hookera coronaria Salisb.

Dark blue. Bulb, solid; coated. Scape, slender; five to twelve inches
tall. Leaves, linear; grass-like; nearly equalling the scape; drying
early. Inflorescence, an unequal umbel. Flowers, dark blue; erect on
rather long pedicels; funnel-form; six-cleft to about two-thirds their
length. Stamens, fertile stamens, three, alternating with three white,
sterile staminodia; borne on the throat of the corolla. Habitat, dry
fields and hillsides. Blooming period, June-July.

In late June and July when the hillsides are turning brown from
the drought, the harvest lilies begin to appear. This plant is a lover
of dry ground, and the scapes come up where the soil is cracked with
the heat, and baked almost to the consistency of brick. It does not
seem possible that any plant could exist, much less grow and blossom
in such a situation, yet in this dry soil the flowers thrive and retain
their fresh beauty for a long time. The secret of the plant's hardiness
is a deep-seated bulb, rich in nutriment; a secret long ago discovered
by the Indians, who found in these bulbs an attractive substitute for

HARVEST CLUSTER-LILY

bread. They are, indeed, very palatable, being tender and mealy when cooked, and, with the addition of butter, equal to the best potatoes. Only their small size hinders them from becoming extremely useful.

WHITE CLUSTER-LILY. WHITE BRODIAEA
Hookera hyacinthina (Lindl.) Kuntze

White. Root, a solid bulb. Leaves, few; all basal; linear. Scape, upright; slender. Flowers, in an umbel; perianth segments united; six-lobed; spreading; the tube shorter than the lobes. Stamens, six, on the throat of the perianth. Habitat, moist meadows. Blooming period, June to August.

With its graceful flowers, each petal of which is centrally marked with a greenish vein, the white cluster-lily is a pleasing variation from the usual blues and purples of the genus. Its favorite habitat is in moist meadows and fields, and its blossoming season varies from early June in the valley to as late as the middle of August in some of the high mountain meadows. The tall slender scapes appear, as in all *Hookeras,* after the grass-like leaves have withered, and in this species they are from one to two feet tall. The individual flowers are carried upright on short, slender pedicels, and each of the six widely spreading lobes of the perianth bear a short fertile stamen. The edible bulb of the white *Hookera* is probably the finest of all, but it is so deeply seated in the ground as to make the task of securing it an exceedingly toilsome one. Perhaps this is just as well, however, for to civilized man the beauty of the flower is worth far more than the food value of the bulb.

BICOLORED CLUSTER-LILY. BICOLORED BRODIAEA
Hookera bicolor (Suksdorf)

Blue. Root, a coated, solid corm. Leaves, grass-like; keeled. Scape, erect; stout; straight; ten inches to two feet tall. Inflorescence, an umbel. Flowers, erect, or finally nodding; tubular; six-cleft for about one-third their length; tube blue; lobes light blue or white, spreading. Stamens, six, in two rows; filaments of the inner row winged. Habitat, dry hillsides and plains. Blooming period, May and June.

Nothing can exceed the grace, and the soft delicate coloring of this,

WHITE CLUSTER-LILY　　　　　　　　　*Hookera hyacinthina*

[12]

our rarest and most beautiful cluster-lily. The drooping flowers have white or light blue lobes, and the tube—longer than the lobes—is of a darker shade, making a combination that is very pleasing to the eye.

This flower, formerly considered a resident of Eastern Washington only, finds a place in this book through the fortunate discovery of a small colony of the plants in the foot-hills of Linn County, and a similar one in Benton County, Oregon. The illustration, therefore, is from the first flowers of this species ever found outside the state of Washington.

To be walking along familiar paths and suddenly find a strange or unknown plant is one of the supreme delights of the botanist, and when that plant proves to be a rare visitor from distant regions, and moreover, of exceptional interest and beauty, it is indeed a red-letter day.

HOOKER'S ONION
Allium acuminatum Hook.

Rose-purple. Bulb, coated; outer coats marked with polygonal reticulations. Leaves, small; terete; onion-scented. Scape, terete; three to six inches tall. Inflorescence, an umbel. Flowers, perianth six-cleft to base; outer segments longest, and with spreading tips; inner segments shorter, and slightly toothed. Stamens, six. Habitat, dry gravelly soil. Blooming period, May and June.

Wandering one day across a gravelly prairie, I was delighted to find what I at first took to be a new cluster-lily of pleasing color, and considerable beauty. Hastily picking the blooms, and wishing to use both hands to dig some of the bulbs, I held the freshly picked stems in my mouth, and immediately became aware from the pungent taste that it was a species of wild onions that I had found. This garlic-like flavor, and a perianth without elongated tube, but with the divisions separated to the base, from two of the chief distinguishing marks between the cluster-lilies and the onions. The unpopular association of the name onion has excluded them from the pages of many popular flower books, a real misfortune, for in beauty and grace many of them rival the finest *Hookeras*.

The flowers of this species are extremely long lived, and may often be found among the dried summer grasses, looking bright and fresh, when the supporting scape has shriveled to a mere brittle straw, or

BICOLORED CLUSTER-LILY   *Hookera bicolor*

[14]

has even separated entirely from the root. The flowers are a bright rose-purple, sometimes varying to a clear soft pink.

The reticulations of the thin outer coating of the bulb of this species are the surest means of identification. Many wild onions have reticulated bulb coats, but in this one they are distinctly different from all others, being polygonal, or many-sided in form, looking under a microscope like the meshes of a fine silk veil.

NODDING ONION

Allium cernuum Roth.

White or pink. Roots, clustered; narrow; coated. Leaves, linear; grooved; onion-scented. Scape, slender; six to twenty inches tall. Inflorescence, a nodding umbel. Flowers, campanulate; six-cleft to the base; carried on slender pedicels. Stamens, six; longer than the perianth. Habitat, in dry soil, and on rocks.

This common wild onion grows from a long, narrow bulb whose outer coat is fibrous and not reticulated. The nodding flowers are white or pink, and the stamens are exserted, that is, longer than the perianth, and projecting from its somewhat campanulate throat.

All species of wild onions were known and used as food by the Indians of the Pacific Coast. In the journals of Lewis and Clark frequent mention is made of wild onion roots as an article of food and commerce. They also mention them as a remedy for the flatulence induced by eating large amounts of camas, and from them they prepared poultices for the treatment of sick Indians as well as for injured members of their own party.

NARROW-LEAVED ONION

Allium attenuifolium Kellog

Pink or white. Root, a coated bulb; outer coats marked with rows of V-shaped reticulations. Leaves, narrowly linear. Scape, round; eight to twelve inches tall. Inflorescence, an umbel; dense; many-flowered. Perianth, six-cleft; spreading. Stamens, six. Habitat, variable; found in low, rich fields or in sand-filled cavities on rocks. Blossoming period, May and June.

This, our most beautiful wild onion, may be found in a great va-

HOOKER'S ONION   *Allium acuminatum*

riety of situations. In growth, too, it varies in form from rather small flat umbels of pure white bloom, to crowded, close-packed spheres of the brightest pink. The flowers are especially beautiful if cut when half opened and kept in water, then the whole head retains its freshness for weeks, and opens out in marked perfection. Persons unacquainted with the plant often contend that such a beautiful flower can not be an onion, but a taste of the stem or root soon silences their unbelief.

The outer bulb coats of this species are reddish, and the reticulations, seen easily with a low-power lens, are composed of fine parallel, V-shaped lines.

CAT'S-EARS
Calochortus tolmiei Hook & Arn.

White. Root, a coated corm. Stem, slightly branched; eight to fourteen inches tall; declined or upright. Leaves, linear. Flowers, one to five; terminal or on short branches. Petals, three; broad; very hairy within; each bearing a noticeable gland at the base. Sepals, three; narrow; without noticeable pit at base. Stamens, six. Anthers, basifixed. Fruit, a noticeable three-winged, three-celled oval pod. Habitat, dry meadows and hillsides. Blooming period, May and June.

One of our prettiest and most graceful flowers is the white maraposa lily, or cat's-ears. This modest flower though less showy than some of its kindred, has a soft pleasing beauty all its own. The satin-like petals need no color to add to their charm, for their very spotlessness endears them to us as no gaudy show could. That such a plant should deign, each spring, to grace our commonest cow-pastures with its presence is one of the wonders of nature's generosity. It is a plant of dry hillside meadows, blooming from early May to June. The flowers are borne singly, or by twos and threes, on slender stems from six inches to a foot and a half high, and sway easily in the wind, looking like pearly white butterflies, which, in fact, is just what the California name "mariposa" means. Our Oregon name of cat's-ears is easily understood if you look at the inside of the flowers, which are soft and hairy like a kitten's ear. Still another name for this plant is sego lily, and under that name a similar species is the State Flower of Utah, dear to the hearts of the people through history and association. When the first settlers reached that state this flower greeted them

NARROW-LEAVED ONION   *Allium attenuifolium*

[18]

amidst the drought and desolation; then, from the Indians, they learned to use its root for food, and thus it became to them a symbol for both beauty and sustenance. In Zane Gray's book, "The Rainbow Trail," he gives to his heroine, a beautiful child reared amidst desolate surroundings, the name of "Sego Lily."

Sego, or seego, is an Indian word. The Shoshone name of camas is "pah-see-go," or water sego, to distinguish it from this species of sego which grows on high land. Sego seems to be a general name for certain kinds of food, for they also use it to designate dried apples or peaches. All species of *Calochortus* have edible bulbs, and some of them are among the Indian's choicest delicacies.

Purdy's Cat's Ears. *Calochortus purdyi* Eastwood. This species differs from the preceding one by having the gland of each petal covered by a small scale. The petals also have a distinctly purplish tint, and they are, if possible, even more beautifully furred within. A rather rare species.

ALPINE CAT'S-EARS
Calochortus subalpinus Piper

White. Very similar to *C. tolmiei,* but smaller. Sepals, marked by a conspicuous purple pit at base. Habitat, alpine meadows. Blooming period, July and August.

This slender species of cat's-ears will be found in alpine and subalpine regions of the Cascade Mountains from Mount Adams in Washington to The Three Sisters in Oregon. The principal features that distinguish it from the lowland form are its smaller size, cream-colored or yellowish hairs within the flower cup, and a small, distinct purple pit at the base of each sepal. On Crescent Mountain, Oregon, it grows along the trail just below the forest look-out, at an altitude of approximately six thousand feet. Its companions are such mountain flowers as the valerian, western wall-flower, squawgrass, and several species of pentstemon.

WILD TIGER-LILY
Lilium columbianum Hanson

Orange. Root, a scaly bulb. Stem, leafy; upright; one to eight feet. Leaves, whorled; oblanceolate. Flowers, few to many on slender

CAT'S EARS

Calochortus tolmiei

petioles near the summit of the plant; perianth, six-parted, the segments recurved; orange; spotted with dark brown. Anthers, versatile. Style, simple. Stigma, capitate; slightly three-lobed. Habitat, low rich soil along streams, or in moist woods. Blooming period, from June in the valleys to August at high elevations in the mountains.

Our common tiger-lily is always attractive, and when at its best it is a truly magnificent plant. Its rich orange, brown-spotted blooms are borne in loose spreading panicles of from two to twenty flowers. Ehe six equal divisions of the perianth are strongly recurved, and the loosely swinging, versatile anthers shed an abundance of bright yellow pollen—a delight to children who coax the unwary to smell the flower, and then giggle at their unsuspecting victim's yellow nose. The root, as in all true lilies, is a large scaly bulb. It is edible, and was highly prized by the Coast Indians. This plant is a lover of rich, moist bottom-lands, but it is not entirely restricted to such locations, as it may be found on hillsides, and in the mountains to an elevation of three or four thousand feet.

WASHINGTON LILY
Lilium washingtonianum Kellog

White or pinkish. Root, a scaly bulb; large. Stem, upright; usually simple; three to six feet. Leaves, whorled. Flowers, funnel-form; three to forty; very fragrant; perianth lobes somewhat spreading, white, finely dotted. Stamens, six. Anthers, versatile. Habitat, open woods and meadows in the mountains. Blooming period, June to August.

In the mountain heights, often within sight of perpetual ice and snow, grows this delicate white flower of the Easter lily type, such as might more properly be associated with sunny Bermuda. Surely, this is the queen of our native lilies. It bears its regal clusters upon upright stems from three to six feet tall, and often whitens extensive meadows with its blooms. The flowers are white, turning pink or rose-colored with age, and are very fragrant, often revealing their presence by their scent when they might otherwise be passed unnoticed. The range of this plant is from the Columbia River southward throughout the Cascade and Sierra Nevada Mountains, and it is unfortunate that it has no commonly accepted name throughout its range. In the north it is known as the Mount Hood lily; in

WASHINGTON LILY　　　　　　　　　*Lilium washingtonianum*

California as the Shasta lily; in southern Oregon as the Mount Pitt lily; and in the central Willamette Valley as the Santiam lily. In intermediate points it bears other local names, each region hoping thus to gain virtue by adopting this flower as its own.

This lily may now be found in gardens throughout the country, and is a great favorite wherever grown.

RICE ROOT
Fritillaria lanceolata Pursh

Brown and green. Root, a white, bell-shaped bulb, thickly covered with plump, ricelike scales. Stems, simple; arching; eight to twenty inches tall. Leaves, root leaves ovate, tapering at both ends; stem leaves whorled; lanceolate. Inflorescence, a raceme. Flowers, campanulate; nodding; rank-scented. Stamens, six. Anthers, basifixed. Stigma, three lobed; the lobes recurved. Capsule, acutely angled. Habitat, dry prairies and hillsides. Blooming period, March to May.

This graceful flower bears so many common names that each person may call it differently and still be right. The name rice root, and Indian rice come from the fact that its large bulbs are covered with plump, white, rice-like scales; chocolate and brown lily, as well as speckled-hen and snake lily come from its peculiar color and markings; mission bells and bronze bells from its graceful shape; and sourdough lily from its peculiar odor, and from the fact that it grows in the land of the "sour-doughs."

We would scarcely suspect this plant of having food value, but the North-coast Indians, who let little that was edible escape them, dug and boiled the roots for food. Among some of the tribes boiled riceroot was an important feast dish, and designs representing the bulbs were woven into their baskets, and carved upon their cedar boxes. Among some California tribes, however, it was believed that if the roots were dug it would cause the acorns to fall from the oak trees. As acorns were their most important bread supply, they naturally followed this superstition and thus saved the acorns! I have found the bulbs, when cooked, quite palatable. They are very tender and delicate, and except for a slightly bitter taste they could scarcely be told from genuine rice. With cream, or butter and sugar, they are very fine.

GIANT DOG-TOOTH VIOLET

Erythronium giganteum

The flowers of the rice root secrete nectar freely; so much so that at times it actually drips from the mouth of the drooping bell.

Indian Rice. *Fritillaria camtschatcensis* (L.) Ker-Gawl. This is a more northern species having its flowers less mottled; capsules obtusely angled; and rather broader leaves. Its range is from northern Washington, northward.

GIANT DOG-TOOTH VIOLET
Erythronium giganteum Lindl.

Cream-color, or pale yellow. Root, a narrow, deep-seated corm. Leaves, a pair; basal; broadly lanceolate; mottled. Scape, erect; four to fifteen inches tall. Flowers, one to six; perianth segments, six; outer three narrowest; inner ones auriculated and with yellow, orange or brown markings at the base; all much recurved and sometimes turning pinkish with age. Stamens, six. Pistil, three-lobed; the lobes recurved. Habitat, open woods and brush-land. Blooming period, April-May.

There is a single species of *Erythronium,* native of Europe; three species are found east of the Rocky Mountains, and eleven or twelve are native of the Pacific Coast. Not only does this region excel in the numbe of species, but in beauty of tint, and in the size of the flowers. The present species bears the specific name of *giganteum,* and it is truly the giant of its kind. I have found single flowers measuring when extended over six inches from point to point. Other plants which bear smaller flowers make up in the number of blooms what they lack in size—four to ten flowers on a single stem. In the number and size of the flowers they are extremely variable, however, and in many neighborhoods single-flowered plants, with blooms only an inch or two across appear to be the rule. The name dog-tooth violet seems to refer to a fancied resemblance of the root to a dog's tooth. A Nez Perce Indian girl informed me that their name for the plant is "bear's tooth." Other local names are spring lily, Easter lily, fawn lily, lamb's-tongue, deer's-tongue, adder's-tongue, curly lily, and chemise lily.

From coast to coast the roots of the dog-tooth violets have been esteemed as food by the Indian tribes, but only along the North Pacific are they plentiful enough to be a really important article of diet. Among the Kwakiutl Indians of British Columbia they are especially

PINK DOG-TOOTH VIOLET   *Erythronium johnsonii*

valued, and are eaten either baked, boiled, or stewed, stirred into a plastic mass with a liberal portion of fish or whale oil. Besides cooked roots, one of their writers states that—"Some women and men eat the roots raw when it is a hot day, for the *Erythronium*-roots are cool inside when they are eaten raw, and they have a milky taste."

PINK DOG-TOOTH VIOLET
Erythronium johnsonii Bolander

Pink. Root, a deep-seated corm. Leaves, two; basal; ovate; obtuse; large; mottled. Flowers, usually one, but sometimes several; on slender scapes; perianth segments nearly equal; narrowly lanceolate; outer ones obtuse; inner ones auriculated and marked with orange at the base. Stamens, six. Filaments, white; much dilated at base. Anthers, yellow. Style, longer than the stamens. Stigma, three-lobed, the lobes recurved. Habitat, open woods. Blooming period, March to May.

As I write this article the botanists of the Coast have not yet agreed on the proper specific name for this flower. Since, then, the recognized authorities are uncertain, my choice of a name may be as correct as any. A name, at its best, is merely a key by which we may unlock the doors of thought concerning any subject, and if the doors swing wide open under some other impulse, the key is not needed. To the non-technical flower lover, then, the key to this flower is its color—the softest, purest pink imaginable, both inside and out, except that the base of each division of the perianth is marked with golden yellow. This shade of pink in a flower of this type is both unusual and striking, and once seen can never be forgotten. This exquisite and unique blossom is at home on the western slopes of the Coast Range, from Lincoln to Tillamook Counties, in Oregon, and probably northward into Washington; also on Vancouver Island.

YELLOW DOG-TOOTH VIOLET
Erythronium parviflorum (Wats.) Goodding

Yellow. Leaves, not mottled. Flowers, commonly only one; bright yellow.

The yellow dog-tooth violet, or glacier lily as it is sometimes called, grows in alpine meadows from British Columbia southward

CAMAS   *Quamasia quamash*

into Northern California. The leaves are not mottled; the segments of the perianth are bright yellow, paler or greenish at the base, and are rather narrow. It is the smallest of our North Coast species. The flowers are quite fragrant.

AVALANCHE LILY
Erythronium montanum Wats.

White. Leaves, not mottled. Flowers, one to several; white; perianth segments broadly lanceolate, each with an orange base.

This species of dog-tooth violet grows abundantly, and covers large areas in the alpine meadows of the Cascade Mountains. Its flowers are pure white with an orange spot at the base of each petal, and grow on a rather stout scape in racemes of from one to six blooms. The leaves, as in the preceding species, are not mottled.

What pictures the very name "avalanche lily" presents to mind— mountain meadows nestling at the very foot of some perpetually white peak, where, in sheltered nooks the snow-banks remain all through the summer; chipmunks and marmots busy among the rocks; Clark's crows dashing here and there, their black and white plumage contrasting strongly with the dark foliage of the spruces; everywhere the sense of silence and aloofness that the high altitudes seem to give, and all about, in ranks and hosts, the white Erythroniums, nodding in the breeze. No region of the world can surpass this West Coast Country in the beauty of her mountain flowers.

CAMAS
Quamasia quamash (Pursh) Coville

Blue. Root, a deep-seated, coated bulb. Leaves, all basal; linear; smooth. Scape, stout; ten to twenty inches tall. Inflorescence, a loose raceme. Flowers, ten to thirty; blue or white; on stiff pedicels, each accompanied by a tapering bract; perianth six parted, the segments unevenly spreading, and twisting and falling separately with age. Stamens, six. Anthers, versatile. Fruit, a dry, three-lobed capsule. Seeds, numerous; black. Habitat, moist soil, often among rocks. Blooming period, April to June.

Of all the food plants used by the Western Indians the camas was the most important and widely known. There is more romance and adventure clustered about the camas root and flower than about almost any other American plant. Hardly one of the early Pacific explorers but records how at some time the camas has saved him from extreme hunger, if not from actual starvation, and in the traditions of the Indians it was given a prominent place; many mythical tales are told of its origin and uses.

The plant prefers to grow in moist or even wet situations. Tracts, sometimes miles in extent, were covered and made blue by its spikes of hyacinth-like flowers. Its root, the part used for food, is a smooth, onion-like bulb, plump and nutritious, forming as near a substitute for bread as anything that was available to primitive cooks.

The camas fields were tribal property, jealously guarded against the trespass of rival clans. Ware were sometimes caused by disputes over questions of possession or boundary, nor could the Indians understand why the white man was privileged to usurp these possessions, and destroy the camas meadows with his plow. The Nez Perce War under the able leadership of Chief Joseph, was a final desperate protest against these trespasses upon their fields.

That the Indians still love camas is testified to by the following directions for cooking the root, given me by a young Nez Perce girl, herself a direct descendent of Chief Joseph: "We make a hole in the ground," she states, "line it with flat stones, and build a fire upon them. When the stones are red-hot we rake out the coals, and cover the hot stones with a certain kind of wild grass found only in the mountains. Then upon the grass we place the camas, and over this place another layer of grass. We then cover all, first with gunnysacks, and then with dirt, and over all we build a fire which is kept burning for two nights and a day. The pit," she further stated, "must not be opened or poked into during this time, or the camas will be spoiled." So delicate was the operation of tending the camas pit, that only the oldest and most experienced women of the tribe were trusted with its care. The modern Nez Perce eat their camas with sugar and cream, luxuries of which their forefathers, of course, knew nothing.

LEICHTLIN'S CAMAS
Quamasia leichtlinii (Baker) Coville

Blue. Similar to *Q. quamash,* but larger and stouter. Flowers, blue or white. Perianth segments regularly disposed, twisting together and about the capsule with age.

Most of what has been said about the preceding species applies equally well to this plant. Both species are inclined to produce white-blossomed specimens, but this tendency seems most pronounced in the present species. The chief distinguishing feature between them is that in *quamash* the divisions of the perianth are unequally arranged, some turning upwards, others downward, thus making a one-sided flower, and in wilting each segment twists, and falls separately. In *leichtlinii,* on the other hand, the flowers are symmetrical, and in wilting all the segments become twisted together about the capsule.

As a garden flower Leichtlin's camas has been found very satisfactory, and improved varieties of it are now offered by florists both here and in Europe.

The roots of all species of camas grow deep in the soil, and it is a difficult task, even with the aid of a good shovel, to secure them. A strong answer to those who picture the Indian's life as one of perpetual idleness is the fact that they secured a large part of their living by digging these deep seated bulbs, and that with no better tool than a crude, pointed stick, and at a season of the year when the ground was baked almost to the hardness of brick.

Although some have ridiculed the idea, declaring boldly that "the camas bulb is not pie fruit," there seems to be unquestionable evidence that the early settlers on the coast did make camas pies. So far, actual proof as to how it was done seems to be lacking, yet the solution is, perhaps, very simple. Camas bulbs, crushed in an old-fashioned iron mortar such as every emigrant train carried, and then stewed or simmered for a long time, take on almost the consistency and taste of stewed pumpkin. The rest, to any ingenious housewife, would be obvious. Camas pies, then, were the Northwestern pioneer equivalent to the far-famed New England pumpkin pie.

So abundant was the camas in the early days that the settlers often depended on it for summer hog feed. Only after they had made a satisfactory growth on this self-harvested food were the animals brought home to be fattened on cultivated grains.

DEATH CAMAS   *Zigadenus venenosus*

DEATH CAMAS
Zigadenus venenosus Wats.

Yellowish-white. Root, a shallow coated bulb; poisonous. Stem, slender; leafy; ten or twenty inches tall. Leaves, linear; keeled; roughish. Inflorescence, a close, bracted, terminal raceme; many-flowered. Flowers, small; perianth segments marked at the base by a conspicuous yellow gland. Capsule, cylindrical. Seeds, numerous; brown. Habitat, wet meadows. Blooming period, May and June.

Death camas has an evil reputation both for man and beast on the Pacific Coast. The Indians knew and dreaded it, the danger coming from its resemblance to the true camas of this region. To them it was a special menace, since it grows in identical situations favored by the edible camas, which was, and still is, one of their favorite foods. In spite of their knowledge of the plant, cases of poisoning, often fatal, were not uncommon.

In Indian medicine the plant seems to have had a prominent place. The pounded bulbs were applied as a poultice to cure boils, for rheumatism, for bruises and sprains, and to relieve pain in general. It is also said that unscrupulous medicine men "mixed the root with a little tobacco, to give a person a severe nausea, in order to secure a heavy fee for making them well again."

Although the use of camas as a food has not become general among the white inhabitants of the Coast, many people, as a novelty, enjoy digging and eating the roots in a raw state, and children are sometimes poisoned through failing to distinguish the edible from the deadly plant.

As long as the fruiting capsules and stem remain upon the plant they are quite easy to distinguish. The capsules of the death camas are much smaller and more closely set upon the stem, and the scapes are more slender than in *Quamash;* the leaves, too, are narrower, roughish, and folded lengthwise into a sharp keel, while those of the true camas are smooth and remain flat. The bloom of the death camas is very attractive, being white, each section of the perianth bearing a pale yellow gland at the base. The many-flowered scape rises to a height of from six inches to two feet. In the Willamette Valley it blooms about the middle of June, and the flowers are rather short lived.

As a stock poisoning plant death camas is one of the worst. Horses

and cattle are often made sick, usually without fatal results, but among sheep the fatalities from eating it are often very high—in badly infested regions as much as twenty per cent of the flocks, annually. Hogs, on the other hand, are not affected by the poison of the plant, and even appear to relish and thrive on it, which has given it among its common names that of "hog potato." Other names locally applied to this plant are lobelia, poison sego, poison grass, alkali grass, water lily, and soap-root.

Zigadenus elegans Pursh. This is a somewhat rare species here. The flowers are greenish, and the leaves are broad, flat ,and glaucous.

WESTERN STENANTHIUM
Stenanthium occidentale Gray

Brownish-purple. Root, a narrow bulb. Stem, sparingly leafy; ten to eighteen inches tall. Leaves mostly basal; linear-lanceolate; eight to twelve inches long. Inflorescence, a raceme or narrow panicle. Flowers, narrow brownish bells. Perianth segments, six; narrow, recurved. Stamens six. Styles, three. Habitat, stream banks in the mountains. Blooming period, from April onward, according to altitude.

The bronze bells of the western stenanthium are quite narrow, and measure from a third to a half an inch in length. These flowers are rather inconspicuous, but are rendered attractive by a pleasantly spicy odor. A shy mountain flower, very partial to mossy stream banks.

ALPINE BEAUTY
Clintonia uniflora (Schult.) Kunth

White. Root, a slender rhizome. Leaves, basal; few, obovate; tapering at base; soft; thin; somewhat pubescent. Flowers, white; solitary; on a weak, slender scape. Perianth, six-parted; segments thin and soft; spreading. Fruit, a blue berry. Habitat, woods in the mountains. Blooming period, May to August according to altitude.

This beautiful mountain flower has been most unfortunate in the names bestowed upon it, for it was first handicapped by the name of Clinton, a New York politician. Then Mrs. Henshaw, a Canadian writer and evidently a staunch Royalist, farther blighted it with the

Clintonia uniflora

ALPINE BEAUTY

flat and futile name of "Queen-cup." The name alpine beauty, bestowed upon it by Prof. Flett, is not entirely satisfactory, but it has
at least the virtue of being appropriately descriptive.

The white clintonia is distinctly a mountain flower. In the subalpine forests of Oregon and Washington, and northward, the plants
often carpet the whole earth with their thin, soft, attractive leaves.
From May to August, according to the altitude, each plant sends
up a single fragile, lily-like flower. In the form of its leaf and flower
there is a suggestion of the dog-tooth-violet, but both are far more
fragile and delicate.

MOTTLED TRILLIUM
Trillium chloropetalum (Torr.) Howell

White. Root, a short, bulbous rhizome. Stems, stout; simple; upright; six to eighteen inches tall. Leaves, ovate; very broad; three, in
a whorl at the summit of the stem; mottled. Flowers, solitary, sessile; at the center of the whorled leaves. Sepals, three; green. Petals,
three; white; upright; narrowly lanceolate. Stamens, six. Anthers,
bastifixed. Pistil, three-lobed. Stigmas, curved and convoluted on their
inner edges. Habitat, moist woods. Blooming period, March to May.
This species is a week or two earlier than *Trillium ovatum*.

The trillium is also called wake-robin because its flowers as har-
bingers of spring are supposed to wake the robin into renewed activ-
ity and song. This is scarcely true in our mild Pacific climate, for
here the robins are frequently "awake" and lively throughout the
entire winter, yet as John Burroughs says, "When I have found the
wake-robin in bloom I know that the season is fairly inaugurated,
not merely with the awakening of the robin—but with the universal
awakening and rehabilitation of nature."

The trilliums belong to that branch of the lily family distinguished
by having creeping, underground root-stalks in the place of scaly
bulbs, but in the wake-robin this root-stalk is so short and thick that
it appears as a solid bulb or corm. The name trillium means triple,
and refers to the fact that all parts of the plant are in threes—three
leaves, three sepals, three petals, twice three stamens, and a three-
lobed pistil. *Trillium chloropetalum* may be easily known by the fact
that its solitary white flower is sessile, that is, it has no stem of its
own, but sits down closely against the centre of the three broad leaves.

WESTERN TRILLIUM

The petals of this species are rather narrow, and not very showy, and the broad leaves are mottled with spots of reddish brown. The amount of coloring in the leaves is greatly influenced by the amount of sunshine that reaches the plant, those growing in deep shade often appearing quite pale.

WESTERN TRILLIUM
Trillium ovatum Pursh

White. Root, a short, bulbous rhizome. Stem, simple; erect; six inches to two feet. Leaves, three; sessile; in a terminal whorl; three to six inches wide; not mottled. Flowers, white, becoming purple with age; solitary; slender pediceled; at centre of whorled leaves. Sepals, three; green; lanceolate. Petals, three; rather broad; one to three inches in length. Stamens, six. Anthers, basifixed. Stigma, three-lobed, the lobes recurved into a "curl." Habitat, moist woods. Blooming period, March to May.

Trillium ovatum differs from *Trillium chloropetalum* by having its handsome, showy flowers raised on a slender stem an inch or two above the plain, unspotted green leaves. The fresh flowers of this species are a clear creamy white, but as they grow older and pass maturity the petals often become tinged with some shade of purple, becoming at length very dark.

A notiable feature of our coast flora is the immense fields of trillium sometimes encountered. One patch of the western trillium of which I know contains at least fifty acres of closely growing plants. Not only is this locality remarkable for the number of individual plants, but, because of the richness of the soil, they there grow to unusual size. Some, indeed, have become too large and coarse to be attractive, and appear almost as caricatures of their kind.

The roots of the various species of trillium have been used as medicine, principally for poultices, both by the whites and Indians.

FETID ADDERS-TONGUE
Scoliopus hallii S. Wats.

Greenish-purple. Leaves, two; basal; thin; oblong; smooth; blotched with brown or purple. Flowers, several; borne singly on weak-slender pedicels. Sepals, three; lanceolate; green and purple.

FETID ADDERS-TONGUE   *Scoliopus hallii*

Petals, three; narrowly linear. Stamens, three. Stigma, three-lobed; lobes narrow. Habitat, moist stream banks in the mountains. Blooming period, early spring; usually in March.

The fetid adders-tongue is a peculiar little plant whose mottled leaves somewhat resemble those of the showy dog-tooth violets. This plant, however, sends up from one to eight weak, curving scapes, each scape bearing a single curiously formed, rather pretty, green and purple, but bad smelling flower. Found in the mountains along moist stream banks in Western Oregon.

SQUAW GRASS
Xerophyllum tenax (Pursh) Nutt.

White. Root, a short, woody rootstock. Stem, simple; upright; leafy below. Leaves, basal; densely tufted; very numerous; linear; forming dense hummocks. Inflorescence, a tall, dense raceme. Flowers, small; white. Perianth segments, six; spreading. Stamens, six. Habitat, dry mountain meadows or at lower altitudes northward. Blooming period, May to August according to altitude.

This plant is a magnificent feature of open woods and meadows in our mountains. Even when it is not in bloom the large crowded hummocks of tough, wiry leaves are very noticeable, but when it bursts into flower, putting forth great plume-like spikes of delicate creamy bloom, it is a sight never to be forgotten. I have seen patches of this plant covering fifty or sixty acres, of almost pure growth, every plant bearing from one to three snowy plumes, three, four, or even five feet in height.

One day while skirting a large field of this grass on a high, inaccessible peak, I was surprised to notice unmistakable evidence of an Indian encampment. Over the ground, everywhere, were scattered chips of obsidian, with here and there an imperfect arrow. How did these come here, and why did the ancient people choose this inconvenient spot, far from water, for setting up their camp? The answer is very simple; they came to gather squaw grass leaves, which were much used, and were an article of extensive commerce throughout the West long before the whites ever came to this coast. From the leaves the natives constructed hats, pouches, cups, baskets, and even water-tight cooking vessels. "Their baskets," writes Doug-

SQUAW GRASS   *Xerophyllum tenax*

las, "were formed of cedar bark and bear grass so closely interwoven with the fingers that they are water-tight without the use of gum or rosin; some of them are highly ornamented with strands of bear grass which they dye of several colors, and interwoven in a great variety of figures; this serves them the double purpose of holding their water, or wearing on their heads."

I have been reliably informed that in early spring bears seek the open hillsides where these plants grow and dig up the roots for food. The same informant said that the roots boiled in water make a very good substitute for soap, and that he had often used them for that purpose. These two items explain two vernacular names for the plant, those of bear grass, and soap grass. The name elk grass, also often given it, is less clear, but since squirrels and chipmunks cut down the fresh flower stalks and eat them, it is equally to be supposed that elk may also relish them. The name squaw grass comes, of course, from its use in basketry, but its truly aboriginal name, current among the Indians of the Columbia Rapids where a large trade in the prepared leaves was carried on, was *quip-quip*.

OREGON FAIRY BELLS
Disporum oreganum (Wats.) B. & H.

White. Root, a slender rootstock. Stems, branching; leafy; one to three feet tall. Leaves, alternate; sessile; ovate; taper-pointed. Flowers, white; nodding at the ends of the branches; narrowly campanulate; the lobes spreading at the apex. Stamens, six; longer than the perianth and protruding beyond its lobes. Pistil, as long as the stamens; slender. Stigma, entire. Fruit, a golden-yellow berry. Habitat, moist woods. Blooming period, April-May.

Between the fairy bells, false soloman's seal, and twisted-stalk, there is a strong family resemblance, especially in foliage, but each has its own peculiarity in the manner of bearing its blooms. The Oregon fairy bells are tall branching plants, and the flowers are borne singly, or in clusters of twos and threes at the extremity of the branches, often completely hidden beneath the broad leaves. In form they are bell-shaped, wide at the mouth and narrow at the base; the stamens, and simple, slender style extend considerably beyond the lobes of the perianth. The leaves are alternate, distinctly veined,

OREGON FAIRY BELLS   *Disporum oreganum*

SMITH'S FAIRY BELLS   *Disporum smithii*

TWISTED-STALK   *Streptopus amplexifolius*

sessile or slightly clasping, and have a long tapering point. The flowers are followed by an oval, golden-yellow berry, that has given to the plant one of its common names—that of gold-drops.

Smith's Fairy Bells. *Disporum smithii* (Hook.) Piper. Similar to the above, but may be distinguished by its flowers, which are broad at the base and narrow at the throat, and with included stamens and pistil, and a three-lobed stigma.

TWISTED-STALK
Streptopus amplexifolius (L.) DC.

White or greenish. Root, a rhizome. Stems, branching; one to three feet tall. Leaves, alternate; sessile; clasping and heart-shaped at the base, tapering at the point. Flowers, solitary in the axils of the leaves; drooping on slender, thread-like pedicels; each pedicel with a curious sharp twist, or kink near the center. Perianth, narrowly campanulate; acutely lobed; lobes spreading. Fruit, a brilliant scarlet berry. Habitat, moist woods. Blooming period, May-June.

In similar places, and very much resembling the fairy bells, will be found the slightly larger plants of the twisted-stalk. At first we might think them identical, but when we raise the leafy branches to look for the flowers we at once perceive our mistake, for those of this plant are borne singly in the axils of the leaves. Look closely at the thread-like stem on which each greenish-white flower is suspended, and you will at once see why the name "twisted-stalk" has been given it, for between the plant and the flower, in each slender pedicel, there is a peculiar kink-like twist that both explains the name, and establishes its identity. If found late in the season, the flowers will be replaced by oblong, bright red berries, but the twist in the stalk still remains.

Simple-Stemmed Twisted-Stalk. *Streptopus curvipes* Vail. This is a similar unbranched species, found commonly in low mountains, and having rose-colored blossoms.

GREEN, OR INDIAN HELLEBORE
Veratrum viride Ait.

Greenish yellow. Rootstocks, short; thick; poisonous. Stem, stout;

WHITE HELLEBORE   *Veratrum californicum*

leafy; two to five feet tall. Leaves, sessile; clasping; ovate; strongly veined and plaited. Inflorescence, a drooping panicle. Flowers, small; greenish yellow. Habitat, wet meadows and swales in the mountains.

Among the Indians of the North Coast no plant was more highly valued for its magical potency than this. It was truly "skookum medicine," if we may judge from their myths and legends, which record endless instances of its marvelous use and powers. According to their stories, the possession of a small piece of the root insured the bearer against all evilly intentioned spirits, as well as the supernatural beings which were ever lying in wait to annoy them. At night, while spearing seals or porpoise, should a sea-monster rise up to threaten them, a bit of the root chewed and spit upon the water would immediately cause it to disappear. If the rain failed, so that no salmon came to the rivers, hellebore was, with much ceremony, thrown into the water. "For this is the strong rain caller of the Indians." A piece of the root carried by a person would even ward off the dangerous powers of those terrible creatures. "The Land-Otter People," whose delight, it was believed, was to steal away men's minds, and make of them pitiable creatures, half man, half beast. Its power was even strong enough to restore to life whole families of people whose disorganized skeletons had been recovered from the maw of a devouring monster. Surely, this is a valuable plant to have about!

The green hellebore is a tall, rank plant of mountain swales and marshes, having handsome, boat-shaped leaves, which are finely veined and plaited, and which lead us to anticipate equally handsome flowers, but in this we will be disappointed, for the long, branching spikes, when they appear, are very disappointing, being first yellowish, and later a bright green. The plant grows to a height of from four to five feet. The root is a drastic poison.

WHITE HELLEBORE
Veratrum californicum Durand

White. Rootstock, thick; short; poisonous. Stem, simple; stout; leafy; erect; three to ten feet tall. Leaves sessile; ovate; plaited in bud. Inflorescence, an upright, branching panicle; the terminal section often very long. Flowers, white; numerous; showy. Habitat, in swamps and swales. Blooming period, June and July.

FALSE SOLOMON'S SEAL   *Vagnera amplexicaulis*

Larger than the green hellebore, and more handsome in every way, is this more southern species. The broad-leaved, tropical looking plants grow from five to ten feet in height, and are crowned at the summit with a great spreading candelabrum of white bloom. Unfortunately, before the flowers open the leaves have often become ragged and wilted, so that the full beauty of the plant is seldom seen. The whole plant is considered to be poisonous, and the root of this and other species have recognized medicinal properties, and are also used as an insecticide. I remember distinctly that as a small boy one of the most distasteful tasks assigned to me was that of sprinkling the current bushes with powdered white hellebore root to rid them of worms. The gathering of hellebore root is a considerable industry in regions where it is abundant.

FALSE SOLOMON'S SEAL
Vagnera amplexicaulis (Nutt.) Greene

White. Rootstock, stout; fleshy. Stem, simple; leafy; arched or declining; ten to thirty inches long. Leaves, alternate; sessile; ovate; taper pointed. Inflorescence, a compact terminal raceme. Flowers, numerous; minute; waxy; sweet-scented. Fruit, a berry; light red, sprinkled with darker dots; edible. Habitat, moist woods. Blooming period, April-May.

In late April and early May, this, the largest of our two species of Solomon's seal, will be found in its prime in moist, open woods. It is a pleasing and decorative plant; each stem rising from the ground in a graceful leafy curve, terminating in a close-flowered pyramidal panicle of minute, waxy bloom. The height of the plant is from one to three feet; the leaves are broad, sessile, and opposite, with prominent parallel veins. The flowers produce in late summer a small cluster of spherical, red-dotted berries, edible, and much relished by bears.

STAR-FLOWERED SOLOMON'S SEAL
Vagnera sessilifolia (Baker) Greene

White. Rootstock, slender. Stem, slender; leafy; arching or declined; ten to twenty inches long. Leaves, alternate; sessile; clasp-

WILD LILY-OF-THE-VALLEY   *Unifolium bifolium kamtschaticum*

ing; lanceolate to ovate; pointed. Inflorescence, a loose, few-flowered terminal raceme. Flowers, about one-fourth inch across. Perianth, segments spreading. Fruit, a berry. Habitat, moist woods. Blooming period, April-May.

The star-flowered Solomon's seal is a dainty, small plant that often covers the forest floor in immense tracts in Western Washington and Oregon. Like the larger species, it grows with simple curved stems, but the terminal flowers are larger, and star-like. They are borne in a loose, few-flowered zig-zag cluster, usually not more than ten or twelve flowers to the raceme.

The root of this species was held in high esteem as a cure for wounds by some of the early explorers, who learned its use from the native tribes. Captain Fremont called it "The best remedial plant known among the Indians." At the present day the pounded root is still much used by some of the Inland tribes as a remedy for rheumatism.

WILD LILY-OF-THE-VALLEY
Unifolium bifolium kamtschaticum (Gmel.) Piper

White. Rootstock, slender. Stems, upright; five to ten inches tall. Leaves, root leaves, roundish; heart-shaped at base; stem leaves, usually two; pointed; heart-shaped or saggitate at base. Inflorescence, a terminal raceme. Flowers, small; white; sweet-scented. Fruit, a red, edible berry. Habitat, moist woods. Blooming period, April to June.

This dainty, sweet-scented flower is common in shaded places from Alaska, southward to California. The blossoming plants grow from five to ten inches tall, and bear two broadly heart-shaped leaves, above which rises a slender raceme of minute, waxy flowers. Unlike most members of the lily family, who delight in threes, all parts of this plant are grouped in twos, or its multiple;—two leaves, a four-parted perianth, four stamens, and a two-lobed stigma. The red berries that follow the blossoms are also two-celled, and each cell is two seeded. These berries are edible, and are used as food by the Indians from Vancouver Island to Alaska, though not always plentiful enough to be of great importance in their diet.

TOUGH-LEAVED IRIS

Iris tenax

TOUGH-LEAVED IRIS
Iris tenax Dougl.

Purple. Rootstock, slender. Stems, simple; slender; bearing a few bract-like leaves. Leaves, mostly basal; tufted; linear; grass-like. Flowers, solitary, showy. Perianth, of six clawed divisions; the three inner, commonly designated as standards, narrowest, erect or in-arched; the three outer, called falls, broad and spreading. Stamens, three, opposite, and hidden beneath the petal-like divisions of the pistil. Pistil, three-parted; petal-like; opposite to, and resting upon the three arched falls. Habitat, dry prairies and hillsides. Blooming period, April to June.

Most species of Iris grow in wet situations, but this one prefers sunny, open uplands and there it often tints whole hillsides with its blooms. In color it is extremely variable, usually purple, but ranging through the darker shades to mauve and lavender, and in the lighter shades to tints bordering on pink with an occasional pure white specimen. In flower or bud it is equally pleasing and decorative.

Its range is quite limited, being restricted solely to the humid portions of Washington, Oregon and Northern California. Within these narrow limits, however, it is very abundant, being one of our most common and typical flowers.

Several species of northwestern iris provided fibre from which the Indians made light, but exceedingly strong ropes, nets, and snares, and this is one of the species so used. Indeed, the specific name *tenax* refers to the tenacity or toughness of that fibre. The botanist Douglas writes of these ropes as follows: "The snare is used in taking elk, and long, and black tailed deer, and in point of strength it will hold the strongest bullock and is not thicker than the little finger." Such cords took much patience to make, and were valued very highly.

Iris tenuis Wats. This is a rather rare little iris of restricted range, found only in the Cascades of Northwestern Oregon. Its stems, usually two flowered, in height about equal the leaves. The flowers are white, marked with yellow and purple.

BLUE-EYED GRASS   *Sisyrinchium idahoense*

BLUE-EYED GRASS
Sisyrinchium idahoense Bicknell

Blue. Stem, slender; flattened; six to twelve inches tall. Leaves, narrow; grass-like; tufted; upright; rather stiff; shorter than the stems. Inflorescence, umbellate, but only one or two flowers of the umbel ever opening at the same time; umbel accompanied by two small, linear bracts. Flowers, small; six-parted; rotate; star-like. Stamens, three. Filaments, united nearly to the apex. Habitat, moist meadows. Blooming period, May-June.

> "What impulse stirs the feathery grasses,
> And dips along their wavering line?
> While, as the sudden tremor passes,
> Two strange, sweet eyes look up in mine!
> - - - - - - O rare blue eyes!"

The flowers of the blue-eyed grass last but a single day, but there are always new buds opening, so that their blooming season is fairly long. We call it a grass, but, in truth, it is more nearly an iris, as a close examination of the flattened stems and the form of the flowers will clearly indicate. Imagine this plant increased to sufficient size, and it would be a fit companion for the royal Japanese iris that we so much admire.

The botanical name of grass-flower, if literally interpreted means "Idaho hog's snout"! It is, at times, fortunate that we, as a people, are too ignorant—or perhaps too wise—to accept seriously all the outlandish names that dry scientists have seen fit to inflict on our lovely flowers; and that when the common people pluck a blossom, they think in terms of poetry, rather than in musty Latin or Greek.

There are a number of other species of blue-eyed grass common throughout this region, but since all are very similar, a separate description of each would be superfluous.

YELLOW-EYED GRASS ·
Hydastylus borealis Bicknell

Yellow. Stem, slender; margins winged; five to ten inches tall. Leaves, linear; grass-like; much shorter than the stems. Flowers, yellow; small; on slender pedicels from a bracted spathe. Petals, six; narrow. Stamens, three. Filaments, united for about half their length. Anthers, versatile. Habitat, moist fields.

GRASS WIDOWS   *Olsynium grandiflorum*

Very much resembling its common blue-eyed cousin, this bright little flower raises its golden stars among the grasses close along the Pacific Ocean throughout the length of the North Coast States, and on into British Columbia. The foliage, when dried, turns black and leaves a purple stain.

GRASS WIDOWS

Olsynium grandiflorum (Dougl.) Raf.

Reddish purple. Stems, compressed; mostly solitary; four to ten inches tall. Leaves, narrow; linear; grass-like. Flowers, on short, slender pedicels; one and one-half inches across. Perianth, of six equal divisions; ovate; narrowly pointed. Stamens, three; shorter than the style; broadened and united at the base. Stigma, three-cleft. Ovary, three-celled. Habitat, dry open hillsides. Blooming period, May to June.

To the best of my knowledge no popular description of this flower has thus far been published, and I fear I shall not be able to do it justice, for it would take the mind of an artist, and the pen of a poet to picture it fittingly. In line and pose it has the grace of the finest iris, with an added supple daintiness to which no iris can attain. Light and lissom as its near relative, the blue star-grasses, it has added to this the attraction of large showy flowers, and graceful drooping buds. In appearance it is ever fresh and charming, for though its flowers last but a single day, each morning finds new buds unfolding, and raising their bright, unscarred faces to greet the coming sun. This is a rare plant west of the Cascades, and is usually found in dry, well-drained meadows, or rocky hilltops. One of the few places where I have found it abundant is on the brow of a precipitous butte. Here, where all about the abrupt slopes fall away for hundreds of feet, it abounds, and in this breezy eyrie the starry blossoms dance and flutter like purple butterflies. East of the Cascades, where, at Celilo the botanist Douglas discovered it in 1826, it is considered a common flower.

Just why the name "grass widow" should be given to this flower, I can not tell, but by inference it may be supposed to originate in the fact that each stem bears but a single flower at a time—a flower widow, alone but not dejected—a widow who enjoys her single state,

MOUNTAIN LADY SLIPPER

since it gives her the privilege of dancing, and smiling, and winking at every passer by.

ORCHID FAMILY

MOUNTAIN LADY'S SLIPPER
Cypripedium montanum Dougl.

White. Root, perennial; thick; fibrous. Stems, erect; leafy; glandular-pubescent. Leaves, alternate; large; oval; clasping at base; acuminate; many nerved. Flowers, white; large; showy. Petals, three; one a slipper-shaped lip, large and showy, the other two, brown; linear; twisted. Sepals, three; brown; linear; the two beneath the lip united almost to the point. Anthers, yellow; two fertile ones narrow, borne on the sides of the column; one sterile; broad; conspicuous; spotted with red. Habitat, well drained open woods and brush-land. Blooming period, May.

The rare white lady's slipper is the loveliest of all our coast orchids, and attracts attention and comment wherever seen. To know this flower is to love it. Of all our orchids, this most nearly fulfills the tradition of its family, whose name is a synonym for rare and exotic beauty. Some day while walking through open woods or brushland you may find this sly plant, and you will know it at a glance by its white, pouch-like flowers, like dainty Indian moccasins hanging out to dry and whiten in the sunlight. The flowers are of a peculiar construction; the lip, or slipper, is supposed to represent an enlarged and modified petal. This lip is accompanied by a number of slender, curiously twisted brown appendages, that represent other petals and sepals. The flowers are delightfully sweet-scented.

In every language, from Greek to Chinook, the likeness of the flower to a shoe is recognized. *Cypripedium,* the botonical name of the genus means "The shoe of Venus." The Cherokees call the plant "partridge moccasin." Other names by which they are locally known are "Venus' shoe," "Noah's ark," "Whip-poor-Will's shoe," and from the medicinal properties of the root, "nervine," and "nerve-root."

STRIPED CORAL-ROOT   *Corallorhiza striata*

[62]

STRIPED CORAL-ROOT
Corallorhiza striata Lindl.

Red. Root, branching; coral-like. Stems, red; tufted; rather stout; simple; upright; six to twenty inches long. Leaves, reduced to small, scattered, scale-like bracts; red. Inflorescence, a simple, many-flowered raceme. Flowers, on short pedicels, accompanied by narrow bracts. Sepals and petals, conspicuously striped with red. Lip, fleshy; ovate; bearing two short ridges near the base. Habitat, deep coniferous woods. Blooming period, April-May.

The coral-roots belong to a parasitic group of orchids, and cannot maintain life except by drawing nourishment from the roots of other plants, or from freshly decayed organic matter. Because of this mode of life they have lost most of their foliage, for their leaves have become mere sheathing scales, reddish instead of green. The whole plant, too, is of a pale reddish color, suggesting a fungus rather than a flower. The blossoms which grow on clustered spikes are of peculiar form, and are distinctly and evenly striped with red. The striped coral-root is a common plant, but as it grows only in the deep shade of fir woods, it is often overlooked, and is not as well known as it should be. The roots of this plant, which are responsible for the name, are knobby and branched, resembling a piece of branched coral.

SPOTTED CORAL-ROOT
Corallorhiza maculata Raf.

Reddish-purple. In general like *C. striata,* but the flowers not striped, and bear a pointed spur. The flower spur, in this species is wholly attached to the ovary. Lip, broad; three-lobed at base; conspicuously spotted with reddish purple. Habitat, deep woods. Blooming period, April-May.

In general habits, form, and manner of growth, the spotted coral-root closely resembles the preceding species, but the stems and flowers are brownish-purple in color, and the white lip is spotted with purple. Both species bloom in early May, but I usually find this species about a week later than the striped form.

Merten's Coral-Root. *Corallorhiza mertensiana* Bong. Similar to the above, but with the spur free from the ovary for about half its length. In mountain woods; common.

PHANTOM ORCHID   *Cephalanthera austinae*

[64]

PHANTOM ORCHID
Cephalanthera austinae (Gray) Heller

White. Stems, simple; erect; white; ten to twenty inches tall.
Leaves, reduced to small white, sheathing bracts. Inflorescence, a
terminal raceme. Flowers, waxy-white; sometimes with a golden
throat; sweet scented. Sepals and petals, oblong-lanceolate. Lip, short;
saccate at base. Habitat, moist woods. Blooming period, May-June.

The day when this slender, waxy orchid is found may well be
marked with a red letter upon your calendar, for it is one of the
rarest of our flowers, as well as one of the most interesting. In color
the whole plant is a pure waxy white, except that within the throat
of the flower there is a lovely spot of golden yellow. As its manner
of growth and appearance indicate, it is a saprophyte, and its leaves,
reduced to sheathing scales, are entirely lacking in chlorophyl. Pick
it, and you will find that the flowers are delicately and exquisitely
scented—a perfume sweet and rare—unlike that of any other plant
of which I know. If you are fortunate you may find this rare flower
in thick woods from Washington, southward to Central California,
but it is no where abundant. It is truly a phantom, for which you may
seek for years, and then, when least expected it suddenly stands before you in some dim forest aisle, a vision of soft white loveliness,
that once seen can never be forgotten.

DEER-HEAD ORCHID, CALYPSO
Cytherea bulbosa (L.) House

Rose-purple. Bulb, solid; ovate. Stem, simple, bearing sheathing
scales; upper scale extending as a slender bract above and behind the
blossoms. Leaf, one; basal; broadly ovate; appearing in autumn.
Flowers, solitary; sweet-scented. Sepals and petals, erect; lanceolate.
Lip, saccate; slipper-shaped; prolonged below into two spur-like projections; bearded within. Habitat, mossy coniferous woods. Blooming period, April-May.

So lovely is the perfume of this plant that we may imagine that
the botanist who named it was reminded of Shakespeare's lines:

> ". . . Sweeter than the lids of Juno's eyes
> Or Cytherea's breath, . . ."

I shall never forget my first glimpse of this flower. That was

DEER-HEAD ORCHID   *Cytherea bulbosa*

[66]

nearly thirty years ago. At that time I was a newcomer from the East, and the fir woods of Oregon were a revelation to me. Walking through the hills one day in early spring, I came out unexpectedly upon the edge of a cliff, and was startled by the scene before me. Directly below, framed in giant firs and fringed with graceful alders, was a tiny blue pond, and in the distance was a magnificent view of the inhabited, open valley. Then, by chance, my eyes strayed to my feet, and there, all about me I saw a numberless host of tiny, rose-colored, slipper-like blooms, nodding in the breeze. Stooping to pick one of the flowers I was greeted by a fresh, spicy fragrance such as I had not known that any flower possessed. The beauty of the place and the flowers, combined with the element of surprise, and most of all, the new, refreshing scent, made a lasting impression on my mind. Lacking text books, yet eager to name my new find, I showed it to some of my friends, and was informed that it was the "deer-head orchid." That name has been my favorite for the plant ever since. The name lady's slipper so often given to this species does not properly belong to it, but only to members of the genus *Cypripedium,* and the more specific name of "Chinese lady's slipper," sometimes used, seems to me to be an unnatural affectation and, moreover, suggests the untrue idea of an Asiatic origin.

These flowers delight in the full shade of fir woods where they stand embedded, not in soil, but in deep *Hypnum* mosses. Often they will be found growing in close ranks upon the mossy trunks of fallen trees.

HEART-LEAVED TWAYBLADE
Ophrys cordata (L.) R. Br.

Greenish-purple. Stem, slender; simple; erect; three to seven inches tall. Leaves, two; opposite; ovate-cordate; sessile. Inflorescence, a slender, terminal raceme. Flowers, small; inconspicuous. Habitat, moist woods. Blooming period, May-June.

The twayblades are inconspicuous forest plants with small, dull-colored flowers borne in simple, terminal racemes. Each plant has a single pair of broad, opposite leaves, borne below the inflorescence, at about the middle of the stem, and in this species these leaves are heart-shaped, giving to the plant its specific name.

HEART-LEAVED TWAYBLADE　　　　　*Ophrys cordata*

[68]

Northwestern Twayblades: *Ophrys caurina* (Piper) Rydb, is similar to the above, but larger, and with broadly ovate, not heart-shaped leaves. It is found in the mountains, and blooms from May to August, according to the altitude.

WHITE-FLOWERED BOG ORCHID
Limnorchis leucostachys (Lindl.) Rydb.

White. Stem, simple; leafy; erect; from ten to thirty inches tall. Leaves, sessile; clasping; lanceolate; reduced in size towards the summit of the stem. Inflorescence, a rather dense, tapering raceme. Flowers, sweet-scented; white. Perianth divisions, small; spreading. Lip, lanceolate; small. Spur, slender; acute; about one-third of an inch in length. Habitat, in marshes. Blooming period, June-July.

A handsome, tall, leafy-stemmed species, found growing in moist meadows and marshes, especially in the mountains. The plant grows from eighteen to thirty inches tall, and bears a tapering spike of white, sweet-scented flowers. Its range is from Alaska to Northern California.

Slender Bog Orchid. *Limnorchis stricta* (Lindl.) Rydb. A similar species, but with green, or greenish-purple blossoms, and a spur shorter than the lip. Abundant and common in marshes.

ELEGANT PIPERIA
Piperia elegans (Lindl.) Rydb.

White. Bulb, a spherical, solid tuber. Stem, slender; bracted; ten to twenty inches tall. Leaves, two to four; basal; broadly ovate to lanceolate; light green; withering before the flowers appear. Inflorescence, a slender, many-flowered spike. Flowers, white; spurred; sessile. Sepals, lanceolate; acute. Lip, linear; obtuse. Spur, slender. Ovary, twisted, so that the flowers are completely reversed. Habitat, dry open woods. Blooming period, July.

In dry, open woodlands, in early spring, you will often find many oval, light green leaves appearing. These leaves strike the eye as being interesting and full of promise for future bloom. They sit close upon the ground, usually in pairs, but occasionally in whorls of three and four, and to even the most inexperienced eye they proclaim that sooner or later a flower scape will rise from their midst, and you wonder, as you wait, what rare or exquisite form it will take. With

ELEGANT PIPERIA   *Piperia elegans*

the dry days of late June no flowers have appeared, and you are disappointed, for the leaves begin to wither. In July, however, a visit to the spot will reveal many slender spikes of greenish-white flowers, although the leaves have now entirely disappeared. The result of our hopes and waiting is rather disappointing, for the flowers are small and not at all showy, but they are not without their points of interest, for each individual bloom is held on the summit of a short, twisted ovary in such a manner that the flowers are turned completely over, and really stand upside-down.

Alaska Piperia; *Piperia unalaschensis,* is very similar to the above, but smaller and more slender, and the flowers have a shorter spur. Besides these there are several other species of *Piperia,* most of them not common.

RATTLESNAKE PLANTAIN
Peramium decipiens (Hook.) Piper

White. Root, fibrous; fleshy. Scape, upright; slender; bracted. Leaves, basal; ovate-lanceolate; evergreen; dark, often marked and blotched with white. Inflorescence, a spike; erect; bracted; one-sided. Flowers, greenish-white. Sepals, lateral ones, free; upper ones united with the petals into a galea. Habitat, coniferous woods. Blooming period, summer.

The conspicuously marked leaf-rosettes that the rattlesnake plantain exhibits throughout the year are unique and attractive, and more noticeable than are the flowers. They are evergreen, and are veined and blotched with white in a way that suggests the mottlings of a snake. It may be for this reason that they have received their common name, but we are also told that certain Indians believed them to be a specific for snake bite, and this may be the true explanation. This plant is a shy bloomer, and often skips a year or two between flowering periods. The flower scapes are from five to ten inches tall, and the greenish-white flowers are loosely scattered along its length, usually in a rather one-sided manner. This orchid shows a decided preference for coniferous woods. When the soil is well drained, it grows upon the forest floor, but in damp situations it seeks a place in the moss on the tops of stumps, or along the summits of fallen and decaying logs. In such places it often forms large colonies.

RATTLESNAKE PLANTAIN

Peramium decipiens

HOODED LADIES' TRESSES
Ibidium romanzoffianum (Cham.) House

White. Root, clustered; tuberous. Stem, leafy below; bracted above; six to twenty inches tall. Leaves, lanceolate to linear. Inflorescence, a twisted, densely-flowered spike. Flowers, white or yellowish; spurless. Habitat, moist swales and stream banks. Blooming period, Mid-July and August.

Mrs. Dana informs us that this name should be ladies' traces, referring to the lacings of a bodice, but to most of us the bloom more strongly suggests a soft, evenly plaited strand of hair, and the name as it is now popularly used is the more pleasing of the two. How perfectly it fits the flower, with its curving line of bloom rising in a spiral twist. This feature alone is sufficient to identify the plant wherever found. It is the latest of our orchids to bloom, and may be found in moist or marshy places from Mid-July, onward. While not a showy plant it is, nevertheless, very interesting; the flowers provide a veritable circular stairway for the bees, up which they love to climb, sipping sweetness at every step.

"CHATTER-BOX." GIANT HELLEBORINE
Epipactis gigantea. Dougl.

Pinkish-purple. Stems, simple; leafy, six to forty inches tall. Leaves, sessile; clasping; ovate to lanceolate. Inflorescence, a terminal leafy raceme. Flowers, showy; greenish, yellow, and purple. Sepals and petals, similar; all separate. Lip, broad; full; constricted near the middle; upper part dilated and petal-like. Habitat, stream banks. Blooming period, July.

The tall leafy stems of this handsome western orchid are a familiar sight along the borders of our swift mountain streams, often growing in crevices in the rocks at the very edge of the rapids, or forming decorative fringes about stone-bordered pools. They make a charming picture in this environment, and one that every observant trout-fisher must carry with him as a treasured part of his vacation memories. The flowers which strongly suggest those of the lady's slipper are green and purple, touched here and there with yellow or gold. The dilated lip is contracted near the centre, and the lower portion hangs as on a hinge—movable with slight pressure. This feature has given to the flower one of its common names, that of "chatter-box."

HOODED LADIES' TRESSES   *Ibidium romanzoffianum*

"CHATTER-BOX"   *Epipactis gigantea*

NETTLE   *Urtica lyallii*

NETTLE
Urtica lyallii. Wats.

Green. Rootstock, stout; spreading. Stems, angled; erect; simple; three to seven feet tall. Leaves, opposite; petioled; broadly ovate; cordate; coarsely toothed; armed with stinging hairs. Flowers, small; inconspicuous; in drooping axillary racemes or panicles. Habitat, low rich land along streams. Blooming period, May-June.

The old tales, wherein a princess breaks an enchantment that has changed her eleven brothers into swans, by clothing them in garments woven from nettles, is not so preposterous as some people think, at least insofar as the spinning and weaving of nettles is concerned. The retting of nettle stalks and the preparation of nettle fibre is an extremely old industry, and has been carried on in Europe and Asia for many centuries. From some species, cloth equal to the finest linen may be made, and only the ease of culture, and the slightly greater yield of flax, now prevents the nettle from being an important economic product. During the past great war, because of the scarcity of industrial fibres, the German Government revived this industry. At one time women and children were paid as much as four pfenning per kilo,—(two and two-tenths pounds), for wild nettle stalks gathered by them in waste land.

Among the American Indians nettle cord was second only in importance to the *Apocynum* or Indian hemp. The North Pacific Indians have an interesting myth to account for the use of this plant. In the olden times, says this tale, the people were starving, for although the salmon were plentiful in the rivers, the Indians had no means of obtaining them. Spider, seeing their pitiful condition, and wishing to help them, changed himself into a man and married one of their maidens. He it was who directed them in gathering and preparing the nettles, and when the cord was completed he taught them in his own cunning way how to weave it into nets.

Steamed nettle roots are a recognized article of diet among our western tribes. I have, myself, eaten this dish, and while the roots themselves are too tough to be palatable, a milk soup prepared with nettle roots has a delicious flavor. Nettle greens are also a good old-fashioned dish both in this country and in Europe.

MISTLETOE   *Phoradendron villosum*

MISTLETOE
Phoradendron villosum Nutt.

Green. Roots, penetrating the bark and wood of the host. Stems, round; brittle; branching; six to eighteen inches long. Leaves, opposite; thick; oblanceolate or obovate; entire; yellowish-green. Flowers, small; inconspicuous; green. Fruit, a pearly white berry, its flesh sticky-viscid; ripening in early winter. Habitat, a parasite on the branches of oak, or occasionally other trees.

If, as we believed by the ancient Druids, mistletoe which grows on the oak is especially potent in virtue and magic, then the North Pacific States are greatly blessed, for our species chooses the oak alone for its host. At the winter solstice, corresponding to our Christmas season, the ancient inhabitants of England gathered the mistletoe with great ceremony, and used it in their winter rites. From these ancient ceremonies come our present custom of hanging the mistletoe on Christmas eve.

In Norse mythology it is recorded that, to save Balder the Good from harm, Frigga, his mother, the wife of Odin, took an oath from the Sacred Elements—Earth, Air, Fire, and Water—that they would do him no harm; but the mistletoe, thought too weak for consideration, and belonging to the rule of none of those elements, was forgotten, and an arrow made from its stem proved fatal to the beloved hero.

The wax-like berries of the mistletoe are filled with an extremely sticky pulp. Birds are very fond of these fruits, and by their help the seeds are widely scattered. The remnants of the pulp quickly glue the discarded seeds to the limbs of the trees on which they are dropped. When the seeds sprout the sharp radicle soon punctures the inner bark of the limb, and from the rich sap the plant draws all its nourishment. In extreme cases, when a tree is thickly overgrown with mistletoe, the unwilling host is so impoverished that it slowly dies, and with it of course, the mistletoe, a victim of its own greed.

BASTARD TOAD-FLAX   *Comandra umbellata*

SANDALWOOD FAMILY

BASTARD TOAD-FLAX
Comandra umbellata (L.) Nutt.

White or pinkish-purple. Root, perennial; sometimes parasitic. Stems, slender; erect; branched; leafy; woody at base; six to nine inches tall. Leaves, alternate; nearly sessile; oblong to lanceolate; entire; pale green. Inflorescence, cymose terminal or axillary. Flowers, small; perfect. Calyx, campanulate; five-lobed; petal-like; bearing a disk or five-lobed shield within its tube. Corolla, wanting. Stamens, five; alternate with the lobes of the disk on which they are borne, and opposite the lobes of the calyx. Anthers, connected to the face of the calyx lobes by a tuft of fine hairs. Habitat, dry open soil. Blooming period, April-May.

This plant is accounted rare in our territory, but may frequently be found in dry open places and along brushy roadsides where its roots find nutriment by sucking the juices from those of other shrubs. The fruit is a hard, nut-like, globular berry. The range of this plant extends entirely across the continent.

BIRTHWORT FAMILY

WILD GINGER
Asarum candatum Lindl.

Red. Rootstalk, stout; branched; hot-aromatic. Leaves, cordate or reniform; entire; long-petioled; reddish beneath. Flowers, solitary, in the axils of the leaves, often hidden beneath moss or litter. Calyx, dark red; spherical; three lobed; the lobes linear and long attenuate. Stamens, twelve. Styles, short; blunt. Stigmas, twelve; forming a crown-like margin about a central depression. Habitat, moist woods. Blooming period, April to July according to altitude.

Wild ginger is permanently associated in my mind, as it so often is in nature, with vine maple canyons. Leaving the open trail you turn towards the sound of running water. As you advance through the thickening vegetation the light fades until you are in a dim half twilight, and the way becomes more difficult through the tangled, contorted trunks of this dwarf tree. Here is the nearest approach to a jungle that the northern half of the temperate zone affords. You

WESTERN WILD GINGER

struggle, and climb, and crawl, until you are breathless, and almost discouraged of ever extricating yourself. Then, suddenly, you find yourself in a tiny arched glade beside a tumbling brook. Above you the tender young maple leaves spread a wide canopy, and where the sun strikes strongly they shed a translucent green light into the dimness below. Beneath your feet in the thick moss the whole glade is carpeted with the pointed, heart-shaped, aromatic leaves of the wild ginger, each pair of terminal leaves bearing close upon the ground a single, dark red, spider-like flower.

The wild ginger grows close upon the ground, spreading by sprawling rootstocks which usually grow through the leaf-mulch or soft moss surrounding the plant, rather than through the soil. The leaves are firm, shiny green, red beneath, and petioled, and the flowers are not raised above the ground, but rather, are often completely covered by leaves or other litter. The flowers have no petals, and the three lobes of the dark red calyx are long and tapering. The whole plant, stem, roots, and leaves, is permeated with a warm, pleasant, ginger-like flavor. The volatile oil found in the plant is said to be used in the manufacture of perfume.

BUCKWHEAT FAMILY

SULPHUR FLOWER
Eriogonum umbellatum Torr.

Yellow. Stems, woody; branched; five to eight inches tall. Leaves, spatulate; green above, woolly-white beneath. Inflorescence, a simple umbel, accompanied by an involucre of leafy bracts. Calyx, six-parted, tapering to a slender stipe-like base. Habitat, rocky soil at high altitudes. Blooming period, July-August.

On high exposed peaks where the trees, from the fury of the storms take on one-sided, contorted forms, you will find the hardy little sulphur flowers. They grow in crevices in the rocks, or in niches in the cliffs, where it does not seem possible that any living thing could find sustenance, and make a brave showing with their tufted mats of spatulate leaves, and close umbels of bright yellow flowers. Many species of *Eriogonums* have these qualities of hardiness and endurance, and seem deliberately to choose for their home spots where few other plants could exist.

In this species the stems are woody, and the leaves are mostly basal, or, if borne on the stems, spread over the rocks, and seldom rise to any height. From the low trailing branches the slender flower scapes rise to a height of from five to eight inches, entirely naked except for a whorl of leaf-like bracts at the base of the umbel. The flowers consist of a single floral envelope, the petals being entirely wanting, and the sepals colored and petal-like. In color they are from light to bright sulphur-yellow, but are sometimes flecked or tinged with bright red. Because of the altitude at which these plants grow, their blooming season is confined to July and August, for up to that time they are usually covered with snow.

Eriogonum nudum Dougl.

White. Stem, slender; upright; ten to twenty inches tall. Leaves, basal; ovate; obtuse; petioled. Habitat, dry gravelly soil. Blooming period, June.

This species of *Eriogonum* is found from Washington to California, rare in our territory, but more common east and south. The leaves are all basal, oval or oblong in form, and finely hairy beneath. The stems are slender and branching, and are naked except for obscure papery sheathes at the joints. From six to twenty flowers form head-like clusters at the summit of these naked scapes. They are without petals, but the calyx is six-cleft, and white or pinkish, becoming rather dry and papery with age. These curious plants choose the most arid soil for their homes, or, as though that were not enough, may frequently be found growing on the tops of hot bare rocks, exposed to the full force of the summer sun.

MOUNTAIN DOCK
Polygonum bistortoides Pursh.

White. Tubers, thick; fleshy. Stems, slender; upright; simple; ten to thirty inches tall. Leaves, root leaves oblong; acute; petioled; stem leaves few; sessile; much reduced; lanceolate. Inflorescence, a dense, oblong spike. Calyx, white; five-cleft. Petals, none. Seeds, three-angled; smooth; brown. Habitat, moist mountain meadows, or, occasionally, at lower altitudes. Blooming period, July-August.

The stems of the mountain dock are slender and almost grass-like, and the fact that they grow among tall grasses in wet, alpine meadows helps to fix this impression. It is, however, a member of the buckwheat family, and an examination of the base of the plant will reveal its few, narrow, dock-like leaves. The flowers are small, and white or pinkish, and are borne in short, stout spikes at the summit of the stems. The root is a thick, oblong tuber, reported by travelers to be roasted for food both by the Eskimos and Indians of Alaska, but I have found it to be extremely bitter and astringent, and in Henry's Medical Herbal (1814) it is listed as "The strongest vegetable astringent known."

FOUR O'CLOCK FAMILY

YELLOW SAND VERBENA
Abronia latifolia Esch.

Yellow. Root, large; stout; fleshy. Stems, stout; prostrate; sticky. Leaves, thick; opposite; entire; ovate. Inflorescence, a compact umbel, surrounded by an involucre of five bracts. Involucre bracts, ovate. Flowers, sessile. Perianth, salver-shaped. Stamens, three to five. Style, filiform. Habitat, sandy seashores. Blooming period, from May onward.

The yellow sand verbena spreads its prostrate, rubbery stems and fleshy leaves over the sands on ocean beaches, and, by its sticky, viscid secretion, collects to itself enough sand to nearly double its weight, a protection, perhaps, against violent winds that might uproot and tear to pieces a lighter plant. The flowers are sweet-scented, yellow, and borne in attractive verbena-like umbels. The very large roots were an article of food among the coast Indians.

PINK SAND VERBENA
Abronia acutalata Standley

Pink. Stems, prostrate; slender. Leaves, opposite; oblong to ovate; obtuse; entire. Inflorescence, umbellate. Involucre bracts, lanceolate. Flowers, salver-shaped; fragrant. Habitat, seashores.

The pink sand verbena has slender stems, oblong or ovate leaves, and deep rose-pink flowers. It is found along the sea shore from Vancouver Island, southward.

RED MAIDS

PURSLANE FAMILY

RED MAIDS, WILD PORTULACA
Calandrinia caulescens HBK.

Rose-colored. Root, a slender tap root; annual. Stems, branching from the base; succulent; decumbent; three to seven inches long. Leaves, oblanceolate; simple; entire. Flowers, about two-thirds of an inch across; singly or in short racemes; a few only opening at one time in bright sunshine. Sepals, two; green; acute; keeled. Petals, five; obovate. Style, three-cleft. Fruit, a dry, many-seeded capsule. Habitat, dry fields. Blooming period, April to July.

The succulent green leaves and stems of the red maids make pretty, spreading mats in dry fields from April to late June, and on bright sunny days, burst unexpectedly into rose-colored velvety bloom. This plant is a close relative of our showy garden portulaca, and both in manner of growth, and in bloom, shows its truly family character. The flowers are about one-third of an inch across, and are very short-lived, lasting only for a day. Like so many of its family, this plant is a source of human food, for the leaves and stems are edible and make excellent greens. The shining black seeds, also, although very minute, have not been overlooked by the Indians as a food supply, and according to Mr. Chestnut, they are sometimes gathered in large quantities.

BITTER-ROOT
Lewisia columbiana (Howell) Robinson

Rose-red. Root, fleshy; branched. Leaves, oblanceolate to spatulate; fleshy. Scape, three to ten inches tall. Inflorescence, a many-flowered panicle. Sepals, nearly orbicular, with minute, gland-tipped teeth. Petals, numerous; rose-red. Stamens, numerous.

The Lewisia, rock-rose, or bitter-root, is a lovely plant of low growth, with showy, cactus-like flowers, and narrow, fleshy leaves. Its petals are often pleasingly marked with a darker line down the mid-rib. Discovered by the botanist Howell in the Columbia River Gap, the plant is also abundant in the Olympic Mountains, and about many of the higher peaks of the Cascades.

Its near relative, *Lewisia rediviva,* common east of the Cascades, is the state flower of Montana, and after it the Bitter Root Valley and

MINER'S LETTUCE

Claytonia perfoliata

Mountains of the state were named. Its roots, called by the Indians *spatlum,* have considerable food value, and were much used by the early explorers and traders, as well as by the natives.

MINER'S LETTUCE
Claytonia perfoliata Donn.

White. Stems, branching from the base. Branches, simple; upright; succulent; five to eighteen inches tall. Leaves, succulent; basal leaves, long petioled; ovate to spatulate; stem leaves, a pair; united to form a saucer-shaped disk near the summit of the stem. Inflorescence, a loose, slender raceme from the centre of the perfoliate leaves. Flowers, small; white. Sepals, two. Petals, five; minute. Habitat, moist open woods and fields. Blooming period, April to June.

This plant has been a favorite salad among the inhabitants of the Pacific Coast since prehistoric times, and from this use its various names of Indian lettuce, Spanish lettuce, and miner's lettuce may be readily understood. Among the gold miners of '49 it was particularly valued. In the wild rush for wealth they were too occupied to plant gardens, yet they needed, and craved fresh vegetables, and in their dried and salted rations there was the constant menace of scurvy. Seeing the Indians gather the wild lettuce, they quickly adopted it to their needs in many a savory dish of "greens and bacon."

Stephen Powers, in his "Tribes of California," reports the following, concerning its use among the Indians: "Of the wild lettuce a curious fact is noted. The Indians living in the mountains gather it and lay it in quantities near the nests of certain large red ants, which have the habit of building conical heaps over their holes. After the ants have circulated all through it, they take it up, and shake them off, and eat it with relish. They say the ants, in running over it, impart a sour taste to it, and make it as good as if it had vinegar on it." No doubt formic acid, used in this way, is just as wholesome, and quite as palatable as our more usual acetic acid.

In England, where it has been grown for over a century, the plant is known as winter purslane.

This species may be easily recognized by its two upper leaves, which unite to form a shield-like disk at the summit of the stem. From the center of this disk rises a loose, somewhat one-sided raceme of minute white flowers.

INDIAN PINK

Claytonia parviflora Dougl., is a similar species, distinguished from the above by its shorter calyx, longer petals, and smaller seeds— about one half the size of those of *C. perfoliata*.

SIBERIAN MINER'S LETTUCE
Claytonia sibirica L.

White or pink. Root, fibrous. Stem, branching from base; erect; succulent; five to twelve inches tall. Leaves, basal, ovate; contracted at base into long petioles; stem leaves, a pair; opposite; sessile or united at the base. Inflorescence, a loose, bracted raceme. Flowers, on long pedicels. Sepals, two. Petals, five; square-oblong; notched or toothed at the apex. Habitat, open moist woods. Blooming period, March to June.

This pretty little plant was first discovered in Siberia, but it is also very abundant along the American coast line from Alaska to California. As a salad plant it should be more generally known than it is, for its great abundance, and the earliness of its appearance make it exceptionally desirable. The basal leaves are ovate or spatulate, contracted below into a long tapering petiole; the cauline leaves are opposite, and broadly oval, but not united into a disk as in the previous species. The blossoms, though small, are showy, white or pink, five oblong petals, each terminating at the summit in an abrupt notch. The whole plant, leaves, stems, and flowers, is very tender and succulent, and make the finest of early spring greens. Look for it in moderately deep shade, especially in rich, mellow loan along stream banks, where it often covers large areas. The flowers usually begin to appear in March.

PINK FAMILY

INDIAN PINK
Silene hookeri Nutt.

Pink. Root, perennial; stout. Stem, branched; leafy; four to ten inches tall. Leaves, oblanceolate; acute; pubescent with grayish white, soft hairs. Flowers, showy; large; erect; borne in the forks of the branches. Calyx, tubular; five-toothed. Petals, four-lobed; appendaged in the throat; long-clawed. Stamens, ten. Habitat, dry prairies and hillsides. Blooming period, May-June.

FIELD CHICKWEED   *Cerastium arvense*

This is the most showy of our wild pinks, having large, handsome blossoms an inch or two across, and soft, grayish-white foliage.

The name pink, does not come from the color of the flower, as most people no doubt suppose, but from the cut and scalloped margins of its petals. To pink, in early English, was to cut, slash, or scallop. Notice the shape of the petals; a pinking iron, such as our grandmothers employed to make ornamental edgings on leather or felt might have been used to shape them. The flowers of this plant are a soft, pleasing pink color, but the color receives its name from the form of the flower, not the flower from the color.

SCOULER'S CATCHFLY
Silene scouleri Hook.

Pink or white. Stems, upright; simple; viscid; ten to twenty inches tall. Leaves, opposite; sessile; lanceolate. Flowers, short pediceled; in the axils of the upper leaves. Calyx, cylindrical; ten-nerved; five toothed. Petals, long-clawed; two-lobed at summit, the lobes toothed; appendaged in the throat. Habitat, prairies. Blooming period, June.

This small member of the pink family secretes an exceedingly sticky substance that thoroughly covers both leaves and stems. In this insects often become entangled, thus earning for the plant the name of catchfly. This secretion is supposed to protect the nectar and pollen of the flowers from undesirable crawlers, and preserve it for the flying bees and moths that are able to fertilize them. Because of the sticky secretion the plant is sometimes called tar-weed.

MOSS CAMPION. CARPET PINK
Silene acaulis L.

Rose-purple. Root, a large, tapering tap-root. Leaves, numerous; crowded; linear; very short. Flowers, solitary; small; sessile or nearly so. Calyx, campanulate; five-lobed, the lobes obtuse. Petals, five; notched or cleft. Stamens, ten. Habitat, rocky places in the mountains above timber-line.

This stemless, or nearly stemless little member of the pink family forms densely-tufted, flower-covered mats at high elevations in the mountains. As the snow melts away with the advancing summer, close

YELLOW POND-LILY   *Nymphaea polysepala*

behind the receding banks they burst into bloom at higher and higher elevations. One of the hardiest of our hardy mountain dwellers, they are at home and content in a region where the uncertain summer gives them but a few weeks of growing weather; then all is again covered with snow for the remaining nine or ten months of the year.

FIELD CHICKWEED
Cerastium arvense L.

White. Stems, tufted; erect; slender; pubescent; six to eighteen inches tall; nearly leafless above. Leaves, sessile; clasping; linear. Flowers, cymose, in slender pedicels. Sepals, five; oblong; acute. Petals, five; white; deeply notched. Stamens, ten. Styles, five. Habitat, dry open ground. Blooming season, April to June.

The flowers of the field chickweed are prettily star-like in form, since each of the five petals is deeply and noticeably two-cleft. The plant itself reaches a height of from six to eighteen inches, and the flowers are about one half inch in diameter. What they lack in size, however, they make up in numbers for on dry hillsides whole landscapes are at times made white with their bloom.

WATERLILY FAMILY

YELLOW POND-LILY. WOKAS
Nymphaea polysepala (Engelm.) Greene

Yellow. Rootstock, very large; scaly; growing in mud at the bottom of ponds. Leaves, very large; round-oval or heart-shaped; floating on the surface of the water, or held erect above it. Flowers, yellow; globular; fleshy; solitary on long peduncles, at, or above, the surface of the water. Sepals, petal-like; five to many. Petals, many; small; yellow; stamen-like. Stamens, numerous; yellow. Pistil, large; stout. Stigma, marked on the broad upper surface with radiating lines. Habitat, lakes and marshes. Blooming period, May to August.

Our common yellow pond lily is an abundant native in most of the region west of the Rocky Mountains. It is a water lover, thriving best in small lakes and warm, stagnant ponds, where its dark leaves, a foot or more long, float on the surface of the water, or are raised above it on stout flexible stems. The flowers which are bright yellow, sometimes tinged red, usually just reach the surface.

WILD CLEMATIS   *Clematis ligusticifolia*

Wokas, or wokash, is the Indian name of the plant, and is a potent word with which to conjure up scenes of primitive life and industry. "In the thumb month," (July and August), "for Klamath Marsh they will start to gather lily seed. Now has ripened wokash; they gather it for five days. During six days the wokash they grind, cook, rub fine, winnow, make flour. Women only gather wokash, the men hunt mule-deer, antelope. Now they haul home the crushed lily seed." Thus Mr. Gatschet quotes "Klamath Pete," in his native dialect.

Among the Klamaths and to a less extent among other tribes, the ripening of the wokas was the sign for their greatest annual food harvest. The whole tribe would move to the marshes where ceremonial dances were held. During this time the shamen, or medicine men were watching the lily patches, and not until they signified that the seed was ripe and ready to gather, would the dances end and the harvest begin. The Klamath Marsh lily fields contained at least ten thousand acres of wokas. Dr. Newberry, in 1854, reported seeing many hundreds of bushels of wokas pods stored about the marshes, in sule sacks of native workmanship.

BUTTERCUP FAMILY

WILD CLEMATIS. VIRGIN'S BOWER
Clematis ligusticifolia Nutt.

White. Stems, slender; branched; climbing; ten to forty feet long. Leaves, opposite; petioled; pinnately compound, of from five to seven leaflets. Leaflets, ovate; coarsely lobed and toothed. Inflorescence, a loose panicle. Flowers, dioecious. Sepals, white; petal-like; four. Petals, none. Stamens, numerous, their styles becoming long feathery plumes in seed. Habitat, low rich soil along streams. Blooming period, June-July.

To appreciate this plant you must see it at its best in its natural environment, trailing its graceful loops and festoons over the brush, and among the boughs of trees in a sunny bend of some placid valley stream. In such a situation, where russet-backed thrushes love to lurk; where wood pewees call all day long, and the loudest sound to be heard is the rattling challenge of the kingfisher; where cattle stand in contentment, knee-deep in the placid waters beneath the swaying

THREE-LEAVED ANEMONE   *Anemone deltoidea*

[98]

vines; the wild clematis makes a bower fit for any virgin's hopeful dreams. It is, indeed, a beautiful vine; white in June with clusters of star-like flowers; whiter still in August with great plumy masses of silk-winged seeds. It grows from twenty to forty feet in length, and climbs by means of its angled, clasping, leaf-stalks. Often it grows on land that is overflowed in winter, and when, by this means, a vine trailing along the ground, or torn from its support by the rising waters, becomes buried in light soil, it takes root along its entire length, producing new vines at every joint. In this way it propagates rapidly, sometimes covering large areas.

THREE-LEAVED ANEMONE
Anemone deltoidea Hook.

White. Stems, upright; simple; six to fifteen inches tall. Leaves, stem leaves, three; simple; ovate; dentate; in a whorl about the upper portion of the stem. Flowers, solitary; large. Sepals, white; deciduous; soon falling. Petals, none. Stamens, numerous. Pistils, numerous; not woolly. Habitat, moist woods. Blooming period, April-May.

The anemones are slender, delicate plants, named after the Greek God of the Winds, perhaps because they bow before the gentlest breezes. If, as some say, their God sends the zephyr to open their flowers, we also know that at times he is a hard master, for on stormy days the delicate flowers are rushlessly torn apart and scattered far and wide. Before such rude assaults—

"There shiver, in rose-tinted white, the pale anemones."

The three-leaved anemone is one of the sturdiest of its kind, and grows to a height of from seven to fifteen inches. Each plant bears somewhat above the centre of the stem, a whorl of three, broad, sessile leaves, and at the summit a single delicate white flower. These flowers are about the size and shape of thimble-berry blooms. I make this comparison because I first found them blossoming at the foot of thimble-berry bushes, and was much impressed by the resemblance. Their blooming season is from early April, in the valleys, to late July in high mountains.

BLUE ANEMONE

BLUE ANEMONE
Anemone oregana Gray

Blue. Rootstocks, white; slender; deep-seated. Stem, simple; upright; very slender; three to seven inches tall. Leaves, three; whorled; compound. Leaflets, three to five; oblong to ovate; toothed. Flowers, solitary; small. Sepals, blue; petal-like; soon falling. Petals, none. Habitat, moist open woods. Blooming period, April-May.

The blue or Oregon anemone has three petioled leaves, divided into from three to five toothed leaflets, and a single fragile blue flower. It is a slender plant, from four to eight inches tall, and is found in moist woods. This species is not very common in our territory, but is abundant east of the mountains.

Wood Anemone, *Anemone piperi* Brit., much resembles the above, but is smaller and more slender; the flowers are white.

WESTERN ANEMONE
Pulsatilla occidentalis (Wats.) Freyn.

Purplish. Rootstock, thick. Stem, hairy; ten to twenty inches high. Leaves, basal leaves, petioled; palmately divided into many narrow divisions; stem leaves, three; also finely divided. Flowers, solitary. Sepals, purplish. Petals, none. Stamens, numerous; with plume-like persistent styles, very handsome in seed. Habitat, mountain meadows.

The beautiful western anemone or pasque flower is a plant of high mountain meadows. It has finely divided leaves, and mauve or purplish flowers, large and showy. After the flowers have fallen the persistent styles develop into silky, oval plumes, that are very curious and interesting.

MEADOW RUE
Thalictrum occidentale Gray

Green and brown. Stems, leafy; erect; fifteen to twenty inches tall. Leaves, long petioled; ternately decompound; large. Leaflets, ovate to orbicular; dentate at apex; smooth. Inflorescence, a loose panicle. Flowers, dioecious. Sepals, green. Petals, none. Stamens, many; drooping. Filaments, very slender; thread-like. Anthers, brown; linear. Styles, slender; purple. Akenes, clustered. Habitat, moist open woods. Blooming period, April-May.

Although not a showy plant the meadow rue makes up for this lack by its sheer grace and delicacy. The whole plant is a soft harmony of fresh greens, browns, and purples. The leaves are thrice compound and finely divided, seen at first as tightly folded rosettes, but later unfolding and expanding until the whole plant is enveloped in broad, airy foliage, as delicate and graceful as the maiden-hair fern. The blossoms are of two kinds, and grow on separate plants. The pistillate flowers are light purple in color, and consist chiefly of an upright clustered group of akens, each with a slender, purple style. The staminate flowers, on the other hand, are drooping; each consisting of four green, spreading sepals below which numerous brown anthers are suspended on delicate hair-like filaments. The entire effect is that of a plant decked with silken brown tassels. This plant is common from British Columbia to California, and will be found on moist, shady stream banks, especially in the mountains.

Tall Meadow Rue. *Thalictrum polycarpum* Wats. This large handsome plant reaches a height of from three to eight feet, and is much stouter and larger in every way than the preceding species. Its leaves are short-petioled, or the upper ones sessile, and the plant is smooth and hairless throughout. It will be found in moist swales and wet prairies.

FALSE BUGBANE
Trautvetteria grandis Nutt.

White. Stems, erect; ten to thirty inches. Leaves, radical, long petioled; deeply cleft into five to nine palmate segments. Segments, oblong; lobed and toothed. Cauline leaves, few; mostly sessile. Inflorescence, a corymb. Flowers, small; numerous. Sepals, mostly four; small; petal-like. Petals, none. Stamens, many; white. Pistils, many. Habitat, moist mountain meadows.

Like the true bugbane, and the baneberry, whose descriptions are given later, the flowers of the *Trautvetteria* owe their beauty, not to large showy petals, for they have none, but to their numerous white stamens. No confusion need result, however, between these plants, for while the leaves of the bugbane and baneberry are noticeably compound, this plant has simple, broad, deep-cleft, maple-like foliage. A tall handsome plant, growing to a height of nearly three feet, it will be found in rich mountain meadows and along stream banks.

WATER CROWFOOT
Batrachium aquatile (L.) Wimm

White. Stems, immersed; very slender. Leaves, floating leaves reniform-orbicular; deeply lobed; small. Immersed leaves minutely dissected; flaccid. Flowers, white; minute; solitary; floating. Habitat, pools and sluggish ditches. Blooming period, April.

Often in early spring you find pools or slow-flowing roadside ditches literally covered with minute, yellow-centred, white flowers, and tiny floating, roundish and lobed leaves. This plant is the water crowfoot. The whole effect, in miniature, is that of a lake covered with white waterlilies. So perfect is the mimicry of this fairy lake that it seems we only lack the gift of second sight to discern elfin boats gliding across the waters, or snowy swans preening themselves among the shallows. To know that the water beneath these plants teem with tiny fish, helps to complete the illusion, for it is in just such pools as these that the tiny, nest building stickleback makes his home.

If we examine closely, we find that the plants have, besides the orbicular, floating leaves, an abundance of a different form—narrow, and finely dissected—submerged below the surface of the water. If taken from its native element the whole plant collapses into a slimy, unattractive mass, impossible to arrange in any pleasing form.

WESTERN BUTTERCUP
Ranunculus occidentalis Nutt.

Yellow. Stems, slender; seven to fourteen inches tall. Leaves, basal leaves orbicular; cordate; deeply cleft or parted, the several parts acutely lobed. Stem leaves divided into entire, linear segments. Flowers, golden-yellow. Sepals, five; reflexed. Petals, twice as long as the sepals. Stamens, numerous; yellow. Pistils, numerous. Fruit, a cluster of dry akenes. Akenes, armed with a strong hook. Habitat, open fields and hillsides. Blooming period, March to June.

From the middle of March, onward, until warm weather is well established, our fields and meadows are starred and sprinkled with this, our commonest buttercup. No fairy gold could be brighter than the burnished petals of this plant, and from coast to mountains it spreads its blooms everywhere with a lavish hand. While preferring

WESTERN BUTTERCUP

moist soil, this species does not restrict itself entirely to such situations, but blooms as well on dry hillsides and upland meadows. I
have seen whole valleys and their surrounding slopes literally gilded
with its blossoms. A few years ago while tramping through the hills
I emerged upon the edge of such a valley which shone forth as a
veritable "Field of the cloth of gold." Acre on acre of lowland spread
away, a solidly massed carpet of yellow buttercups—and to make the
scene unique, down the centre of the valley, where the soil was
wettest, flowed a perfect river of the blue of camas blossoms, winding
and curving across the plains. The whole gold and blue picture was
so bright as to be visible for miles from the surrounding mountains.

The leaves of the western buttercup are prettily veined and lobed,
and usually appear in January. The ripened akens are armed with a
stout hook which at times makes them rather unpleasantly prominent
by clinging to woolen garments.

BIRD'S-FOOT BUTTERCUP
Ranunculus orthorhynchus Hook.

Yellow. Stems, erect or spreading; sparingly leaved above; branching; ten to twenty inches tall. Branches, hollow; somewhat fleshy.
Leaves, petioled; pinnately divided into narrow, linear segments. Inflorescence, axillary or terminal. Flowers, yellow. Sepals, yellow; reflexed; ovate; acute. Petals, five; burnished; often marked on the
outside with reddish orange. Stamens and pistils, many. Habitat, wet
open places. Blooming period, April-May.

The bird's-foot buttercup will be found blooming in early April,
and loves a soil that is well saturated, though not flooded with water.
The leaves, which give the plant its name, are finely cleft and divided, the lower ones with long clasping petioles, the upper smaller and
nearly sessile. The flowers are borne on long, slender stems, and
usually consist of five strongly reflected sepals, and five to many shiny,
golden petals. The tendency to multiply petals is very marked in this
species, and some flowers are decidedly double. Many plants also have
their petals strongly tinted with orange-red on the outside.

TALL LARKSPUR   *Delphinium trolliifolium*

[106]

SWAMP BUTTERCUP
Ranunculus alismaefolius Geyer

Yellow. Stems smooth; stout; erect. Leaves, radical, long, petioled; cauline mostly sessile. Sepals, small; five; yellow. Petals, thick; five or more. Habitat, shallow water in swales and ditches. Blooming period, April-May.

This is a stout, erect plant, found growing in swampy fields and roadside ditches, where its roots are covered with water. It has hollow, succulent stems, and grows to a height of from one to three feet. The light green leaves are tapering and lanceolate, and from three to eight inches in length. The flowers are yellow, and an inch or more across, and are of firm, slightly fleshy texture. They bring to my mind a suggestion of the well-loved marsh-marigold of the eastern states.

TALL LARKSPUR
Delphinium trolliifolium Gray

Blue. Root, perennial; elongated; fascicled. Stems, stout; erect; hollow; three to seven feet tall. Leaves, light green; thin; orbicular; palmately cleft and lobed. Inflorescence, a loose, terminal raceme. Sepals, blue; the lateral ones long spurred. Petals, four; two spurred; two very small. Stamens, numerous. Habitat, moist woods and stream banks. Blooming period, May-June.

It is unfortunate that this beautiful plant should be such a menace to livestock, for our pleasure in its beauty is marred by the thought of the destruction that it works among the cattle ranging in the forest. While gathering the flowers to illustrate this volume, I was struck by the sheer loveliness of its handsome broad leaves, and graceful blue spires, but even as I reached to pick them I stumbled over the whitened, bleaching bones of a cow, no doubt killed by the plant's poison. There is no rational excuse, however, for the fear of touching or picking the plant, which some persons seem to have. Judging from the amount required to kill cattle, it would be necessary for a person to eat two or three pounds of the leaves to produce serious results, an amount that no sane person would think of consuming. There is, therefore, no reason save the thought of the unfortunate cattle, to prevent our enjoying its beauty, gathering it, or even growing it in our gardens. Indeed, there is no evidence to make us think that the

LOW LARKSPUR

Delphinium menziesii

many beautiful cultivated *Delphiniums* are less poisonous than this.

The tall larkspur is most often found in shady spots, along streams, or in moist woods. It grows from three to seven feet tall, its leaves are round, broad, and handsomely cut and slashed; the stems are hollow, and the whole plant, especially in early spring, is lush and succulent.

Medicinally and otherwise the species of larkspurs have been put to various uses. An extract of the plant may be used as a substitute for the drug, aconite. The powdered seeds have, since ancient times, been sprinkled on the head to free the hair from lice. In Australia the leaves and stems are sometimes placed about gardens to poison the swarms of locust which would otherwise consume the growing vegetables.

Glaucous Larkspur; *Delphinium glaucum* Wats. This plant differs from the above by having paler blue flowers, short pedicles, (shorter than the flowers,) and glaucous stems and leaves.

LOW LARKSPUR
Delphinium menziesii DC.

Dark blue. Roots, tuberous. Stems, slender; erect; branching; ten to thirty inches. Leaves, dark green; palmately parted; the divisions deeply lobed and cleft. Inflorescence, a raceme. Flowers, pediceled; dark blue; spurred. Sepals, five; blue; petal-like; the upper one forming a slender spur. Petals, four; two-spurred. Stamens, many. Follicles, three. Habitat, open fields. Blooming period, May-June.

The low larkspur, unlike its taller relative, prefers dry open country and full sunshine. It may most often be found on sunny hillsides, or about the borders of dry fields.

West of the Cascade Mountains the tall larkspur is the most serious menace to livestock. Owing to local conditions the low species, though equally poisonous, does comparatively little damage. East of the mountains, on the other hand, the low larkspur is the most troublesome plant, and "riding for poison," that is, herding stock away from badly infested areas, is often part of the ranchman's spring routine.

Delphinium menziesii ochroleucum T. & G., is a handsome white or cream-colored variety of the above species, local in the Willamette

COLUMBINE   *Aquilegia formosa*

Valley. I have found it especially plentiful about the town of Philo-math, Oregon. In everything save the color of the flower it is almost identical with the blue form.

COLUMBINE
Aquilegia formosa Fisch.

Red. Stems, erect; branching; one to three feet tall. Leaves, ter-nately compound; green above, lighter beneath. Leaflets, cuneate; lobed. Flowers, drooping. Sepals, five; petal-like. Petals, five; with open, yellow throat, the limbs extending backward in long, slender, scarlet spurs, tipped at the summit with a blunt honey-gland. Sta-mens, numerous; exserted. Pistils, five. Habitat, fields and copses. Blooming period, from April in the valleys to August in high moun-tains.

The scarlet trumpets of the wild columbine provide a welcome feast for the hummingbirds and long-tongued butterfles, who, alone can gather the deep-hidden sweets. Children and bumblebees, how-ever, defeat the flower's purpose by biting open the swelled honey-gland from above, thus stealing the abundant nectar. No plant sur-passes this in its airy grace of flower and leaf. The name columbine refers to a dove, and points to a fancied resemblance between the spurred flower and four doves about a shallow dish. Jean Ingelow, with her usual airy touch has thus expressed the thought—

> "O Columbine, open your folded wrapper,
> Where two twin turtle-doves dwell."

Mr. Gibbs, an explorer of 1853, tells us that the roots of the columbine are edible, and were eaten by the Indians; however, it be-longs to a rather dangerous order, and any experiment along this line should be made with extreme caution.

Yellow Columbine, *Aquilegia flavescens* Wats., is a rare mountain species having its flowers wholly yellow.

WILD PEONY
Paeonia brownii Dougl.

Dark red. Root, perennial; woody. Stem, upright; branched; smooth; eight to fourteen inches long. Leaves, smooth; ternately or

palmately compound. Flowers, solitary; nodding; one to two inches across; dark red or purplish. Sepals, green. Petals, five or more; thick; leathery. Stamens, numerous. Habitat, high mountains.

It has never been my good fortune to find this plant, but luckily we may describe it in the words of David Douglas, its discoverer, who first saw it at a high altitude in the Blue Mountains of Oregon. "That which gratified me most," he writes, "was a beautiful *Paeonia,* with a flower that is dark purple outside, and yellow within, blooming on the very confines of perpetual snow, while it grows poor and small on the temperate parts of the mountains, and wholly disappears on the plains below."

Of this plant Mr. J. S. Newberry, also writes: "The flowers of this plant are erect, but when the seed is nearly ripe the stocks which support the carpels curve downward and outward until the carpels themselves rest on the ground accurately inverted.—Near the base of Mt. Jefferson, Oregon, at an altitude of five thousand feet, I found large surfaces covered with this plant which had already been touched with frost. Of the hundreds of clustered pods, all were inverted and resting on the ground, completely covering the seeds."

MARSH MARIGOLD
Caltha asarifolia DC.

Yellow. Stems, decumbent; rooting at the nodes; smooth; succulent; leafy. Leaves, reniform. Flowers, few; yellow. Sepals, six to eight; petal-like. Petals, none. Stamens, numerous; Pistils, several. Habitat, marshes and bogs near the coast.

Those who have known the glowing golden flowers and lush foliage of the eastern marsh marigold will be delighted to learn that in our coastal marshes it is represented by a similar species. The stems of this plant are decumbent, and the flowers rather few.

Caltha biflora DC. and *Caltha leptosepala* DC.; white marsh marigolds, are two rather small, white flowered species found in wet meadows in the mountains.

BANEBERRY
Actaea spicata arguta (Nutt.) Torr.

White. Stems, simple; slender; erect; one to three feet tall. Leaves, ternately compound. Leaflets, ovate; coarsely toothed. Inflorescence,

BUGBANE   *Cimicifuga elata*

a short, ovate raceme; dense. Flowers, small; white. Sepals, small; petal-like. Petals, small. Stamens, numerous; white. Fruit, a bright scarlet (sometimes white) berry. Habitat, moist copses. Blooming season, April-May.

A common, abundant plant in bushy thickets and along roadside copses, especially in the low mountainous regions of Western Oregon and Washington. In form and manner of growth it bears a marked resemblance to the more strikingly handsome bugbane, but the plants are much smaller and less branched, seldom exceeding a height of two feet. The flowers are borne in smallish round-topped clusters. Late in July and August the plants are most noticeable, for at that time they ripen their shiny scarlet berries, giving a touch of brilliant color to our roadside. The berries are undoubtedly poisonous, but not, as some fear, extremely so, and in nowise dangerous to touch or handle.

BUGBANE
Cimicifuga elata Nutt.

White. Stems, erect; three to six feet. Leaves, large; ternately compound. Inflorescence, a slender, tapering raceme. Flowers, white; small. Sepals, small; falling as soon as the flowers open. Petals, one to eight; sometimes none; small; clawed. Stamens, white; numerous. Habitat, moist open woods and copses. Blooming period, May to July.

Counted a rare species on the Pacific Coast, there are, nevertheless, rich shady woods within our borders where these handsome plants comprise a major part of the undergrowth. The almost shrubby stems grow to a height of from three to six feet, broadly forked, and clothed with extremely large, handsome, ternately compound leaves. The ultimate divisions of the leaves are maple-like, dark green, broad, and strikingly veined. In late May or June each plant puts forth shapely, tapering spires of fluffy white bloom that seem in every way appropriate to this noble plant, and lend a grace and beauty that is seldom equalled. The beauty of the flowers is due to their numerous spreading stamens, for the sepals fall as soon as the blossoms open, and the petals are minute.

The roots of the closely allied bugbane of the East, *C. racemosa,* are an article of commerce, recognized according to the U. S. Dis-

OREGON GRAPE   *Berberis aquifolium*

pensatory as a remedy for hysteria, rheumatism, and dropsy, and there is every reason to think that our western plants have like qualities, and are of equal value.

BARBERRY FAMILY

OREGON GRAPE

Berberis aquifolium Pursh

Yellow. Root, woody; yellow. Stem, erect; shrubby; two to ten feet tall. Wood, yellow. Leaves, pinnate; alternate; stiff; evergreen; shiny. Leaflets, five to nine; dentate; the margins undulate, and armed with stiff, spiny points. Inflorescence, terminal or axillary racemes. Flowers, numerous; yellow. Sepals, six; petal-like. Petals, six; each with two glands at the base. Stamens, six; sensitive. Stigma, peltate. Fruit, a dark blue berry with a heavy bloom. Habitat, open woodlands. Blooming period, March to May.

The Oregon grape is the state flower of Oregon. It is, as most people know, not a grape, but a barberry, yet its clusters of dark berries are grape-like, and produce a fine jelly of real wild-grape flavor. It is not strange, therefore, that the early pioneers, remembering the purple-clustered vines of the Mississippi Valley, called it a grape.

Before America was discovered the Indians were using this fruit, and also making a yellow dye by steeping the twigs and bark in water. Not only did the plant provide them with food and dye, but they also used large quantities of the root for medicine. The white man has learned the value of this medicine, and every year many tons of Oregon grape roots are dug and marketed. For this reason, and because the evergreen leaves are very popular for decorating purposes, the plant has been nearly exterminated in the vicinity of our larger towns. Fortunately, it multiplies very rapidly, otherwise Oregon's state flower might be in grave danger.

The flowers of the Oregon grape are borne in close clusters at the summit of the stems, and are one of our earliest blossoms, appearing in late March. They are yellow in color, and quite attractive. Those who think of all plants as lifeless, inanimate things, have a surprise in store for them the first time they examine closely the flowers of the Oregon grape. In fair weather, when the blossoms

VANILLA-LEAF   *Achlys triphylla*

[118]

fragrance while wilting. A substitute for vanilla has been extracted from the leaves, but the amount is too small to be of commercial importance.

The flowers of the vanilla-leaf are borne on tall wiry scapes, and grow from the roots among the abundant leaves, but apparently not connected with them. These flowers have neither petals or sepals, but consist solely of numerous naked stamens and pistils. The plant is common in fir woods from sea-level nearly to the summit of the Cascades.

INSIDE-OUT FLOWER
Vancouveria hexandra (Hook.) Morr. and Done.

White. Stems, slender; smooth; erect; one to two feet tall. Leaves, two to three times ternately compound. Leaflets, thin; cordate at base; angled. Inflorescence, a loose panicle or raceme. Flowers, white; drooping; on slender pedicles. Sepals, six; petal-like; reflexed. Petals, six; opposite the sepals, but smaller; strongly reflexed. Stamens, six. Habitat, open woods. Blooming period, May-June.

One would scarcely suspect this slender, delicate plant of being closely related to the shrubby Oregon grape, yet such is the fact. The leaves are much divided, light and delicate, and with their stiff wiry stems are suggestive of the meadow rue or maidenhair fern. The loose- many-flowered scapes like the leaves are slender and wiry. Each individual blossom is about half an inch long, and they are curious in that all parts—sepals, petals, and stamens—are in sixes, and are arranged one before the other, and the petals and sepals are turned abruptly backward until the flower is truly inside out. The flowers are waxy-white, and firm in texture.

POPPY FAMILY

CALIFORNIA POPPY
Eschscholtzia californica Cham.

Golden yellow. Root, annual. Stem, erect or declining; branched from the base; smooth; succulent; glaucous; six to twelve inches tall. Leaves; petioled; ternately cut and divided into linear lobes. Flowers, large. Petals, four. Calyx, a narrow, conical cap, splitting lengthwise and falling as the flower unfolds. Stamens, numerous, Stigma, divid-

Bikukulla formosa

WILD BLEEDING HEART

ed into narrow, linear lobes. Capsule, narrow; elongated; splitting forcibly and scattering the seeds at maturity. Habitat, open prairies. Blooming period, from May until frost.

The California poppy is a typical southern plant that has strayed northward as far as the Columbia River in Oregon, and east of the mountains, into Washington, but it is not known to occur in Western Washington except as it has escaped from gardens. Even in the Willamette Valley, where it is common, it is restricted to the lower portions along the river. Near the foot-hills, with less than one hundred feet of increased altitude, it entirely disappears, though self-seeding and thriving from year to year when planted in gardens.

The golden blossoms of the California poppy so covered the hills that the first explorers called California "The Land of Fire." Certain conspicuous poppy-covered hills were so brilliant that they served as landmarks and beacons to the early mariners, visible far out to sea.

This is a plant of sunshine, opening only on bright days, and closing each night. From this habit it has received among the Spanish Californians the name of "dermidera," or the drowsy one. Like the true poppies it has the power of making others drowsy, for the juices contain a narcotic principal which has been used by physicians to some extent. The Indians recognized this quality in the plant, and as a cure for tooth-ache they would put a small piece of the root in the cavity of the offending molar.

When the buds first appear they are enclosed in a peculiar conical cap, which is really the calyx, but when the flower unfolds, this calyx, instead of opening with the petals, as in most flowers, is cast off, and falls to the ground. Children love to pull off these little caps and watch the tightly folded petals expand.

WILD BLEEDING-HEART
Bikukulla formosa (Andr.) Coville

Pink. Rootstock, creeping; stout. Leaves, ternately compound, the segments pinnately incised. Inflorescence, a loose drooping raceme. Flowers, pink; drooping. Sepals, two; small and scale-like. Petals, in two pairs, the outer largest; saccate; spurred at base, and with spreading tips. Inner pair, smaller. Stamens, six; in two sets. Habitat, moist low woods. Blooming period, March to May.

Capnoides scouleri

The delightful, little wild bleeding-heart may be instantly recognized by its resemblance to the cultivated bleeding-heart of old fashioned gardens. Though not so showy in form and color, our wild plant lacks none of the charm and grace which the garden plant possesses, and its soft, modest tints are even more pleasing. It is a lover of low, cool woodlands, and is very abundant from British Columbia to California.

Capnoides scouleri (Hook.) Kuntze

Pink. Rootstock, thickened; spreading. Stems, scaly at base; two to four feet tall. Leaves, radical, very large; cauline, smaller; few; all decompound; thin. Inflorescence, a raceme. Flowers, pink and purple. Sepals, two; small. Petals, four; the outer largest, slightly united into a one spurred corolla; inner petals narrow; keeled. Stamens, six; in two sets. Habitat, moist woodlands in deep shade. Blooming period, April-May.

In moist, shady canyons, sometimes at low levels, but more frequently at rather high altitudes in the mountains, will be found this the most beautiful plant of the bleeding-heart family. It is a shy flower, never flaunting itself in the public eye, and therefore is little known, and has no well-recognized common name. Its great compound leaves are a wonderful sight, finely cut and fern-like, but they are soft and feathery, and of a light green color unknown to any fern. The flowers stand in showy, upright racemes at the summit of the plant, and are quite distinctive, each flower having a purplish limb surmounted by a single very long, pink or rose-colored spur.

MUSTARD FAMILY

SPRING BEAUTY
Dentaria tenella Pursh

Rose-purple or pink. Root, tuberous; edible. Stem, smooth; erect; four to twelve inches tall. Root leaves, orbicular; crenately lobed; reddish beneath. Stem leaves, three-parted; the segments linear. Inflorescence, a few-flowered raceme. Flowers, rose-purple. Sepals, four; green. Petals, four; spreading. Stamens, six; unequal; one pair shorter. Pod, elongated. Habitat, moist woods and thickets. Blooming period, March to June.

This is not the spring beauty of the East, which is an entirely

SPRING BEAUTY *Dentaria tenella*

different plant. Our spring beauty belongs to the cress or mustard family, the flowers of which are all characterized by having four petals, a fact which gives them their family name of *Cruciferae,* meaning "a cross." The foot leaves of this plant come up scattered here and there over the ground as though in no wise connected with each other or with the flower stem. The creeping rootstalks from which they spring are white, with tuber-like swellings at short intervals that give to the plant the name *dentaria* meaning toothed. These roots are edible, as are the leaves and stems, and eaten with bread and butter they make a tasty sandwich. Their favorite habitat is on moist, rocky hillsides, and the edges of brush or hazel thickets.

Nothing is more charming and spring-like after a dark rainy winter, than to come unexpectedly upon a group of these nodding beauties, swaying in the breeze on some sunny slope. They have a freshness and grace that makes them loved by all.

MOUNTAIN TOOTHWORT
Dentaria macrocarpa Nutt.

Pink-purple. Stems, succulent; rather weak; ten to eighteen inches tall. Root leaves, thin; smooth; pinnately three to five parted, the divisions toothed or lobed. Otherwise as *D. tenella,* but larger in every way and the blossoms darker.

The rare mountain toothwort may be easily known by its resemblance to its smaller relative, the spring beauty. In form the flowers are the same, but those of this species are larger, and usually of a somewhat darker shade. The basal leaves are divided into from three to five large leaflets, quite variable in form, some broad and toothed, others narrow and with unbroken regular outlines. The plants are somewhat coarse and succulent, with scarcely strength to stand alone, and at the slightest excuse they are apt to recline on the ground or lean against other supporting vegetation. This rather rare flower will be found, if at all, in deep bushy canyons, and in my experience, shows a decided preference for north slopes where the sun seldom reaches. It is uncommon here, but I have been fortunate enough to find it both in the Cascades and Coast Ranges. East of the Cascades it is considered more common. Like all of its genus it is cress-like and sprightly in taste, and the soft, succulent stems are very appetizing.

CUCKOO FLOWER   *Cardamine pratensis*

CUCKOO FLOWER
Cardamine pratensis L.

White. Rootstock, somewhat tuberous. Stems, upright; six to twelve inches tall. Leaves, pinnately divided; the lower ones largest. Leaflets, seven to thirteen; entire; rounded. Inflorescence, a short raceme. Habitat, in mud or shallow water. Blooming period, April-May.

In form and appearance there is often a marked resemblance between this plant and the common spring beauty. In the shape and arrangement of the flowers, especially, they are strikingly alike, but while the blossoms of the spring beauty are a bright rose-purple, these are pure white. Among children it is commonly known as water-pepper, from the biting, pungent flavor of the leaves, in which again, they resemble the spring beauty. The plants often fill roadside ditches with their snowy bloom.

ANGLED BITTER-CRESS
Cardamine angulata Hook.

White. Stems, slender; simple; upright; one to two feet tall. Leaves, cut and divided into from three to five leaflets. Leaflets, oblong to triangularly ovate; coarsely toothed. Flowers, white, in a short raceme. Petals, four. Stamens, six; unequal. Pods, linear. Habitat, moist woods. Blooming period, May.

The slender plants of the angled bitter-cress will be found growing in moist woods and on stream banks near the coast or in the mountains. The white, four-petaled flowers proclaim it at once to be a member of the mustard family, and the rather large, sharply angled leaflets of its pinnate leaves will help to distinguish this species from others of this rather difficult genus. The blossoms appear from April to June.

WILD WALL-FLOWER
Erysimum asperum (Nutt.) DC.

Yellow. Root. a single tap-root. Stem, upright or reclining, stiff; angled; usually simple; one to three feet tall. Leaves, small; lanceolate; dentate; sessile. Inflorescence, a corymb, lengthening with

WILD WALL-FLOWER   *Erysimum asperum*

age. Flowers, yellow. Petals, four; clawed; lateral pair gibbous at base. Stamens, six; unequal; one pair shorter. Habitat, dry open hillsides, usually at high altitudes. Blooming period, April to August according to altitude.

The golden yellow blooms of the wild wall-flower are a conspicuous feature of our high mountain meadows, and in rare instances they will be found at low levels in the valleys. I have found them in both situations, and have never failed to be pleased with their attractive brightness. The blossoms are at times very fragrant. Widely distributed, the range of this plant extends as far east as Ohio, and from Saskatchewan to California.

Erysinum capitatum (Hook.) Greene. A very similar species. This is a somewhat larger plant than the preceding, having greener leaves, a capitate stigma, and lenticular seeds.

SUNDEW FAMILY

ROUND-LEAVED SUNDEW
Drosera rotundifolia L.

White. Leaves, in a spreading rosette at the base of the scape; round; long petioled; the blade covered with gland-tipped hairs. Inflorescence, a one-sided raceme; curled in bud. Scape, simple; leafless; slender; three to seven inches tall. Flowers, small; white; opening only in full sunlight. Sepals, petals, and stamens, five each. Habitat, spagnum bogs. Blooming period, June-July.

> "Warm stilly place, the sundew loves thee well,
> And the greensward comes creeping to thy brink,
> And the golden saxifrage and pimpernell
> Lean down their perfumed heads to drink."

This picture, drawn by the sympathetic poet, is exactly true of our coast sundew as I have found it, save that our saxifrage is white, not golden, and it is the false pimpernell, *Hypericum anagalloides,* that here spreads its flowers about the borders of the bogs. This is one of our most curious plants, for the leaves of the sundew—perfect jewels—are beset with fine bristles, each bristle tipped with a shining, dew-like globe of a reddish secretion. It is all very beautiful, but the purpose is to attract tiny curious insects to their death. Drawn to the leaf the insect alights to investigate, and is immediately held

ROUND-LEAVED SUNDEW *Drosera rotundifolia*

fast on the sticky surface. Then, little by little, the leaf blade enfolds and crushes its victim, and extracts and digests its edible juices, after which it again opens and awaits the coming of another luckless fly.

One would scarcely expect a plant like this of having practical uses, but we read on good authority that, "The whole plant is acrid, curdles milk, and has a reputation for removing corns, bunions, and warts." In the Mediterranean regions this plant, blended with brandy, sugar, and raisins was made into a sweet cordial called *rossolis*.

STONECROP FAMILY

STONECROP
Sedum spathulifolium Hook.

Yellow. Stems, decumbent; five to ten inches long. Leaves, spatulate; broad; glaucous; fleshy; along the stem or in close rosettes at the ends of the branches. Inflorescence, a one-sided cyme. Flowers, sessile. Sepals and petals, of equal number, usually four or five. Stamens, twice as many as the petals. Habitat, on rocks. Blooming period, May.

The stonecrop spreads its crowded rosettes of fleshy leaves over the dry rocks, apparently finding an abundance of nourishment from the tiny pockets of soil that have accumulated in the cracks and seams of its rocky support. This manner of life might give us the idea that the plant required but little moisture, but this is a fallacy, for if you watch it through succeeding wet and dry years, you will find that like most vegetation the season of abundant rainfall shows a marked increase in the thrift of the plant. It is perfect drainage, not drouth, that these flowers seek, and although by the storage of moisture in their fleshy leaves the stonecrop can survive a long time with little moisture, it responds quickly and gratefully to an abundant rainfall.

Sedum divergens Wats., has smooth, bright green foliage, oval in form but nearly as thick as broad, growing in rosettes at the tips of the branches. The flowers are yellow, borne in close clusters.

Sedum stenopetalum Pursh, has green, lanceolate leaves. The stems are upright, from two to five inches tall. Flowers, yellow.

STONECROP   *Sedum spathulifolium*

[134]

SAXIFRAGE FAMILY

MODESTY
Whipplea modesta Torr.

White. Stems, shrubby; slender; trailing; one to two feet long. Leaves, opposite; ovate; slightly toothed. Inflorescence, a cyme; terminal on naked pedicels. Flowers, small; white. Calyx, campanulate; five-cleft; lobed; petal-like. Petals, five. Stamens, ten. Habitat, open woods. Blooming period, April to June.

A low, almost trailing shrub with pretty clusters of sweet-scented flowers at the ends of the slender twigs. The leaves are opposite and somewhat hairy. Found in open woods from Washington southward, and very abundant in low mountains.

RED-FLOWERED CURRANT
Ribes sanquineum Pursh

Red. Stems, shrubby; upright; branching; four to eight feet tall. Leaves, cordate; three to five lobed; serrate; aromatic. Inflorescence, a raceme; slender; drooping. Flowers, pink to red. Calyx, cylindrical; with spreading lobes; red. Petals, erect; clawed; pink or white. Fruit, globular; black, with a heavy white bloom; insipid. Habitat, dry open woods. Blooming period, April-May.

In late March the wild currant bursts into bloom, covering every bush with crimson panicles, and with it come a host of rufous hummingbirds, brilliant in glittering coppery mail, to buzz and twitter and chase each other noisily from bush to bush. These two brilliant friends are sure and inseperable in their springtime tryst, and together make one of our most colorful and animated pictures. A full-blooming shrub of this species shimmering in the sunlight through the dim, dark arches of a fir forest, has a glowing, etherial quality, as though woven of soft-tinted gossamer, and floating lightly in the golden atmosphere.

In color the flowers range from pale pink to brightest crimson. The whole plant—leaves, stems and blossoms—is strongly permeated with a spicy, aromatic scent, giving it the occasionally used name of incense shrubs. This plant bears an abundance of fruit, but it is insipid, dry, and scarcely edible.

Flowering currants and skunk cabbage are inseperably connected

RED-FLOWERED CURRANT   *Ribes sanguineum*

[136]

in my memory of my first view of the West, for as I traveled down the Washington Coast on my initial trip, every swale was circled with the crimson, drooping blossoms of the currant, and lighted with the flame-like yellow spathes of the skunk cabbage, both new to me, and equally charming.

SYRINGA
Philadelphus gordonianus Lindl.

White. Stems, shrubby; branching; erect; six to twelve feet tall. Leaves, opposite; ovate; dentate to entire. Inflorescence, cymose. Flowers, numerous; white; heavy-scented. Calyx, top-shaped; four to five lobed. Petals, four; convoluted in bud. Stamens, twenty or more. Styles, three to five; united at base. Habitat, forest borders and stream banks. Blooming period, June-July.

In early June our lowland thickets are perfumed with the rich fragrance of the syringa, and in this month of brides and orange blossoms the creamy white flowers are a favorite substitute for the more conventional blooms. The flowers in purity and fragrance, are quite worthy of this honor, and are perhaps more commonly known as mock-orange than syringa.

Throughout the Northern Hemisphere, in Europe, Asia, and North America, there are many species of *Philadelphus.* Some of them have been introduced into cultivation and somewhat improved, but few are more beautiful, and none more fragrant than our own wild species. A syringa, *P. lewisii,* is the state flower of Idaho, discovered there by Captain Lewis on his famous trans-continental trip.

From a utilitarian viewpoint, the syringas were much valued by the Indians. The young, straight shoots were a favorite material for arrows. Bows were made from the larger, stiffer stems, but were not highly valued on the Coast, where the yew, bow-wood *par excellence,* was so common. Dr. Cooper, in 1853, also reports that he found the Indians using the macerated leaves as a substitute for soap, and a trial recently made shows that they are capable of producing a rather thin lather.

SYRINGA   *Philadelphus gordonianus*

FRINGED GRASS OF PARNASSUS
Parnassia fimbriata Koenig

White. Stem, simple; scape-like; eight to fourteen inches tall, bearing a single clasping leaf. Leaves, basal, cordate to reniform; petioled. Flowers, solitary. Calyx, deeply five-cleft. Petals, five; fringed at the base. Stamens, five. Habitat, in mountain bogs.

The slender, single-flowered scapes of the fringed grass of Parnassus rise to a height of from eight to fourteen inches, and should be unmistakeable, since each bears above the centre a single, heart-shaped, sessile, clasping leaf. The basal leaves are smooth and glossy. The showy, white flower is nearly an inch in diameter, with five white petals, fringed at the base, and with a peculiar cluster of sterile stamens opposite each petal. This is a charming flower of moist mountain meadows, and if, as the name indicates, the Muses in their Parnassian Heights play amidst such "grass" we need not wonder that inspiration follows their footsteps.

OREGON SAXIFRAGE
Saxifraga oregana Howell

White. Leaves, all basal; in a spreading rosette; thick; oblong to ovate; toothed; sessile, or tapering to a short petiole. Scapes, stout; leafless; one to two feet tall. Inflorescence, paniculate; pyramidal. Flowers, white; sessile; fragrant. Calyx, deeply five cleft. Petals, five. Stamens, ten. Styles, two. Carpels, two; nearly distinct. Habitat, moist swales and ditches. Blooming period, March to May.

The Oregon saxifrage will be found in wet places about springs, and moist roadside ditches, beginning to blossom in late March. The leaves are thick, oval, rather hairy, and unevenly toothed along the margins. They form small basal rosettes from which the stout, leafless scapes rise to an average height of eighteen inches, though in favorable situations they sometimes grow to three feet or more. The flowers are white and very sweet scented. The range of this plant is from Washington to California.

OREGON SAXIFRAGE   *Saxifraga oregana*

SPOTTED SAXIFRAGE
Saxifraga mertensiana Bong

White. Leaves, all basal; on long, slender petioles; round-cordate; lobed; the lobes toothed. Inflorescence, a loose, spreading panicle; usually bearing bulblets on the lower branches of the panicle. Flowers, white; star-like. Petals, five; ovate; short-clawed; white, with two yellow spots at the base. Stamens, ten; club-shaped. Carpels, two; beaked; divergent in fruit. Habitat, moist cliffs. Blooming period, May-June.

Among the many lovely rock plants which, in our mountains, beautify talus and cliff, none fill a more decorative niche than the spotted saxifrage. Whenever moisture is plentiful—below seeping springs, on moist rocks about waterfalls, or where porous rock has absorbed the melting snow—it clings in the crevices, and spreads a refreshing display of green over all its craggy foothold. Occasionally, too, you will fiind it in shady stream bottoms, rooted, here, in the cracks and splintered crevices of great waterworn logs from the flood-swept wreckage. This plant has an interesting mode of propagating itself, in that the flower stems bear an abundance of small red bulblets which finally separate from the mother stem and produce other plants. This feature is extremely variable; plants in some localities producing bulblets freely, while in others they are entirely absent. This feature has led some botanists to believe that there are two distinct species.

DOTTED SAXIFRAGE
Saxifraga bronchialis L.

White. Stems, tufted; ascending; four to eight inches tall. Leaves, coriaceous; lanceolate; sessile; closely crowded on the branches. Flowers, few or solitary. Petals, oblong; white; marked with orange dots. Stamens; ten; subulate. Habitat, on rocky cliffs.

The lanceolate leaves of this little saxifrage are stiff and leathery, and closely crowded on the branches. The low, closely tufted plants often cover large tracts on the rocks in moist places. The flowers are white, dotted with red and yellow. In our territory this species is represented by two varieties, *austromontana,* and *vespertina,* the latter found at low altitudes, the former, high in the mountains.

SPOTTED SAXIFRAGE

Saxifraga odontoloma Piper

White. Leaves, all basal; reniform; coarsely dentate; long petioled. Scape, four to sixteen inches tall. Flowers, white; panicled. Petals, five; orbicular; clawed. Stamens, ten; spatulate. Habitat, along mountain streams.

With round or kidney-shaped, evenly toothed leaves, all basal, one to three inches broad. Flowers, white, in panicles, on scapes fifteen inches or less tall. The five white petals are roundish.

Saxifraga bongardi Presl.

White. Stem, three to ten inches tall. Leaves, in basal rosettes; short petioled; lanceolate to spatulate; toothed above. Inflorescence, a loose panicle. Flowers, white, interspersed with leafy bulblets. Sepals, reflexed. Petals, five; clawed; lanceolate; unequal; white, spotted at base with yellow. Habitat, along mountain streams.

The loose panicles of this pretty mountain flower are borne on very slender, graceful stems. The small, white flowers are sometimes replaced by bulblets. The leaves are mostly basal, somewhat stiff and thick, and oblanceolate in form.

WESTERN SAXIFRAGE
Saxifraga occidentalis Wats.

White. Root, perennial; woody. Leaves, all basal; whorled; coriaceous; obovate to broadly spatulate; evenly serrate above the middle; tapering to a short, broad petiole at base. Inflorescence, a panicle; bracted. Scape, branched; three to ten inches tall. Flowers, small; white. Calyx, five-parted; rotate. Sepals, oval. Corolla, rotate. Petals, five; oval. Stamens, ten. Styles, two; distinct. Carpels, divaricate; reddish. Habitat, on moist rocks. Blooming period, March to May at low altitudes.

This is a pretty leathery-leaved species found commonly in moist rocks in the Cascades.

FOAM-FLOWER
Tiarella unifoliata Hook.

White. Stem, simple; upright; five to ten inches tall. Radical leaves, ovate; cordate; petioled; three to seven lobed; the lobes dentate. Cauline leaves, one; small. Inflorescence, a slender, terminal

WESTERN SAXIFRAGE

Saxifraga occidentalis

panicle. Calyx, campanulate; five-parted. Petals, five; filiform. Stamens, ten; long and slender. Styles, two. Habitat, coniferous woods. Blooming period, June to September.

In moist woods, and in the mountains to an altitude of four thousand feet, this little plant of the saxifrage family is a familiar sight. The plants are from five to ten inches tall, with a few prettily lobed, long petioled leaves at the base, and a single small leaf at about the middle of the stem. At the summit of the slender scape it bears a delicate panicle of white, foam-like flowers. A peculiar feature of these flowers are their petals, which are so narrow and thread-like that they might easily be mistaken for antherless stamens. The sepals are white and petal-like. A very abundant plant, sometimes completely carpeting the forest floor; from this it has earned another of its popular names, that of Nancy-over-the-ground.

Tiarella trifoliata L., is a similar species, but with trifoliate leaves, the central leaflet lobed and toothed.

WOODLAND STAR
Tellima parviflora Hook.

White. Stem, slender; simple; upright; six to eighteen inches tall. Leaves, radical, on slender petioles; round-cordate; three to five lobed or parted; lobes cut or toothed. Cauline, few; small; three-parted; the divisions three-cleft. Flowers, white or pink; clustered or elongated into a simple raceme at the summit of the scape. Calyx, obconic, with acute, triangular lobes. Petals, clawed; deeply three-cleft. Stamens, ten; included. Styles, two or three; short. Habitat, moist open ground. Blooming period, April-May.

A delicate little plant with a few roundish, finely cleft leaves, and a slender, nearly naked stem, bearing at the summit a few pretty white or pinkish blossoms. The attractive flowers each have five petals, each petal deeply three-cleft, making a fifteen rayed, star-like circle. The plant grows from five to twenty inches tall, and will be found in rocky or gravelly places. Its range is from British Columbia to California.

WOODLAND STAR   *Tellima parviflora*

FRINGE-CUPS
Tellima grandiflora (Pursh) Dougl.

Green or red. Stems, clustered; tapering; upright; bearing a few reduced, sessile leaves. Basal leaves, petioled; round-cordate; two to four inches across; lobed and toothed; often veined with red or brown. Inflorescence, a simple raceme. Calyx, inflated; campanulate; green. Petals, laciniate; green, pink, or becoming red with age. Stamens, ten; short; included. Styles, two or three; short. Habitat, moist woods. Blooming period, April-May.

The showy leaves of the fringe-cups make pleasing borders in our woods on moist stream banks or about springs. The basal leaves are long-petioled, nearly orbicular in outline, and prettily wavy-margined. They grow in close clusters, and the larger ones are often richly mottled and veined with red or brown. The tapering flower scapes are ordinarily a foot or two tall, but in favorable situations may reach a height of five feet. The petals are five in number, green or pink, and while not showy are very prettily formed, being pinnately divided into small, delicate lobes.

Sweet-Scented Fringe-Cup, var. *odorata.* This is a very beautiful variety of the above, having more showy racemes of nearly white flowers that are exquisitely perfumed. Their scent is almost identical with that of the trailing arbutus of the East. This variety is extremely plentiful along the highways within the gorge of the Columbia River.

SLENDER THEROFON
Therofon elatum (Nutt.) Greene

White. Stems, slender; erect; sparingly leafy; ten to twenty inches tall. Leaves, round-cordate; five to seven lobed; incised and toothed. Stipules, reduced to bristles. Inflorescence, loosely paniculate. Calyx, campanulate. Sepals, five. Petals, five; white; soon falling. Stamens, five; opposite the sepals. Styles, two. Carpels, diverging. Habitat, stream banks. Blooming period, June-July.

This is another of those white-flowered, saxifrage-like plants so numerous and puzzling to the beginner, and so useful in training him in the rudiments of observation. Without them we could never make the progress necessary to reach the really difficult forms.

SLENDER THEROFON   *Therofon elatum*

[148]

The slender therofon makes delicate lacy bowers along mountain streams, and tempts us to pick it, but it is useless to yield to this temptation, for no sooner is it plucked than it promptly sheds most of its small white petals, and leaves us with nothing for our pains but a bunch of bare uninteresting stems.

Large Therofon. *Therofon major* Gray. This is in every way a stouter, larger plant than the former. The broad, dark green foliage forms attractive verdant patches among the rocks closely bordering our mountain streams. The bases of the rather stout petioles are noticeably dilated, and the stipules are either parchment-like or green and leaf-like. The upright or arching stems grow to a height of from twenty to thirty inches, and bear the white flowers in loose flattish panicles.

LEAFY-STEMMED MITREWORT. BISHOP'S CAP
Mitella caulescens Nutt.

Green. Stems, simple; slender; tapering; seven to fourteen inches tall. Basal leaves, ovate; cordate; coarsely five to seven lobed; the lobes dentate. Cauline leaves, similar but smaller; one to three. Inflorescence, a slender, simple raceme. Calyx, five lobed; broad. Petals, five; pinnately divided into from five to nine very narrow divisions. Stamens, five or ten; short. Styles, two. Habitat, moist shady woodlands. Blooming period, May-June.

Though considered rare, the leafy-stemmed mitrewort will sometimes be found in great abundance. Certain narrow canyons of the Cascades are literally fringed with it, and it carpets the ground in a most decorative manner. Even before the flower scapes appear, the basal leaves are very attractive, and with the coming of the slender, tapering racemes and delicate greenish flowers the picture is complete. The finely cut petals of these flowers are wonderful in their delicacy, and remind one of some of the forms assumed by snowflakes, but these are five-pointed, translucent green snowflakes, such as no chilly storm cloud ever dropped. After the flowers are gone the plants send forth slender runners, by means of which they multiply. The range of this species is from British Columbia to Oregon.

Five-stemmed Mitrewort. *Mitella pentandra* Hook. The characteristics of this small mitrewort are its five stamens borne opposite

LEAFY-STEMMED MITREWORT   *Mitella caulescens*

[150]

the petals, and broad, heart-shaped leaves with wavy margins—all basal.

OVAL-LEAVED MITREWORT. BISHOP'S CAP
Mitella ovalis Greene

Green. Stems, leafless; six to eighteen inches tall. Leaves, all basal, petioled; oval or reniform; slightly lobed; toothed. Inflorescence, a slender, simple raceme. Flowers, small; greenish-yellow. Calyx, short; broad; saucer-shaped; five-lobed. Petals, five; pinnately divided. Stamens, five or ten; short. Styles, two. Habitat, moist woods near the coast.

The leaves of this mitrewort are all basal, and are oval or reniform, somewhat lobed, and with a wavy or toothed margin. The scapes are about ten inches tall, and rather one-sided. The same star-like form distinguishes this flower as in the other species of mitrewort.

YOUTH-ON-AGE
Leptaxis menziesii (Pursh) Raf.

Purplish brown. Stems, clustered; simple; slender; erect; fifteen to twenty inches tall. Radical leaves, cordate; acute; lobed and toothed; petioled. Cauline, smaller; nearly sessile; reduced upwards to floral bracts. Inflorescence, a slender raceme. Calyx, purple-veined; cylindrical; narrow; unequally lobed. Petals, four; filiform; recurved; brown. Stamens, three; exserted. Habitat, rich moist woods. Blooming period, April to June.

The maple-like leaves and wand-like scapes of this plant are gracefully attractive. The flowers, however, are not especially beautiful, since the calyx is the most conspicuous part, and this is a dull purplish or brown in color. It is narrowly cylindrical in form, and from its throat protrude the four very narrow, thread-like petals, and three slender stamens. Perhaps the most interesting feature of this plant, and that to which it owes its name, is the manner in which the young plants appear. These spring from the base of the leaf blade— perfect duplicates of the parent in form and beauty, but very small. As the old supporting leaf fades, these minute plants send rootlets into the ground, and so produce a new generation.

ALUM ROOT

ALUM ROOT
Heuchera glabra Willd.

White. Stems, slender; erect or declining; one to three feet tall. Leaves, thin; glabrous; orbicular; cordate at base; lobed; the lobes acute; serrate. Cauline leaves, similar; smaller; nearly sessile. Inflorescence, a slender open panicle. Flowers, white; very small. Calyx, top-shaped; five-lobed. Petals, five; minute; clawed. Stamens, five; exserted. Styles, two. Habitat, banks and moist rocky cliffs. Blooming period, April to June.

On level ground are fine airy panicles of the smooth alum root stand erect, but on banks and declivities they often decline or hang outward, and when the slanting sun catches them, they shine like a curtain of soft silver lace. The leaves also have their own particular style of beauty, for they are often finely marked and mottled with reds and browns. The homely name of alum root is given them because their large woody root is very astringent.

Heuchera micrantha Dougl., a similar plant but with the foliage more or less hairy, and the leaf lobes rounded.

UMBRELLA-PLANT
Peltiphyllum peltatum Engler

Pink or purplish. Rootstalks, stout; spreading. Leaves, all basal; long petioled; orbicular; peltate; eight to twelve lobed; very large. Inflorescence, a branching panicle. Scapes, naked; ten to forty inches tall. Flowers, pink or purplish; about one half inch across. Petals, five; rounded. Stamens, ten. Stigma, capitate. Carpels, two; distinct; spreading; reddish. Habitat, on rocks, in and about mountain streams. Blooming period, early spring.

A big leaf—a very big umbrella-like leaf—is the most characteristic feature of this fine plant. A leaf so big that it may literally be carried and used for a sun-shade on sultry days. The plants grow on the borders of our rapid mountain streams, or even within the stream itself, their stout creeping rootstalks finding a foothold in the crevices of the rocky bed. No more effective bordering for a stream could well be imagined. Having found the leaves, one naturally begins to look for the blossoms that accompany them, but this is useless, for the flowers come up, and have wilted, long before the leaves

UMBRELLA-PLANT

Peltiphyllum peltatum

make their appearance. The ripening carpels found with the leaves in May are pretty, however, being two-lobed, and reddish-purple in color. In autumn, too, the leaves are changed by the frost into rich, deep colors. It is said that the Indians were very fond of the young leaf and flower stems of this plant, and for this reason they are sometimes called Indian rhubarb. If they were so used it must have been only when very young and tender, for I have found them exceedingly tough and tasteless.

ROSE FAMILY

BITTER CHERRY
Prunus emarginata erecta (Presl.) Piper

White. Stem, a slender tree; twenty-five to sixty feet tall. Bark, brown or grayish, marked with conspicuous lenticles. Leaves, ovate; minutely serrate. Inflorescence, a few-flowered cyme. Petals, five. Stamens, numerous. Fruit, a drupe; bright red; small; bitter. Habitat, open woods. Blooming period, April-May.

The bitter cherry is a slender, upright tree, at times reaching a height of sixty feet, and with a trunk from twelve to eighteen inches in diameter. These are extreme sizes, and in high mountains or arid regions it is often only a small shrub. The bark is smooth, reddish in young trees, but becoming gray with age. The blossoms, which appear with the leaves in April, are borne in loose, few-flowered corymbs. The numerous stamens have dark-tipped anthers, and are very prominent. The fruit is small—about the size of a pea—and is red, and exceedingly bitter. The local names of bitter cherry, and quinine cherry refer to this quality of the fruit.

CHOKE-CHERRY
Prunus demissa (Nutt.) Dietr

White. Stem, shrubby, or becoming small trees. Bark, brown; smooth. Leaves, oblong or oblong-oval; cuneate at base; serrate. Inflorescence, a many flowered raceme; erect or nodding. Calyx, hemispheric. Petals, five. Stamens, numerous. Pistil, one. Fruit, a fleshy drupe; edible. Habitat, open woods and prairies. Blooming period, May.

CHOKE-CHERRY   *Prunus demissa*

In early May the choke-cherry bursts into bloom, covering every slender twig to the tip with crowded snowy blossoms. No plant that I know is more lavish with its flowers and fruit, and could we but find some Burbank with skill to remove the "pucker" from its juice, we would have an excellent fruit. Even as it is the fully ripe cherries have a pleasing flavor, and when dried and prepared in Indian fashion lose their disagreeable astringency and become a wholesome food. Pemmican prepared of buffalo meat mixed with choke-cherries was one of the most important winter stores of the plains Indians. On our own coast this dish was made of choke-cherries and pounded salmon-bellies. To prepare this fruit the Indians beat it, seeds and all, upon flat stones, so that the edible seed, as well as more or less of the finely ground shell was included in the food. When not fully ripe the cherries are so puckery and astringent as to be unfit for food, and small children, especially, should be cautioned against partaking of them too freely, as cases of death have resulted from eating the unripe fruit in large amounts. When fully ripe they are dark red, or nearly black, and birds and bears are then extremely fond of them.

OSO-BERRY
Osmaronia cerasiformis (T. & G.) Greene

White. Stems, shrubby; clustered; six to twelve feet tall. Leaves, alternate; ovate; simple; entire. Inflorescence, a bracted, nodding raceme. Flowers, polygamo-dioecious; rank-scented; white. Calyx, campanulate; lobed; the lobes about half as long as the utbe. Petals, five; alternate with the lobes of the calyx; spatulate. Pistil, one. Fruit, blue-black; scantily fleshed; insipid or rather bitter. Seed, large; flattened. Habitat, low rich woods. Blooming period, January to May.

As I write of this plant, on a rather chilly thirty-first day of January, the room in which I am seated is scented with the rank smell of its blossoms, for this is one of the earliest of our spring flowers, rivalled in this respect only by the modest blue grouse flower. A few warm days in late winter are sufficient to cause the soft green leaves of this plant to push forth, and with the leaves, from the same buds, appear drooping panicles of closely folded green flower buds. Some of these buds open almost at once, but many of them linger on from week to week, and the plant's blooming season is thus extended over a con-

OSO-BERRY   *Osmaronia cerasiformis*

siderable period, or from January to May. The oso-berry is a shrub from six to twelve feet in height. It will be found growing in moist, rich lowlands. The leaves are ovate, alternate, and entire in outline. The young foliage has a characteristic smell and when crushed, somewhat like that of fresh watermelon rind, and the flowers, like many early blossoms that depend on flies, rather than bees for fertilization, are strongly rank-scented. From this they receive their common name of skunk-bush. Other common names are Indian plum, and Indian peach. Oso, in Spanish, means bear, so that this is simply another "bear-berry."

The fruit which ripens in June is first orange, and later bluish-black with a heavy bluish bloom. The pedicels supporting the clusters are often handsomely tinted in oranges and reds, and in contrast with the ripening fruit they make an attractive color scheme. Each individual fruit is a flattish drupe, in which a single horny seed is encased in sweetish black pulp. Although they are edible they are rather insipid.

HAWTHORN. THORN-APPLE
Crataegus douglasii Lindl

White. Stem, branching; shrubby or becoming small trees. Leaves, elliptical or obovate; toothed or incised. Inflorescence, an umbel. Flowers, white; heavy-scented. Calyx, campanulate; persistent. Petals, five; on the calyx. Stamens, five to twenty. Styles, one to five; distinct. Fruit, a small pome; black. Seeds, large; horny. Habitat, low rich woods. Blooming period, May.

> ". . . . The ragged hawthorn
> Dips its prickly bud of perfume
> In the wave."

The black hawthorn will usually be found growing along stream bottoms, although not always as close to the water as the above verse suggests. The hawthorn was the English mayflower, from which the historic ship Mayflower was named.

> "The fair maid, who, the first of May
> Goes to the fields at break of day,
> And washes in dew from the hawthorn tree
> Will ever after handsome be."

WILD CRAB-APPLE   *Pyrus diversifolia*

Ours is a shrub or small tree with very spiny branches, and dark green, toothed leaves. The flowers appear in close corymbs, and are creamy white. The fruits are clustered, black, and contain a number of hard bony seeds. Although seldom used the fruit makes good jelly. It is sweet but rather insipid. The Indians used it to a considerable extent.

WILD CRAB-APPLE
Pyrus diversifolia Bong.

White. Stems, a small tree; fifteen to twenty feet tall. Bark, smooth and grayish in young trees, rough and scaly on old trunks. Leaves, ovate to lanceolate; serrate; somewhat three lobed. Inflorescence, a cyme. Flowers, white; fragrant. Calyx, persistent; lobes lanceolate; as long as the tube. Petals, five; orbicular; abruptly short clawed. Stamens, twenty. Styles, united at base. Fruit, a pome; oblong; clustered; acid. Habitat, along stream bottoms. Blooming period, May.

This is the only species of wild apple found in the West. It varies from a tall shrub to a small tree, seldom over twenty-five feet in height, or with a trunk over a foot in diameter. The blossoms are borne in loose cymes, are a beautiful waxy white, and are very sweet-scented. The fruit that follows appears in loose clusters. These little apples are oblong in form, and measure scarcely three fourths of an inch in length. They are extremely sour, but are excellent for jams and jellies.

Few plants are more frequently mentioned in Indian mythology than this. Its fruit was among the most highly valued delicacies. To report that—"In the house were many boxes of wild crab-apples mixed with grease," was equivalent to a statement of wealth and extreme luxury. The wood of this plant was also greatly valued. It is very compact and tough, and was used by the natives as a material for the manufacture of wedges. Before the white men came to the Coast the Indians were living in comfortable cedar houses, some of them of great size, and the whole work of constructing them—felling the trees, cutting them into lengths, and splitting out the immense planks—was done with no other tools than a stone axe, a stone hammer, and wedges of crab-apple wood.

SERVICE-BERRY   *Amelanchier florida*

MOUNTAIN ASH

Pyrus sitchensis (Roem.) Piper

White. Stem, shrubby, or a small tree; five to twenty feet in height. Bark, smooth; brown. Leaves, pinnate. Leaflets, four to six pairs; oblong; acute; serrate; shiny. Inflorescence, a flat topped cyme. Flowers, white; small. Calyx, subulate; one to three lines long. Petals, five; orbicular; two to three lines long. Stamens, numerous. Fruit, a bright red, berry-like pome. Habitat, mountain forests. Blooming period, May onward, according to altitude.

The mountain ash, or American rowan, is our west coast representative of the European rowan tree—symbol of ambition and aspiration. In Northern Europe a single twig of the rowan tree was deemed sufficient protection against all evil spirits. Ours is a mountain shrub or small tree, seldom exceeding eighteen feet in height. It has pretty pinnate leaves, smooth brown bark, and broad, flat cymes of white flowers in spring, followed by bunches of bright red fruit. This fruit is much loved by the birds, especially the robins and varied thrushes.

SERVICE-BERRY

Amelanchier florida Lindl.

White. Stems, clustered or branching from the base; shrubby, or becoming a small tree. Bark, smooth; gray. Leaves, oblong; rounded or cordate at base; toothed above the middle; deciduous. Inflorescence, raceme. Flowers, white; abundant. Calyx, campanulate; five-parted; persistent. Petals, five; oblanceolate; soon falling. Stamens, twenty. Styles, three to five; united below. Fruit, black; sweet; edible. Habitat, open woods. Blooming period, April.

Our name, service-berry, is a corruption of the old botanical name, *Sorbus,* formerly applied to this genus, and it is probable that the English name of savoy, given to the European species, comes from the same source. The service-berry in its various forms grows from coast to coast, and throughout its range carries a number of local names. It is the shad-bush in New England, because it blossoms at the season of the annual run of shad. In the middle west it is the June-berry, from the ripening of the fruit in that month. In Western

OCEAN-SPRAY

Canada it is the saskatoon, a name of Indian derivation. Among the early western explorers it is often spoken of as the mountain pear.

With us it is a branching shrub or small tree from fifteen to thirty feet in height, but at the northern extremity of its range, and in high mountains, it is much reduced and dwarfed, often only a foot or two in height. Among the Indians from the plains to the Pacific the straight, slender shoots were much desired as a material for arrow shafts. The fruit was also one of their staple articles of food, either fresh or dried, or mixed with pounded meat as pemmican. Very few of the early Oregon explorers but speak of its great value to the natives, or were themselves glad to assuage their hunger by its use. Lewis and Clark speak of a kind of native bread made of these berries mixed with the pounded seeds of balsam-root and lambs-quarter. The berries are sweet and pulpy, with small seeds and are covered with a thick bluish bloom. Pies made from them are excellent, but are improved by the addition of a little acid.

The Klamath Indians trace their origin from this plant, according to one of their myths. In this story "Old Martin" caused the first people to be made from service-berry bushes.

OCEAN SPRAY. ARROW-WOOD
Holodiscus discolor (Pursh) Maxim.

White. Stems, clustered; shrubby; erect; five to fourteen feet tall. Bark, grayish-brown. Leaves, alternate; ovate; lobed and toothed; cuneately narrowed at base to a winged petiole. Inflorescence, a large, loose panicle. Flowers, minute; white. Calyx, five-lobed; white. Petals, five; rounded; one to two lines long. Stamens, twenty. Pistils, five. Habitat, brushy tracts and open woods. Blooming period, June-July.

The popular name of ocean spray very fittingly describes the plumy panicles of this beautiful shrub. The slender, graceful stems, tipped with foam-like flowers in June, are very plentiful, yet we can never tire of their dainty loveliness. Each individual bud as it appears is a tiny, perfect sphere, and when they burst into bloom they form a cascade of flowing, creamy beauty. The plants attain a height of from eight to twenty feet, and when grown to perfection make an imposing show. Unfortunately, their popularity is often their destruction, and about towns, especially, the bushes are often mutilated and broken by the hands of careless vandals. This is one of the In-

STEEPLE BUSH

Spiraea douglasii

dian arrow-woods, for the straight young shoots made almost perfect arrow shafts.

STEEPLE BUSH
Spiraea douglasii Hook.

Rose-red. Stems, tufted; shrubby; upright; three to seven feet tall. Bark, smooth; reddish-brown. Leaves, oblong; serrate; short petioled; tomentose beneath. Inflorescence, a pyramidal, terminal panicle. Flowers, rose-red; minute. Calyx, campanulate; lobes, ovate; acute; as long as the tube. Petals, five; obovate; short clawed. Stamens, exserted; numerous. Habitat, swales and borders of ponds. Blooming period, June.

Our commonest spiraea, with its soft pyramidal clusters of bright pink flowers is a beautiful plant. In our own state it is not yet appreciated as it should be, for it seems a part of our nature to disregard the beauty close at hand and value only that which has come from afar. Recently a prosperous farmer of my acquaintance, wishing to improve his grounds, bought a number of highly recommended shrubs from an eastern nursery, paying a liberal price for them. When the plants bloomed he was much chagrined to find that they were nothing but the common steeple bush, already very abundant in fence corners and waste land about his place. Yet in this case the nurseryman had in no wise over-stated the beauty of the flowers, as many satisfied customers in other localities could testify.

The steeple bush grows in moist low land throughout our territory, and is a typical plant of our humid coast region at low altitude. The flowers are very small and closely crowded, and the numerous pink stamens give to the cluster a soft, fuzzy appearance very pleasing to the eye.

Menzie's Steeple Bush. *Spiraea menziesii* Hook. This is a very similar species, but smaller, and with leaves smooth (not woolly) beneath. It is rare in our limits, but common east of the Cascades.

BIRCH-LEAVED SPIRAEA
Spiraea lucida Dougl.

White. Stems, shrubby; branched; one to two feet tall. Leaves, ovate; lobed and toothed above the middle; narrowed below. Inflor-

GOAT'S BEARD   *Aruncus aruncus*

escence, a flat-topped corymb. Flowers, small; white. Calyx lobes, short; triangular; five; reflexed. Petals, elliptical. Carpels, five. Habitat, dry ground in low mountains.

This is a low branching shrub with reddish, brittle stems and showy, flat-topped clusters of creamy-white flowers. You will find this spiraea along roadsides in the mountains at low altitudes. Like the steeple-bush, the stamens are numerous, and give to the flower cluster a soft, fluffy appearance.

PARTRIDGE FOOT. ALPINE SPIRAEA
Lutkea pectinata (Pursh) Kuntze

White. Stems, shrubby; decumbent; caespitose; slender. Leaves, alternate; three-parted; the segments again lobed and parted. Inflorescence, a short raceme. Sepals, five. Petals, five. Stamens, numerous. Pistils, five; distinct. Habitat, high mountain meadows.

This little spiraea-like plant forms dense mats close to the ground in high mountain meadows. Its finely cut leaves are very moss-like, a characteristic that should make identification very easy. In suitable places the plants cover large areas.

NINEBARK
Opulaster opulifolius (L.) Kuntze

White. Stems, clustered; shrubby; upright or arching; five to ten feet tall. Bark, thin; flaky; loose; peeling in many layers at the base of old stems. Leaves, alternate; ovate; cordate; serrate; three to five lobed; deeply veined; pubescent beneath. Inflorescence, a hemispheric, umbel-like corymb. Flowers, white; numerous; showy. Calyx, five-cleft; persistent. Petals, five; orbicular. Stamens, numerous. Anthers, red; conspicuous. Pistils, one to five. Carpels, two to five; red; showy. Habitat, low rich soil. Blooming period, May.

In the journals of Lewis and Clark this shrub is commonly spoken of as "seven bark," but ninebark is now its more commonly recognized name. On old mature stems the parchment-like bark will easily peel off—layer after layer—the number of them by no means confined either to seven or to nine. On very old stems twenty or more may frequently be counted. The dainty white flowers appear in

THIMBLE-BERRY   *Rubus parviflorus*

rounded, compact umbels in early May. Asa Gray, lacking his usual clear discernment calls them—"White flowers of no beauty," but the popular name of bridal-wreath proves that Gray was for once mistaken in his verdict. Each flower has many slender stamens, each stamen tipped with a noticeable red anther, quite striking and decorative. The lobed carpels—bright red in color—that follow the blossoms, are also quite attractive.

GOAT'S BEARD
Aruncus aruncus (L.) Karst

White. Root, perennial. Stem, herbaceous; erect; glabrous; three to eight feet tall. Leaves, large; ternately decompound; leaflets, thin; ovate to lanceolate; doubly serrate; plaited. Inflorescence, a loose panicle. Flowers, minute; sessile; white; dioecious. Petals, five; spatulate. Stamens, numerous. Filaments, longer than the petals. Habitat, moist woods. Blooming period, May to July.

This is a plant of world-wide distribution, growing in cool rich woods from Alaska to Oregon in the West, eastward to New York, south to Georgia and Missouri, and in Northern Europe and Asia. It is a handsome spiraea-like herb, growing to a height of from three to ten feet. Its thrice pinnate leaves, and its bright green, taper-pointed and sharply serrate leafllets are attractively and deeply veined. The large open panicles, often two feet or more long, are borne at the summit of the plant, and are composed of slender pencils of minute, closely set white flowers. This plant is sometimes cultivated in gardens as an ornamental, and for this use deserves wider recognition. In nature it often forms dense banks and thickets in just such locations as a landscape gardener would choose were he planting it for the best possible effect.

THIMBLE-BERRY
Rubus parviflorus Nutt.

White. Stems, shrubby; upright; smooth; three to eight feet tall. Bark, green; on young shoots, becoming reddish-brown and flaky with age. Leaves, large; palmately five-lobed; serrate; strikingly veined. Inflorescence, terminal; few-flowered. Flowers, white; perfect; one to two inches across. Calyx, five-cleft. Petals, five; large; white; crape-like. Stamens, numerous. Carpels, many; tomentose. Fruit, a cap-like berry; flat; red; edible. Habitat, open woods and brushy tracts. Blooming period, May-June.

In nature's garden, her shrubby borders at the edge of the forest, surrounding lakes, bordering streams, or banking the base of cliffs— "tying them to the ground," in the language of the gardener—are among the most beautiful of all her floral features. There are spiraeas and syringas, ocean spray and *Ceantothus,* snow-berries and mahonias, with every available space between filled with glossy ferns, goats' beard or *mertensia.* None of these have a more prominent place, or are more essentially beautiful than the spreading, pale-green thimble-berry with its broad-lobed leaves, and delicate crepe-like flowers. The blooms of the thimble-berry can best be likened to soft crinkled tissue-paper. They are in form much like an extremely fragile wild rose. The fruit is flat and thin, and to me seems rather insipid, though highly praised by some writers. Both the berries and the tender early shoots were eaten by the Indians. Unlike most species of *Rubus* this plant is not at all thorny or prickly.

WILD BLACKBERRY. DEWBERRY
Rubus macropetalus Dougl.

White. Stems, weak; trailing; armed with sharp, curved prickles; six to thirty feet long. Leaves, three to five-foliate; serrate. Flowers, dioecious. Calyx, prickly. Petals, five; white; those of the staminate flowers much the larger. Stamens, many. Carpels, many. Fruit, a fine, well-flavored dewberry; black; oblong. Habitat, fence rows along new fields, and in burns and slashings. Blooming period, May-June.

> "Above the graves the blackberry hung
> In bloom and green its wreath,
> And harebells swung as if they rung
> The chimes of peace beneath."

Whittier's lines might have been written in Oregon, where, often, in our pioneer cemeteries the trailing blackberries have overgrown the ground, and draped themselves across the leaning stones.

This is the "green bryor" of Lewis and Clark, of which they said: "It rises perpendicularly to a height of four or five feet, when it descends in an arch becoming procumbent or rests on some neighboring plant or shrub—The frute is a berry resembling the blackberry in every respect and it is eaten when ripe and much esteemed by the natives.—This bryor retains its leaf or foliage and verdure until late in December."

This species has the pistilate and staminate flowers on different plants. The sterile, or staminate flowers are much the larger and more showy, so that where the most flowers are seen the least fruit will be found. No one who has gathered and eaten our common wild blackberry needs a recommendation for its fruit. It is the finest and richest in its genus. Some people consider it a trifle too acid, but when it is fully ripe even this can not be held against it. Wherever lumbering operations have been carried on it springs up as though by magic, and flourishes for a number of years, and although people come from miles to secure the fruit, literally tons of these delicious berries waste ungathered each year.

SALMON-BERRY
Rubus spectabilis Pursh

Reddish-purple. Stem, shrubby; armed with weak prickles; two to five feet tall. Leaves, trifoliate. Leaflets, ovate; serrate; often lobed; the principal veins somewhat prickly. Flowers, solitary; perfect; red-purple. Petals, five; ovate. Stamens, many. Fruit, red or golden-amber; raspberry-like. Habitat, moist woodlands. Blooming period, April to August.

There are three possible reasons why this plant came to be called salmon-berry. The first is from the fact that, in the fishing taboos of the Chinook Tribes, the salmon-berry held a large place. Coyote, according to one of their myths, was fishing for salmon, but had no success:

"Coyote scolded. 'Why have those salmon disappeared?' "

"Oh, you foolish Coyote. Do you think it is the same here as at Clatsop? Do not throw salmon ashore so that the head is downward. It is taboo. When you kill a salmon go and pick some salmon-berries. When you have caught many salmon put salmon-berries in the mouth of each."

The second possible reason is that the bark, which is astringent, was used by the early explorers as a remedy for certain digestive disorders brought on by eating too largely of salmon.

NUTKA ROSE   *Rosa nutkana*

The third reason is the clear salmon-yellow color of some of the fruit. These light colored berries are the best for eating. The dark red variety, while extremely beautiful when ripe, is ordinarily not so well flavored.

The young, tender shoots of the salmon-berry are edible, and were much used by the tribes of the lower Columbia. Salmon-berry shoots were usually eaten with fish spawn, or oil. In cases of necessity, however, they were eaten without dressing. David Douglas writes that "they (six Indians who were with him on a difficult trip) had paddled forty miles without any food except the young shoots of *Rubus spectabilis.*"

NUTKA ROSE
Rosa nutkana Presl.

Rose-pink. Stems, shrubby; erect; two to five feet; prickles abundant, strongly recurved. Leaves, alternate; pinnate; leaflets, five to nine; oval; doubly serrate. Rachis, glandular; prickly. Flowers, two to three inches in diameter; mostly solitary; fragrant. Calyx, five-cleft, tipped with foliaceous appendages; persistent. Fruit, bright red; globose. Habitat, open woods and brush-land. Blooming period, May-June.

Roses are the flowers of romance and chivalry, but our western rose has a different role in lore and folk-tales. It is the fruit, not the flower whose tales are told, and its association is that of dark and hopeless tragedy. Rose hips were a famine food of the western tribes, a supply of nutriment to sustain life against the time of actual starvation. To read, "It was winter and they were eating rose hips, which was all the food they had," is to realize the culmination of Indian misery. Often the early explorers suffered the same extremes of want. Nathaniel Wyeth, near Walla Walla, in 1832 wrote: "We found some poor horses in charge of a squaw and some children. They had no food but rose hips of which we made our supper." Townsend, in 1833 records: "Having nothing prepared for supper today I strolled along the stream and made a meal of rose buds." In camp that same night he found the botanist, Nuttall, making a meal of boiled owl.

LARGE-LEAVED AVENS   *Geum macrophyllum*

[176]

CLUSTERED ROSE
Rosa pisocarpa Gray.

Deep pink. Stems, slender; erect or sometimes trailing over other growths; three to fifteen or more feet long. Prickles, few; slender; straight. Leaves, serrate. Flowers, in corymbs; one to two inches in diameter. Otherwise much as *R. nutkana*.

The clustered rose is taller and more slender than the last species. Its stems are slender and rather weak and are inclined to sprawl over any convenient support or even to climb into the limbs of surrounding trees, sometimes to a height of from fifteen to twenty-five feet. The flowers are rather small. This rose will often be found associated with the nutka rose and it is not always easy to distinguish the two kinds. It is said to grow at greater altitudes in the mountains than our other common roses.

REDWOOD ROSE
Rosa gymnocarpa Nutt.

Rose-pink. Stems, shrubby; armed with prickles; one to four feet tall. Leaves, pinnate. Leaflets, five to nine; small; elliptical to oblong; serrate. Flowers, spicy-scented; about the size of a dime. Sepals, lanceolate; decidious. Petals, five; broad. Stamens, many. Fruit, smooth; red; oblong. Habitat, open woods and brush land. Blooming period, May.

The redwood rose is the smallest and daintiest of its kind. Its tiny flowers, often no larger than a dime, might be mistaken for a dwarfed flower of the nutka rose, but the sepals lack the long leaf-like tips of that species, and the scent is quite different, being delicate and spicy, though some specimens are entirely lacking in scent. The plants are small—two feet or more high—and they are fond of light shade. As the name indicates, this species extends its range southward into the redwood region of California.

LARGE-LEAVED AVENS
Geum macrophyllum Willd.

Yellow. Stems, erect; hairy; one to two feet tall. Radical leaves, lyrate; irregularly pinnate; six to nine inches long; the terminal

GRACEFUL CINQUEFOIL   *Potentilla gracilis*

leaflet very large; the lower ones unequal, sometimes very small; all toothed and lobed. Cauline leaves, sessile; three to five parted; toothed or lobed. Flowers, solitary or in a few-flowered terminal cyme. Calyx, five-lobed, alternating with five bracts. Petals, five. Stamens, many. Styles, many; elongated in fruit, and jointed and twisted at tip. Fruit, orbicular; dry. Habitat, moist fields. Blooming period, April-May.

The large-leaved avens is a rather coarse hairy herb, found growing along roadsides, usually in moist places. The flowers are yellow, borne in close clusters, and surrounded by reduced upper leaves. They have five broad, blunt petals, many stamens, and terminal styles that elongate in fruit, becoming dense spherical heads. These heads are noticeable, for each bristly style is abruptly bent and twisted near the summit, giving the whole a rather distinctive look.

WHITE DRYAD
Dryas octopetala L.

White. Stems, very short; tufted; woody at base. Leaves, alternate; petioled; oblong-ovate; crenately toothed; green above, white beneath. Inflorescence, solitary on slender scapes. Calyx, eight or nine lobed; the lobes lanceolate. Petals, usually eight; obovate. Stamens, many. Styles, persistent; becoming long and plume-like in fruit. Habitat, high mountains northward.

The white dryad, or wood-nymph, as its name indicates, usually, but not always, has eight petals. These are low alpine shrubs, closely allied to the cinquefoil and avens, and like the latter the persistent styles form a decorative ornamentation on the ripened fruit. The range of this plant is in the mountains from Mount Rainier, northward.

GRACEFUL CINQUEFOIL
Potentilla gracilis Dougl.

Yellow. Stems, tufted; upright; slender; ten to twenty inches tall. Leaves, basal leaves long petioled; palmately parted; cauline, few; short petioled; all green above and white tomentose below. Leaflets, three to seven; oblanceolate; pinnately cleft or toothed. Inflorescence, a cyme; few-flowered terminal. Calyx, persistent; of five lobes alternating with five bracts. Petals, five; obcordate. Stamens, numerous. Habitat, dry fields and prairies. Blooming period, May-June.

WHITE HORKELIA   *Horkelia fusca*

The bright yellow flowers of the cinquefoil are such a common sight along our roadsides that we often disregard their simple beauty. Gene Stratton Porter, through one of her characters, expressed the thought that all decorative artists were unaware of the existence of any other flowers save the conventional rose and violet. In this opinion I agree, and I further recommend the various species of cinquefoil, with their soft plaited leaves and golden blossoms as plants on which to base new decorative forms.

The name cinquefoil is derived from five, and leaf, because many of them have five-parted foliage. In the present species the leaflets are from three to seven. The flowers in form and substance much resemble those of the wild strawberry, a nearly related plant, but they differ in color, and are borne at the top of slender, upright stems.

Besides the above there are about ten species of cinquefoil found on the North Coast, many of them characteristic mountain flowers, and some of them quite rare.

WHITE HORKELIA
Horkelia fusca Lindl.

White. Rootstocks, perennial; scaly. Stems, erect; simple; twelve to thirty inches tall. Leaves, alternate; soft-downy; pinnately parted; the segments narrow. Inflorescence, a cyme. Calyx, five cleft; the segments alternating with five bracts. Petals, five, truncate; cuneate. Stamens, ten; on the receptacle. Filaments, broad. Styles, several to many. Habitat, dry open soil. Blooming period, May-June.

This is a weedy little plant, scarcely showy enough to be placed with the flowers, yet at times it makes a rather pretty showing with its white, or pink-tinted blooms. In form it very closely resembles the cinquefoils, and with that genus it has at times been classified. Its range is from Washington to California both east and west of the Cascades.

WILD STRAWBERRY
Fragaria chiloensis (L.) Duch.

White. Stems, extremely short. Leaves, all basal; short petioled; trifoliate. Leaflets, obovate; coarsely toothed; reticulated; tomentose beneath. Inflorescence, few-flowered. Scape, very short. Flowers, ply-

WILD STRAWBERRY

gamo-dioecious. Calyx, silky; the lanceolate lobes alternate with five bracts. Petals, five; orbicular. Stamens, twenty. Fruit, fleshy; fine flavored. Habitat, open prairies and hillsides. Blooming period, April-May.

The wild strawberry is one of our earliest flowers, and on sunny, sheltery banks it will often be found by the middle of February. Dr. McLoughlin, the factor at old Fort Vancouver, makes an even earlier date, for he says: "I have seen strawberries ripe here in December, and in blossom in January."

There are two general types of wild strawberries on the Pacific Coast, a thin leaved, long stemmed form, and a short stemmed, thick leaved form, to which the present species belongs. So short is the scape of this kind, especially in closely grazed pastures, that the process of picking the fruit is very tedious. At times the berries seem literally sunk into the ground. The fruit is of fine flavor, and well worth gathering when found in abundance. The Indians made extensive use of it, for it is the sweetest of our wild fruits, and was a rare change from their acid diet of unsweetened cranberries and wild crab-abbles.

Fragaria crinata Rydb. In this species the leaves are less strongly reticulated, and more hairy. Otherwise very similar to the above.

TALL WILD STRAWBERRY

Fragaria bracteata Heller

White. Scape, slender; upright; leafless; three to eight inches tall. Leaves, all basal; long petioled; trifoliate. Leaflets, ovate; coarsely toothed; pinnately veined and plaited. Flowers, polygamo-dioecious. Calyx, five lobed; lobes alternating with five bracts. Petals, five; orbicular. Stamens, twenty. Fruit, fleshy; somewhat acid. Habitat, open woods and fields. Blooming period, May-June.

That child is to be pitied who grows to manhood never having known the happiness of picking wild strawberries. What pleasant memories the very thought brings forth—long sunny noontime hours in the grassy fields searching out the sweet, luscious fruit—then, at the sound of the calling bell, to rush pell-mell into the little school house, and sing from the old Franklin Square Song Book:

"The strawberries grow in the mowing, Mill May,
And the bobolink sings in the tree;
On the knolls the red clover is growing, Mill May;
Then come to the meadow with me.
Yes, come, the ripe clusters among the thick grass,
We'll pick in the mowing Mill May,
And the long afternoon together we'll pass,
Where the clover is growing, Mill May."

This species bears its fruit on long slender scape, often taller than the foliage. The thin leaves are regularly and deeply veined, and coarsely toothed.

SILVER-WEED. CINQUEFOIL
Argentina grandis (T. & G.) Piper

Yellow. Roots, fleshy; edible. Stems, stoleniferous; creeping. Leaves, odd-pinnate; green above, silvery-white beneath; ten to fifteen inches long. Leaflets, nine to twenty-five, often interspersed with several minute pairs. Flowers, solitary; axiliary. Calyx, five-lobed, the lobes alternating with five bracts. Petals, five; yellow. Stamens, numerous. Habitat, along seashores.

This is a common plant immediately along the sea coast, but rare elsewhere. It is often classed among the cinquefoils which it resembles in many ways. This is the "cinquefoil" that holds so prominent a place in the tales and myths of the Coast Indians from Oregon to British Columbia. The roots are edible, and were so highly prized that they often formed a valued part of the marriage gift. The short upper roots were the food of the common people who dug them, but the long, lower roots were the chief's privilege, given to him by the lower class as a sort of tax or tribute. Indeed, to offer short "cinquefoil" roots to a chief or a person of noble blood was considered a deadly insult, only to be canceled by blood. The favorite "cinquefoil" digging grounds were a family heritage, and each family jealously protected its choice "garden." The roots were dug annually. Temporary houses were erected during the digging season, and the roots were dried for winter use, the chief's portion of long roots being religiously kept separate. At the close of the season, as they were about to depart, the head of the family, standing upright in his canoe offered a prayer to the house as follows:

"Look upon my wife and me, and protect us, so that nothing may happen to us, friend! And wish that we may come back to live in you happily, O house, when we come next year to dig cinquefoil; Good bye."

PURPLE MARSH-LOCKS
Comarum palustre L.

Purple. Stem, stout; ascending; one to two feet tall. Leaves, alternate; pinnate; with large stipules. Leaflets, five to seven; oblong; serrate. Inflorescence, a cyme; few flowered. Calyx, five-lobed; the lobes alternate with five narrow bracts; purple within. Stamens, twenty. Filaments, fleshy. Habitat, in marshes.

Another plant that was formerly classed with the cinquefoils, but it is now segregated into a genus of its own. The distinguishing feature of this species is its large, dark purple flowers, nearly an inch in diameter, quite different from the usual yellow cinquefoils. It has trailing or decumbent stems. It grows in swampy places, or along the borders of ponds in shallow water.

PEA FAMILY

FALSE LUPINE
Thermopsis gracilis Howell

Yellow. Stem, stout; glaucous; twenty to thirty inches tall. Leaves, alternate; three-foliate. Leaflets, oblong-ovate; one to three inches long. Stipules, large; leaf-like. Inflorescence, a terminal raceme. Flowers, papilionaceous; yellow. Calyx, pubescent, the lobes triangular; short. Stamens, ten; distinct. Pod, eight to ten seeded. Habitat, in open woods.

The flowers of this plant much resemble those of a true lupine, but with its clear yellow tints it offers a charming variation from the usual blues and purples of that genus. A further mark of identification will be found in the stamens, which are all distinct and separate, while in the lupines they are more or less united into one or two groups, or "brotherhoods." These are stout, thrifty-looking, upright plants, from fifteen inches to two feet tall. The flowers are borne in loose, terminal racemes.

COLUMBIAN LUPINE
Lupinus columbianus Heller

Purplish blue. Stem, branched; upright or decumbent; from a stout, woody, perennial caudex; twenty to forty inches tall. Leaves, radical leaves rather large; stem leaves alternate, smaller; all palmately divided. Leaflets, six to nine; oblanceolate. Inflorescence, a slender, terminal, bracted raceme; often attended by smaller, lateral ones. Bracts, sublate. Flowers, papilionaceous. Calyx, symmetrical or nearly so. Stamens, ten; monadelphous. Habitat, open gravelly ground. Blooming period, May to August; sometimes producing a second crop of flowers in late fall.

We who live west of the Rocky Mountains in what is known to botanists as "the lupine region," should be well acquainted with this abundant genus. Altogether there are over forty species of lupines within the borders of Washington and Oregon, and at least twenty in the humid western section covered by this book. Unfortunately, while the genus as a whole is well marked, the species are among the most difficult of all plants to determine, and the beginner must usually be content to name a few of the outstanding ones, and know the rest simply as lupines.

The name lupine is derived from the word lupus—a wolf—for the plants were supposed—like a wolf—to devour the fertility of the soil on which they grow. It is true that lupines often predominate in poor shallow soil, but far from being the cause of this sterility they are really soil builders, and are able to grow in such places because, through the nodules on their roots, they can draw fertility from the air, and in passing, leave the soil better, rather than worse. Let us be thankful that a plant as beautiful as this exists to populate and make beautiful the waste and barren places. When viewed from afar or close at hand they are equally pleasing. Each individual spike stands out straight and distinct, and with almost geometric exactness in the arrangement of the flowers, yet most graceful withal. One of the chief beauties of the lupine is its leaf. Each leaflet is folded precisely in bud, and when opened they spread out in a symmetrical, palmate circle, with the individual rays grooved to catch the drops of dew. The fine hairs of the leaf retain just enough air beneath each drop, to give to it a silvery sheen, so that in the morning, or after a shower, each leaf is an exquisitely fashioned, diamond-set ornament such as no silversmith may hope to equal.

Unfortunately, some varieties of lupine are a serious menace to livestock. Sheep, especially, are often poisoned by eating the leaves and pods. This causes the plants to be looked upon with disfavor in the grazing areas of the West.

CHINOOK LICORICE
Lupinus littoralis Dougl.

Blue. Root, fleshy; edible. Stems, decumbent or ascending; leafy; slender; ten or thirty inches long. Leaves, alternate; palmately five to eight parted. Leaflets, oblanceolate; one or two inches long. Inflorescence, a short raceme. Flowers, blue. Corolla, one-third inch or more in length. Pods, linear; ten to twelve seeded. Habitat, sandy beaches along the seashore.

This species of lupine, although perhaps not so handsome as some, is an extremely interesting plant, and its story is intimately woven into the history of the Puget Sound and Columbia River regions. Lewis and Clark in their journals have much to say about it under the name of licorice, and it was they who first recorded the use of the root for food. Twenty years later David Douglas collected and named the plant, and he also speaks of the edible roots, and was himself grateful for its sustenance when other food was exhausted.

The lupines, as is well known, are poisonous plants, and this species is no exception. When the Indians were forced by hunger to eat the roots in a raw state, it is recorded that they were afterwards overcome by a sort of intoxication, from which it took some time to recover. Here is a condensed account of the eating of the raw roots, as given by George Hunt, a Kwakiutl Indian of Fort Rupert: "In spring, when the salmon-berries begin to have buds and the olachen (smelt) first arrive in Knight Inlet, the season arrives when the tribes are hungry. Then the woman first takes her digging-stick and her basket, and goes to the flats back of the house. When she finds the tops of shoots of lupines as they come out of the ground, she puts down her lupine basket and her digging-stick. She pushes the point of her digging stick into the ground close to the lupine shoot, and she pries it up. As soon as the roots come out, she picks them out of the clay and throws them into her basket; . . . Then she takes some of the lupine roots and washes them. As soon as all of the clay is off, she begins to eat the roots, with her husband and children; and they only

MANY-LEAVED LUPINE   *Lupinus polyphyllus*

stop when they have enough. After eating lupine roots for a time they become dizzy, as though they were drunk. When the women and her husband eat too much of the lupine roots they become really drunk. Their eyes are heavy, and they can not keep them open, and their bodies are like dead, and they are really sleepy. Then they go and lie down and sleep; and when they wake up they feel well again, because they are no longer drunk."

It seems that the raw roots were eaten only in time of famine, and cooking, by baking or roasting, dissipated the deleterious principle. In the cooked state it seems to be a good food, and the writer quoted above concludes a long account of its preparation with the words: "Now they do not get drunk, and they do not get sleepy after eating (cooked) lupine roots."

The chinook licorice is a slender, decumbent or creeping plant of beaches and sand dunes. Its leaves are silky, its flowers blue, and the roots long and spreading. It is found close along the seashore from British Columbia to Northern California.

MANY-LEAVED LUPINE
Lupinus polyphyllus Lindl.

Purple or violet. Stems, upright; stout; simple; three to seven feet tall. Leaves, large; long-petioled; palmately divided. Leaflets, of lower leaves, ten to sixteen; upper leaves, six to twelve; from two to six inches in length. Racemes, terminal; one to two feet long; densely flowered. Flowers, violet, purple or sometimes white. Stamens, ten; monodelphos or diadelphos. Pods, about an inch long. Habitat, moist fields. Blooming period, April to June.

The many-leaved lupine is now cultivated as a garden flower throughout the United States and in Europe, and it is the best of the hardy perennial species. Under cultivation many shades and colors have been developed, but the best of them, it seems to me, can not surpass a really fine group of the wild plants in their native fields. It is native to Oregon and Washington, where David Douglas discovered it in 1825. "Nor can I pass," he says, "the beauty, not to say grandeur, of *Lupinus polyphyllus,* . . . covering immense tracts of the low land on the borders of streams, with here and there a white-flowered variety, and growing to a height of six or eight feet wherever the ground was partly overflowed."

CALIFORNIA TEA   *Psoralea physodes*

The leaves are very large; palmately lobed or divided, and spread out from the centre in a dial-like circle. The name sun-dial, commonly given to the cultivated forms, no doubt refers to this form of the leaves.

CALIFORNIA TEA
Psoralea physodes Dougl.

Green, white or purplish. Stems, branching; upright or declining; one to two feet tall. Leaves, trifoliate; dark green. Leaflets, ovate; acute; punctate or glandular dotted. Inflorescence, a short, dense raceme. Flowers, papilionaceous. Calyx, black-hairy; inflated in fruit. Stamens, ten; diadelphos. Pod, membranaceous; one-seeded. Habitat, open hillsides. Blooming period, June-July.

This plant is a near relative of the prairie potato, white-fruit, or *Pomme blanch,* (*Psoralea esculenta*) so often mentioned by the early hunters and explorers on the western plains. Besides this, it is principally interesting as being a source of a tea substitute largely used by the early settlers. The leaves were dried and used the same as the commercial article. They are rather pleasantly aromatic when crushed, and if held to a strong light are seen to be marked with numerous semi-transparent dots. These dots are the receptacles that hold a scented oil, giving to the plants their characteristic smell. The flowers are bean-like, but are small, greenish-white, and not conspicuous.

WILD CLOVER
Trifolium tridentatum Lindl.

Purple. Stem, glabrous; slender; erect; three to fifteen inches tall. Leaves, palmately trifoliate. Leaflets, linear to lanceolate; serrulate. Stipules, lacinate. Inflorescence, an involucrate, flattish head. Involucre, deeply cleft; the lobes cut and slashed. Flowers, papilionaceous. Calyx, five-toothed; the teeth subulate and sometimes again three-toothed. Stamens, ten; diadelphous. Habitat, open hillsides and prairies. Blooming period, May-June.

There are many kinds of clover found growing in the Northwest, but several of them are introduced, cultivated, or semi-domesticated species, and of our native sorts the greater part are small-flowered,

WILD CLOVER

inconspicuous plants. The flowers of the present species are light purple, prettily marked and blotched with dark purple and white. The flower heads are rather flat, consisting usually of a single circle —or at most only a few loose rows—of blossoms. Occasionally, in the spring, and in limited areas, these plants become plentiful enough to make good pasture.

WOOLLY-HEADED CLOVER
Trifolium eriocephalum Nutt.

White. Root, perennial; stout. Stems, soft-hairy; erect; five to ten inches tall. Leaves, palmately trifoliate. Leaflets, oblong to lanceolate; serrulate. Stipules, lanceolate. Inflorescence, a terminal, oblong, many-flowered head. Flowers, white; reflexed. Calyx, five-toothed; the teeth plumose. Stamens, ten; diadelphous. Habitat, open gravelly soil. Blooming period, May-June.

The heads of this interesting clover are soft and velvety, for its white, reflexed flowers are set in calices of downy silk.

AMERICAN VETCH
Vicia americana truncata (Nutt.) Brewer

Violet-purple. Stem, angled; slender; climbing by leaf tendrils. Leaves, pinnate. Leaflets, four to eight; elliptical; truncate; mucronate. Inflorescence, few-flowered; axillary; on long, naked peduncles. Flowers papilionaceous; short-pedicled. Calyx, five-cleft; the teeth short, unequal. Stamens, ten; diadelphous. Styles, slender; hairy at tip only. Pod, glabrous; about an inch long; three to six seeded. Habitat, brushy fields and roadsides. Blooming period, May-June.

> "There was once a nest in a hollow,
> Down in the mosses and knot grass pressed.
> Soft and warm, and full to the brim,
> Vetches hung over it purple and dim,
> With buttercup buds to follow."

You will find the common vetch trailing over bushes and weeds in the waste corners of fields and along highways. The stems are angled and weak, and support themselves by tendrils at the ends of the pinnate leaves. A sure mark of identification for this species is the ovate leaflets which terminate in an abrupt, square end, as though they had been clipped off.

See back end of sheet for picture.

WOOLLY-HEADED CLOVER

GIANT VETCH

Vicia gigantea Hook.

Ocherous. Stems, tall; stout; climbing by tendrils at the ends of the leaves. Leaves, pinnate; six inches or more long. Leaflets, large; oblanceolate; entire; eight to fourteen pairs. Pedicles, shorter than the leaves. Inflorescence, axillary; six to fourteen flowered. Flowers, papilionaceous. Stamens, ten, monadelphous. Style, slender; hairy at tip only. Pod, broad; one to two inches long; three to four seeded. Habitat, open woods or brush land.

The ocherous blossoms of the giant vetch will be found hanging in bushes and over weeds in moist bushy places. They are borne in dense one-sided racemes from the axils of the leaves. The seeds are edible, and were used by the Indians.

CREAM-COLORED PEA

Lathyrus sulphureus Brewer

Cream-colored. Stems, weak; climbing by tendrils at the end of the leaves; two to five feet tall. Leaves, pinnate. Leaflets, three to five pairs; broad; ovate or oblong. Inflorescence, axillary; a raceme. Flowers, papilionaceous; two to twelve; cream-colored or sulphur-colored, becoming brownish with age. Stamens, diadelphous. Style, slender; bent and flattened at the summit; hairy on the inner surface. Habitat, dry brushy tracts. Blooming period, May-June.

The genus *Lathyrus* are commonly known as wild pea, or, more properly, vetchings. They very much resemble the true vetches, and are distinguished from them principally by the form of the style, which in the vetches is round, with a tuft of fine hairs at the extreme tip, while in the vetchlings it is flattened, and has a brush-like tuft of hairs extending for some distance down the concave side. In general, also, the flowers of the vetchlings are larger, some species, like the sweet pea of our gardens being very showy. Our wild species, however, are rather inconspicuous.

The present species should be easily identified, as it is the only vetchling in our territory that has cream-colored or yellowish flowers,

CREAM-COLORED PEA   *Lathyrus sulphureus*

MANY-LEAVED PEA
Lathyrus polyphyllus Nutt.

Purple. Stem, glabrous; stout; branching; climbing by leaf tendrils; two to five feet tall. Leaves, pinnate; large. Leaflets, eight to twenty pairs; thin; oblong; obtuse. Inflorescence, axillary; six to ten flowered. Flowers, papilionaceous; purple. Stamens, ten; diadelphous. Style, flattened and hairy on inner surface. Pods, four to twelve seeded. Habitat, open woods. Blooming period, May.

The many-leaved pea is a luxuriant, showy plant with long pinnately divided leaves of from sixteen to forty leaflets terminating in a small tendril. The flowers are purple, closely crowded in short racemes, and appear in May. Very few of the blossoms ever mature seed. The whole plant is smooth and hairless.

Shaggy Pea, *Lathyrus littoralis* (Nutt.) Endl. The whole plant is densely clothed with long silky hairs. The leaves have from one to three pairs of leaflets and no tendril. A coastal species, common along the ocean shore.

Beach Pea. *Lathyrus maritimus* (L.) Bibel. A thin-leaved, purple-flowered species having from three to five pairs of leaflets. It is common on sandy beaches along the Pacific Coast from Alaska to Oregon, as well as along the Atlantic, about the Great Lakes, and in Europe. The green seeds are sometimes used the same as garden peas.

One-Flowered Pea. *Lathyrus torreyi* Gray. The round, erect stems of the one-flowered pea grow from six inches to a foot tall. The leaflets number from four to six pairs, and are rather hairy. The flowers appear singly, or at times in twos and threes, and are bluish-purple and white, and very fragrant. It is found in woody borders from Washington to California.

BICOLORED BIRD'S-FOOT
Hosackia bicolor Dougl.

Yellow. Stem, branched; glabrous; succulent; erect or decumbent; one to two feet tall. Leaves, odd-pinnate; smooth. Leaflets, five to nine; thin; obovate or oblong. Inflorescence, a flat, spreading umbel. Flowers, four to twelve; sessile; papilionaceous. Corolla, yellow, with white, or occasionally pink wings. Stamens, ten; diadelphous; sessile. Pods, terete; spreading. Habitat, slow shallow streams or pools; growing in the water. Blooming period, May-July.

MANY-LEAVED PEA

Lathyrus polyphyllus

The bicolored bird's-foot makes its home in shallow ponds or along the borders of slowly flowing streams. The flowers are delightfully fragrant and are attractive both in arrangement and color. The bright yellow tubes of the blossoms form a compact, velvety circle, bordered at its circumference by the pure white wings of the corolla. Rarely, mingled with the yellow and white flowers will be found a variety having soft pink wings in place of white. Later in the season, when the flowers have fallen, the long slender pods extend in a radiating circle and look like the naked ribs of a coverless umbrella, or, when fewer in number, like the spreading toes of a bird's foot. This last resemblance has given to the genus its common name of bird's-foot.

CREEPING BIRD'S-FOOT
Hosackia decumbens Benth.

Yellow. Stems, creeping; decumbent; slender; tufted from a perennial woody caudex; villous. Leaves, odd-pinnate, usually of five obovate leaflets. Inflorescence, a flat spreading umbel. Stamens, diadelphous. Pod, curved; few-seeded. Habitat, dry gravelly prairies. Blooming period, May-June.

The odd-pinnate leaflets of the common creeping bird's-foot are usually borne in fives. In texture they are soft and silky; irregular in outline, and from one to two centimeters in length. The stems of this plant are slender and wiry, and creep over the ground in dry gravelly places, a single plant sometimes forming a mat-like tuft of considerable size. The flowers are bright yellow in color, with a few flecks or splashes of red at the base of the petals. The standards are broadly ovate, upright, and slightly reflexed. The two lateral wings are narrow and folded, and extend forward beyond the keel in two noticeable horn-like projections. The flower clusters are arranged in a close, converging umbel, each umbel accompanied by a leafy bract consisting of from one to three leaflets.

PINK BIRD'S-FOOT
Hosackia crassifolia Benth.

Pink or purplish. Root, perennial. Stems, glabrous; erect or decumbent; branching; rather succulent. Leaves, pinnate; light green. Leaflets, nine to fifteen; oblong or ovate; entire; thin. Inflorescence,

PINK BIRD'S-FOOT

an umbel. Flowers, papilionaceous. Calyx, five-toothed; the teeth nearly equal. Stamens, diadelphous. Pod, stout. Habitat, dry open woods. Blooming period, May.

The umbels of the pink bird's-foot are raised on slender stems, and save for the large size of the blossoms, and the fact that they grow in a single row, look rather like a pink clover head. The succulent stems are branched and rather weak, having scarcely strength to stand alone, and often decline upon the ground. This plant is a lover of dry places, and grows plentifully east of the Cascades as well as in California.

GERANIUM FAMILY

OREGON CRANE'S BILL
Geranium oreganum Howell

Purple. Root, perennial. Stems, erect; slender; branching; with long internodes; one to two feet tall. Leaves, long petioled; five to seven cleft; the segments cuneate, incised and toothed. Inflorescence, axillary. Flowers, large. Sepals, oblong-ovate; glandular. Petals, five; obovate; purple. Stamens, usually ten; in two sets, one set shorter. Ovary, beaked; five-lobed; five celled. Habitat, open brushland. Blooming period, May-June.

The seed pods of the common wild geranium are extended in a long beak-like form, from which the plant receives its popular name of crane's bill. The attics of our grandmothers contained many homely herbs and simples comprising a rural *materia medica* of unquestionable value. Among others, were the roots of this plant, which are very astringent. When pounded in an iron mortar they were used to check bleeding, or, internally, as a remedy for diarrhea or dysentery.

The Oregon crane's bill is of very limited distribution, since it is found only in the Willamette Valley. The flowers vary in color from light purplish to nearly pink. White flowered specimens are occasionally found. The crane's bill is one of the most difficult of all plants to photograph, since it wilts and droops almost as soon as picked.

OREGON CRANE'S BILL   *Geranium oreganum*

YELLOW WOOD SORREL
Oxalis suksdorfii Trelease

Yellow. Rootstocks, scaly. Stems, erect; slender; two to four inches tall. Leaves, trifoliate; villous; petioled. Leaflets, obcordate. Flowers, singly or in pairs; on pedicels that about equal the leaves. Sepals, five; nearly distinct. Petals, five; yellow. Stamens, ten; in two sets. Filaments, dilated at base. Habitat, dry open soil. Blooming period, May-June.

Every country child knows the yellow wood sorrel both by sight and taste, for its palatable, acid leaves are a great favorite everywhere. Mr. Fredrick Stack records the fact that sorrel leaves eaten raw are of benefit in certain forms of skin disease. This is in complete harmony with the recently reported fact that raw sorrel leaves contain the greatest percent of vitamins of any green vegetable. Much of the sturdiness of country children, then, may be due to their often deplored habit of eating nature's goodies wherever found. The instinct that causes pussy to roll in the catnip, and leads children to the sorrel patches may be a wiser guide than all the learned physicians. The leaves of the sorrel are neatly folded in bud, and close on dark days and at night. Oxalic acid, useful for certain bleaching and cleaning operations, is a product of the various species of sorrel.

MOUNTAIN SORREL
Oxalis oregana Nutt.

White. Rootstocks, scaly; spreading. Leaves, trifoliate; erect on slender petioles four to six inches tall. Leaflets, obcordate; one to two inches broad. Flowers, solitary. Scapes, usually shorter than the petioles; each bearing two small bracts. Sepals, five; nearly distinct. Petals, five; white, purple veined. Stamens, ten. Habitat, deep woods. Blooming period, May-June.

If you are used, as was I, to the small, delicate wood sorrel of the East, you will be amazed when you first enter the deep coastal forests to find acre on acre of the giant mountain sorrel completely covering the forest floor. It is remarkable not only for its abundance and profusion of growth, but for the size of its foliage which surpasses anything that one could imagine. No plant is more characteristic of

MOUNTAIN SORREL

Oxalis oregana

the humid West than is this. The flowers of this species are borne singly on slender scapes, shorter than the leaf petioles. They measure from two-thirds, to one inch in length, and are white with purple veins.

Oxalis trilliifolia Hook., is a very similar species found in the same habitat, the two kinds often intermingling. It may be easily known by the more numerous flowers—three to eight in an umbel, and raised nearly to the height of the leaves.

SPURGE FAMILY

TURKEY MULLEN
Piscaria setigera (Hook.) Piper

Greenish. Stems, much branched; procumbent; five to twenty inches long. Leaves, opposite or crowded at the ends of the branches; hispid. Flowers, monoecious; greenish; inconspicuous. Seeds, smooth; shiny; gray. Habitat, on dry prairies or gravel banks along streams.

The foliage of the turkey mullen is harsh and rank-scented, and it is no doubt poisonous as is that of most members of the spurge family. This is another of those plants that were used by the Indians to obtain fish. Thrown into pools at the season of drouth, it had a tendency to stupify or intoxicate the fish, and they floated to the surface and were easily caught. The seed of the turkey mullen when ripe is ejected from the pod with considerable force—often to a distance of ten or fifteen feet—the act being accompanied by a sharp snapping sound.

CASHEW FAMILY

POISON OAK
Rhus diversiloba T. & G.

White. Stems, shrubby; slender; upright or climbing by rootlets; one to thirty feet tall. Leaves, alternate; three to five foliate; shiny; dark green. Leaflets, oblong or ovate; obtuse; toothed or lobed. Inflorescence, an axillary, drooping panicle. Flowers, polygamo-dioecious; small; white or greenish. Fruit, white. Habitat, dry open hillsides or gravelly prairies. Blooming period, June-July.

POISON OAK   *Rhus diversiloba*

The poison oak with its glossy, bright green summer foliage—crimson-tinted in autumn—and its masses of minute, starry flowers, would be a very attractive plant were it not that association has rendered it obnoxious. The very beauty of its form has lured many a victim to gather it, to his later profound regret. The plant assumes a variety of forms according to the soil and environment in which it grows. In poor soil, where no support is available for its weak stems, it spreads over the ground by creeping root-stocks, forming a ground cover of slender, shrubby plants from a few inches to a foot in height. At other times it forms close, compact bushes, from two to ten feet in height, or it may climb as a vine high into the trees. In burns and slashings it often forms magnificent pillars by growing about snags and stubs.

The result of touching poison oak largely depends on the physical condition of the individual. Some persons can gather it with impunity, while others experience the direst results from even the slightest touch. A severe case of *Rhus* poisoning is a really serious calamity, entailing intense suffering. Even fatal results have been known to occur when the mouth and throat have become affected. For those who are prevented by this shrub from enjoying out-door life, it is worth knowing that a thorough washing of all exposed parts—hands, face, neck and even ankles if thin stockings are worn—in a solution of baking soda, is an almost sure preventative of oak poisoning. This precaution should be taken as soon as possible after coming in contact with the plants, and it is also advisable, especially for extremely sensitive persons, to avoid handling the clothing worn in the woods without afterwards scrubbing the hands with a soda solution. This simple remedy will save untold suffering if carefully observed.

Even this noxious shrub has its uses, and among the Indians, who appear to have been nearly immune to its poison, the slender stems are used to a considerable extent in the manufacture of baskets. The fresh juice also produces a black stain, used in creating ornamental designs on their utensils. According to Mr. Chestnut, the Pomo Indian name for the plant is *Ma-tu-ya-ho,* meaning literally, Southern fire doctor, and they used the juice to burn out the roots of warts —after first cutting them off—and as a cure for ring-worms. The flowers of this plant are very fragrant and secrete abundant nectar, and the honey gathered from them is said to be of excellent quality.

Ceanothus sanguineus

BUCKBRUSH

STAFF-TREE FAMILY

MOUNTAIN LOVER
Pachistima myrsinites (Pursh) Raf.

Dull reddish. Stems, shrubby; one to three feet tall. Leaves, opposite; leathery; smooth; evergreen; ovate or lanceolate; serrate on upper portion. Inflorescence, axillary. Flowers, brown or purplish red; small; solitary or in small cymes. Sepals, four; united. Petals, four; separate. Stamens, four. Ovary, two celled. Habitat, in woods and thickets, especially in the mountains. Blooming period, March-April.

This is a pretty little evergreen shrub, more noticed for its foliage than for its flowers which are very small. Abundant in the mountains from British Columbia to California.

BUCKTHORN FAMILY

BUCKBRUSH
Ceanothus sanguineus Pursh

White. Stems, shrubby; upright; slender; four to twelve feet tall. Bark, smooth; reddish. Leaves, deciduous; thin; ovate; serrate. Inflorescence, a panicle. Flowers, small; fragrant; all its parts white. Calyx, five-cleft. Petals, five; arched; minute. Stamens, five. Styles, three. Fruit, dry; horny; three-lobed. Habitat, dry open woods. Blooming period, May.

The low, delicate New Jersey tea of the East, of which our Revolutionary ancestors made a drink to replace the tax-cursed English product, is replaced in the West by its near relative, the tall woody buckbrush. This abundant shrub grows to a height of from six to eighteen feet; has slender, reddish twigs; thin, alternate, deciduous leaves, and abundant panicles of white, sweet-scented flowers. As the individual blossoms are very small, the effect is that of a bush covered with soft, fluffy plumes. The whole flower—petals, calyx, and even the slender pedicels that support them—are of a soft, pure white. They appear in early May in the Willamette Valley, but later northward and in the mountains. Early in the season the tender new twigs of the buckbrush have a pleasant taste like wintergreen. This flavor persists until the season's wood hardens, when it disappears, or is hidden under the bitterness of the mature bark. The various species

CHAPARRAL   *Ceanothus cuneatus*

of Western *Ceanothus* are often given the name of wild lilac, and their panicled flowers somewhat warrant this name, but it is more applicable to certain blue-flowered species, mostly natives of California.

Ceanothus peduncularis Greene, is a smaller species with pointed, entire leaves, pubescent on both surfaces, and having blue or white flowers. Its range is from California to Washington.

CHAPARRAL
Ceanothus cuneatus (Hook.) Nutt.

White. Stems, shrubby; erect; closely branched; rigid; two to twelve feet tall. Leaves, small; opposite or whorled; short petioled; oval; scantily dentate; evergreen. Flowers, in axillary umbels; white; minute. Calyx, five-cleft. Petals, five; clawed; hooded. Stamens, five; exserted. Styles, three. Fruit, dry; horny; three-lobed. Habitat, dry gravelly ground. Blooming period, May.

Chaparral is a Spanish-Californian term meaning a dense thicket, and is used to designate any closely growing underbrush, though composed of several species. The Oregon use of the word in connection with this plant is not unwarranted, however, for few shrubs are capable of forming more impassible thickets. The stems are branching, stiff and brittle, and are beset with somewhat thorny twigs so closely interwoven that it is almost impossible to force a passage through them. To this I may add that along the Willamette River, where it is abundant, it is usually twisted and matted with the debris of winter floods into an almost hopeless maze. The leaves of this plant are very small, evergreen, and as shown by the arrangement of the branches, are opposite, though often appearing in confusing whorls. The mark of the twigs is whitish or ashy. The flowers which come in May are usually white, but sometimes bluish. This shrub is not found north of the Columbia River.

CALIFORNIA LILAC
Ceanothus thyrsiflorus Esch.

Blue. Stems, shrubby; branched; five to twenty feet tall. Branches, angled; smooth; brownish. Leaves, thin; oblong; serrate. Flowers, small; in dense compound panicles. Calyx, five-lobed. Petals, five; hooded. Stamens, five. Ovary, three-lobed. Habitat, dry hillsides.

WILD HOLLYHOCK   *Sidalcea virgata*

This southern species is the finest of its genus within our limits. With us it is a loosely branched shrub, from five to fifteen feet in height, but in California it occasionally becomes a tree, as much as twenty-five feet tall, and with a trunk from five to twelve inches in diameter. This is the true "wild Lilac," for its dense terminal panicles are a beautiful pale or light blue and very showy. Although found both in Western Washington and Oregon, the wild lilac is rare here, but in California whole hillsides are tinged with its blossoms.

STICKY LAUREL
Ceanothus velutinus Dougl.

White. Stems, shrubby; stout; forked; three to eight feet tall. Leaves, thick; gummy-coated; evergreen; shiny above; woolly beneath; alternate; oval; obtuse strongly three-veined. Inflorescence, a compound panicle. Flowers, minute. Calyx, five-lobed. Petals, five; arched and clawed. Stamens, five. Habitat, dry hillsides and open woods. Blooming period, May to August, according to altitude.

In dry open woods and in the mountains to an altitude of three or four thousand feet, grows this interesting species of *Ceanothus*, commonly known as sticky laurel, or wild white lilac. The plant is rather stout, with smooth and forked branches, and bears its leaves principally near the ends of the twigs. These leaves are evergreen, coated with a gummy varnish, very glossy above, and somewhat woolly beneath. The whole plant is permeated with a strong aromatic odor. The flowers are white, and very similar to the common buckbrush. Mr. Saunders tells of a novel use for the flowers of this, and other species of *Ceanothus*. They may be used as a substitute for soap, and make a healthful, fragrant, and cleansing lather. This species grows from about the latitude of San Francisco, northward into British Columbia.

MALLOW FAMILY

WILD HOLLYHOCK
Sidalcea virgata Howell

Pink. Stems, weak; slender; ten to thirty inches tall. Basal leaves, long petioled; orbicular; lobed or divided. Cauline leaves, reduced;

three to seven cleft; all stellate-pubescent. Inflorescence, a tapering raceme. Flowers, pink. Calyx, five-cleft. Petals, five. Stamens, numerous; united in a double tube. Habitat, dry open ground. Blooming period, April to June.

The dainty wild hollyhock will be found growing on dry hillsides from late April until June. Not in size or stateliness does it merit this name, but rather in the form and arrangement of its flowers. These are slender, delicate plants, only a foot or two tall, and show none of the stiff formality of the true hollyhock. The basal leaves are long petioled, orbicular in outline, sometimes cut and lobed, at other times nearly entire. The stem leaves are narrowly divided, the lower ones usually five, or from five to seven lobes, the upper ones much reduced. The flowers which are borne in a simple slender raceme are an inch or more across, and bright pink or rose-colored—rarely pure white. There are five petals, blunt or notched at the summit; thin and as delicate as craped silk. These petals are beautifully convoluted and taper-pointed in bud. The stamens are united into a prolonged tube about the pistils, and terminate in a brush-like cluster of many minute anthers. This is a very pleasing plant, but as the flowers wilt almost as soon as gathered, it is not satisfactory for cutting. Found abundantly in the Willamette Valley and southward.

TALL WILD HOLLYHOCK
Sidalcea campestris Greene

Pink or white. Stems, erect; branching above; pale green; two to six feet tall. Basal leaves, petioled; orbicular in outline; palmately five to seven parted; the divisions narrow and unevenly lobed. Cauline leaves, deeply parted into linear divisions. Inflorescence, a terminal raceme. Fruit, several carpels forming a close ring; separating at maturity. Habitat, moist fields and swales. Blooming period, May-June.

This stiff, upright, rather stout species of wild hollyhock grows in wet swales and roadside ditches, often reaching a height of five or six feet. The flowers are almost identical in form and size with those of *S. virgata,* but are pale pink or nearly white in color, and borne in a rather close raceme. The scanty foliage and the stems are pale green. All the leaves, both radical and cauline, are deeply lobed and divided. This plant is not common north of the Columbia River, where its place is taken by the following species.

HENDERSON'S WILD HOLLYHOCK
Sidalcea hendersonii Wats.

Red. Stem, green; glabrous; erect; twenty to thirty inches tall. Leaves, orbicular; five to seven cleft; the segments lobed and toothed. Fruit, smooth at maturity. Habitat, marshes along the seashore, Northward. Otherwise the same as the two preceding species.

This is an erect, bright green species of wild hollyhock, having red or deep rose-colored blossoms. It is a northern species, found from Vancouver Island, southward to Oregon, and especially abundant in marshes near the sea coast.

ST. JOHNS-WORT FAMILY

SCOULER'S ST. JOHN'S-WORT
Hypericum scouleri Hook.

Yellow. Stems, stiff; erect; simple or branched at summit; from a few inches to three feet tall. Leaves, opposite; sessile; partly clasping; oblong; entire; dark dotted on margins; about an inch long. Inflorescence, a cyme. Flowers, half an inch across. Sepals, five; obtuse; persistent. Petals, five; orange yellow; black dotted on margins. Stamens, many; in three clusters. Styles, two to five. Capsule, obtuse. Habitat, in wet places.

All who know the pestiferous goat-weed, Tipton-weed, or field St. John's-Wort—a most obnoxious plant from Europe, and now all too common here—will recognize the present form as belonging to the same genus. The numerous slender stamens in the midst of the bright yellow blossoms would alone proclaim that fact, and the dark-dotted leaves help to make identification certain. Our plants are lovers of moist places, in contrast to the European form which grows in dry fields.

In the Old World many superstitions are found clustering about this family. The flowers are supposed to appear on St. John's Day, (the twenty-fourth of June,) and were used at that time to avert the influences of evil spirits. *"Fuga daemonum"* (devil chaser) was formerly one of its common names.

SCOULER'S ST. JOHN'S-WORT

Hypericum scouleri

[216]

CREEPING ST. JOHN'S-WORT
Hypericum anagalloides Cham. & Schlecht

Yellow. Stems, slender; branching; weak; prostrate; forming mats. Leaves, opposite; entire; sessile; slightly clasping; ovate; small; punctate with dark or pellucid dots. Inflorescence, a cyme. Sepals, lanceolate. Petals, five. Stamens, filiform; fifteen to twenty. Styles, two to five. Habitat, moist places. Blooming period, May to August.

This little flower will be found commonly about springs, along ditches, or in cool spagnum bogs throughout our territory. Its specific name, *anagalloides,* refers to its fancied resemblance to the pimpernel, and thus it receives its common name of "false pimpernell." The stems are weak and prostrate, the leaves small and rather closely set, and the flowers are a pretty shade of salmon yellow.

VIOLET FAMILY

TRAILING YELLOW VIOLET
Viola sempervirens Greene

Yellow. Stems, creeping; slender; smooth. Leaves, evergreen; cordate; orbicular; punctate with brownish dots. Stipules, oval. Flowers, solitary; yellow, veined with brown. Petals, five, unequal; the lower ones spurred; the two lateral ones bearded. Stamens, five; short; conniving and nearly covering the short styles; two posterior ones spurred. Habitat, open woods. Blooming period, February to June.

This is the smallest and daintiest of our three common yellow violets. Its evergreen leaves are smooth and broadly heart-shaped, and the plants spread by slender trailing stems which creep over, and through the moss and fallen leaves in moist woods.

JOHNNY-JUMP-UP
Viola nuttallii praemorsa (Dougl.) Wats.

Yellow. Stems, very short. Leaves, petioled; obovate to lanceolate; crenate; white pubescent. Stipules, scarious; lanceolate. Scapes, longer than the leaves. Petals, five; yellow; not bearded; the lower one spurred. Stamens, five; short; clustered about the style; two of them spurred. Habitat, dry prairies. Blooming period, March-May.

Viola glabella

BRANCHING YELLOW VIOLET

In every part of the world, in English speaking countries, you will find some member of the violet family, either wild or cultivated, bearing the name of Johnny-jump-up. It is a meaningless name, originating no one knows when or how, but it has grown up with the language, and it is so woven into our folk-history, and twined into our childhood memories that no one, even were it possible, would wish to suppress or change it. On the Pacific Slope I have found this name most frequently coupled with the yellow flowers of *Viola nuttallii,* and have so retained it in this book, although perfectly aware that many will differ with me, and claim the name for some other species.

This flower delights in dry prairies, and sunny, well drained knolls, and may be easily recognized by its upright, ovate to lanceolate leaves, which are covered on both sides with soft white hairs. No other description than this is necessary, for the leaves of all our other species are smooth, or nearly so.

BRANCHING YELLOW VIOLET
Viola glabella Nutt.

Yellow. Stems, smooth; branching; five to twelve inches tall. Leaves, broadly cordate; toothed. Flowers, yellow; solitary; axillary. Petals, five; the lower one spurred. Stamens, five; short; clustered about the short style. Habitat, moist woods. Blooming period, March to May.

> "Beneath the spreading maples, old,
> Are shadows, edged and set with gold,
> For yellow violet's shining face
> Makes happy all that darksome place."—L. G. H.

This large yellow violet has thin, heart-shaped leaves, and succulent branching stems. The showy blooms are veined and centred with purplish brown. It often covers large tracts in moist woods and about the margins of thickets.

All of our violets have a peculiar habit that is well worth observing. In spring when the air is cool, and moisture plentiful, they present to our view many showy flowers. A little later they seem to cease blooming, but if we search low down among the leaves we find many new buds forming, and these finally develop seed without ever having opened. These late, cleistogamous flowers really produce more

Viola adunca

BLUE VIOLET

seed than the early, showy ones. It seems as though the plants, after one short, youthful blaze of beauty, had settled down to sedate, thoughtful age, with an eye to utility rather than show.

BLUE VIOLET
Viola adunca Smith

Violet-purple. Stem, short; leafy. Leaves, ovate-cordate; crenate. Pedicels, as long or longer than the leaves. Petals, five; unequal; the lateral ones bearded, the lower one spurred. Stamens, five; short; almost hiding the pistil. Habitat, moist open places. Blooming period, April-May.

To speak of blue violets, is, of course, a misnomer, but in this, as in so many other cases, we understand the English language by what is meant, rather than by what is said.

The violets are the flowers of the poets, the synonym for modesty, and the personification of fragrance, but in this last quality our wild species do not fulfill the tradition, for they are mostly lacking in scent. This species is a small, pretty sort of low growth. The flowers are rather short stemmed, violet-purple, bearded in the throat. The leaves are brown-dotted, heart-shaped, and toothed. It is common in open meadows and roadsides from Alaska to California.

Viola howellii Gray, is a species of more limited range, found only from British Columbia to Oregon. It has broad, dotless leaves and entire stipules. The flowers are violet.

Viola montanensis Rydb., is a short, branching-stemmed species, with very pale violet flowers. Found in mountain meadows.

Viola palustris L., or Blue Swamp Violet, is a stemless species with pale violet flowers. It will be found in swamps from Alaska, southward, its range extending eastward as far as Labrador. It is also a native of Europe and Asia.

BIRD-FOOT VIOLET. HALL'S VIOLET
Viola hallii Gray

Yellow and violet. Stems, short; glabrous. Leaves, five-parted, the lobes again cut and cleft into linear divisions; callus-tipped. Flowers, solitary, on slender peduncles. Petals, five; unequal; the lower one spurred; two upper ones violet; three lower ones yellow. Stamens,

GIANT FIREWEED   *Epilobium angustifolium*

short; conniving about the short style; two posterior ones spurred. Habitat, prairies.

Not found north of the Willamette Valley. The upper petals are dark violet, the lower ones yellow. The plant is almost stemless, the leaves and blossoms rising from spreading rootstocks. The leaves are deeply three-parted, each division also cut and divided into from three to five narrow segments.

EVENING PRIMROSE FAMILY

GIANT FIREWEED. WILLOW HERB
Epilobium angustifolium L.

Rose-colored. Root, perennial. Stems, erect; mostly simple; three to eight feet tall. Leaves, short petioled; lanceolate; acute; simple. Inflorescence, a spire-like terminal raceme. Flowers, on slender pedicels, accompanied by linear bracts. Petals, four; obovate; clawed; spreading. Stamens, eight; in two unequal sets. Stigma, of four recurved lobes. Pod, linear. Seeds, minute, accompanied by abundant silky hairs. Habitat, open burns and slashings. Blooming period, June to September.

The giant fireweed at its best is worthy of our greatest admiration, for its tall stateliness, pleasing flowers, and willow-like foliage make a perfect picture in soft tints and graceful lines.

Some plants are of very local habitat, being limited to a single state, or even county. Others are world-wide in their distribution, and continents and hemispheres are their boundaries. The present species belongs to the latter class, for it truly encircles the globe, being found abundantly throughout Northern Asia and Europe as well as in America. It is a noticeable plant, and every nation where it abounds has taken note of its rosy, tapering spires, and woven it into their life, either in story, song, or homely utility. The Alaska Indians in their cedar huts tell a tale of a terrible one-eyed giant who seeks to deceive the innocent by exchanging useless arrows tipped with fireweed pods for good weapons, thus hoping to gain an advantage and so destroy them. The poet laureate of England sings of the brook slipping softly past—

> ". . . Many a fairy foreland set
> With willow-weed and mallow."

The bee-keepers of our own western states, as well as in Wisconsin and Michigan, hail its flowers as a blessing, knowing that where it abounds every hive will be filled with pure fragrant honey. In Russia, just as we sip our oriental tea for a soothing beverage, so they use the dried leaves of the fireweed. They call it Kaporie tea, and every year many tons of it are prepared and marketed. Even the wood from the seed pods has been used to a limited extent for padding and filling quilts, although it lacks the qualities to make it a really good fibre. Finally, in our own states and in Canada some people seek out the tender young shoots for "greens," a welcome addition to the monotony of early spring diet.

A trip through any lumber producing area of the coast at the right season will reveal great patches of fireweed covering the logged-off lands and the accompanying burns and slashings. As you curve about on the mountains, climbing higher and higher on the narrow grades, brilliant patches of fireweed, many acres in extent, attract the eye across the distant canyons as far as the eye can see. The name fireweed is due to the fact that it springs up so quickly on burned over areas, nor are burned forests the only place where it appears, for when several blocks in my home village were burned, the whole area was soon covered with two or three species of fireweed.

PANICLED FIREWEED
Epilobium paniculatum Nutt.

Pink. Stems, slender; branched; one to two feet tall. Bark, reddish; loose; flaky. Leaves, linear. Flowers, pink; small; terminating the almost leafless branches. Petals, four; notched at apex. Capsule, linear. Seeds, minute; silky-appendaged. Habitat, dry open soil, abundant after fires. Blooming period, June to August.

This is a slender, narrow-leaved, annual form of fireweed. It is quite variable in its habits, sometimes much branched and bushy, at other times with simple, strict stems. The flowers are small, pale pink or sometimes white. The calyx tube is lengthened beyond the ovary.

There are many other species of fireweed in our territory, but they are difficult to classify, and most of them have small, inconspicuous flowers.

Epilobium adenocaulon Haussk. This rather succulent species of fireweed grows in moist places, and in the autumn produces fleshy rosettes of crowded leaves on the crown of the perennial roots. The leaves are ovate-lanceolate, short petioled, and bright green. The flowers are bright pink, and each petal is distinctly notched at the summit.

YELLOW FIREWEED
Epilobium luteum Pursh

Yellow. Stems, one to two feet tall; slender. Leaves, opposite; elliptic to ovate; dentate. Flowers, yellow; in the axils of the upper leaves. Style, exserted. Stigma, four-parted. Habitat, along streams in mountains.

This fireweed is unique in having yellow blossoms, a most unusual feature for this genus. It is a common mountain plant, growing from Alaska to Oregon.

FAREWELL-TO-SPRING
Godetia arnottii (T. & G.) Walp.

Rose-purple. Stems, erect; leafy; simple; from a few inches to two feet tall. Leaves, oblong to lanceolate; entire; becoming crowded at the summit of the stem. Flowers, closely crowded in the upper leaf axils. Petals, four; rose-purple. Stamens, eight. Capsule, short; stout; prominently ribbed. Habitat, dry banks and prairies. Blooming period, June-July.

The persistence with which some plants will live and survive under unfavorable conditions is well illustrated by this species. I have found large tracts of it, year after year, on dry, sterile banks, where every individual was starved and stunted to a height of only an inch or two, while not a plant could be found in much riched soil nearby. Under favorable conditions, it is a slender plant from eight to twenty inches tall, its simple, leafy stem bearing at the summit a crowded cluster of showy rose-purple flowers. The short, stout seed pods are abruptly pointed, as though cut off, and are strongly eight ribbed.

SLENDER FAREWELL-TO-SPRING
Godetia quadrivulnera (Dougl.) Spach.

Dark rose-purple. Stems, slender; simple or branching from the

HERALD-OF-SUMMER

[226]

Godetia amoena

base; erect; one to three feet tall. Leaves, alternate; narrowly ovate
to lanceolate; simple; entire; somewhat folded. Inflorescence, axillary.
Flowers, small; solitary. Calyx, four lobed; lobes free and strongly
reflexed, or splitting along two sides only, and reflexed in two sections. Petals, four; obovate. Stamens, eight. Pistil, one. Stigma, four
lobed, the lobes short and broad. Capsule, sessile; grooved; slender.
Habitat, dry fields. Blooming period, June-July.

This is a slender, sometimes branching species of godetia, found
in dry pastures and fields from Washington to California. The flowers are dark rose-purple, small, and are borne singly in the axils of
the leaves. The sepals, which in bloom are strongly recurved, are
sometimes split into two sections, and sometimes entirely divided and
separate.

HERALD-OF-SUMMER
Godetia amoena (Lehm.) Lilja.

Rose-purple. Root, annual. Stem, slender; upright; simple or
branching; one to two feet tall. Leaves, alternate; short petioled;
linear to lanceolate. Flowers, terminal or in the axils of the upper
leaves. Buds, erect. Calyx, tips united, splitting along one side and
turning back in bloom. Petals, four; obovate; obtuse and slightly
notched at summit. Stamens, eight, in two series. Anthers, yellow;
curved at tip. Stigma, four-lobed. Capsule, slender; long; without
conspicuous ribs; obtuse. Habitat, dry prairies. Blooming season,
June-July.

Of the eight or more species of godetias found within our territory, this is perhaps the showiest, and largest. The godetias are
strictly Western American plants. The genus as a whole has been
given the somewhat poetical name of farewell-to-spring, but the present showy species is distinguished by the specific appelation of herald-
of-summer. In this latitude it distinctly deserves that name, for I
invariably find the first seasonal blooms within a day or two of the
summer solstice. The silky, rose-purple flowers are two or three inches
across, and are variable in color, at times quite pale, at other times
of rich, royal shades, unsurpassed by any bloom. Often the base of
each petal is marked with a deep crimson eye that is very effective.
The plants are usually found along roadsides and fence rows in the
valleys, sometimes making perfect banks of color. Many handsome
cultivated varieties of godetias have been developed from our native

Boisduvalia densiflora

species, and this probably has the honor of being the first one so grown. At Fort Vancouver, in 1826, they were planted in the garden "along with the turnips," and David Douglas reported that under cultivation they grey "very branched and thrifty." From Fort Vancouver this botanist carried them to England, and from there they were distributed to France and Switzerland, and throughout Europe. In our own country they are not yet known as they should be.

The green sepals which completely encase the unopened buds have an interesting manner of bursting along one side only, to release the expanding flowers, and turn back in a single piece, instead of separating and opening as in most blossoms.

While as a genus the godetias are easy to know, the separation of the various species is sometimes difficult. One distinguishing feature of this one is its long, slender seed pods, not prominently ribbed, and its upright buds.

Boisduvalia densiflora (Lindl.) Wats.

Rose-purple. Stem, upright; simple; leafy; ten to thirty inches tall. Leaves, lower leaves lanceolate; upper leaves broader and shorter. Inflorescence, a crowded leafy spike. Flowers, in the axils of the dense upper leaves. Calyx, funnelform; four-lobed. Petals, four; two-lobed. Stamens, eight; in two sets. Habitat, moist fields and ditches. Blooming period, June to August.

A rather pretty little plant found growing in ditches and wet fields. Its alternate leaves are narrowly lanceolate and scattered below, but become broader and densely crowded at the summit of the stem. The flowers are borne in the axils of the upper leaves. They are rose-pink with noticeable purple veins. So far as I have been able to learn this plant has no common name. The seeds which are numerous were gathered for food by the Indians. They are small, but rich and meaty, with somewhat the taste and consistency of flax-seed, and are no doubt quite nourishing.

Boisduvalia stricta (Gray) Greene., is a similar, rarer species having both upper and lower leaves narrowly lanceolate, and with smaller, purplish flowers.

EVENING PRIMROSE
Oenothera biennis L.

Yellow. Stem, upright; simple. Leaves, alternate; lanceolate to oblanceolate; repandly denticulate; the lower ones petioled, the upper ones sessile. Flowers, sessile; in a leafy spike. Calyx, villous; four-lobed; lobes reflexed. Petals, four; obovate; yellow. Stamens, eight; all equal. Ovary, four-celled. Stigma, four-lobed. Habitat, along rivers; commonest near the coast.

The evening primrose, viewed by day, presents to our view the draggled remains of a few wilted flowers, and a number of unopened buds. Watch it at dusk, however, and you may see a few of the largest buds flutter into bloom almost in a moment's time. Usually only a few flowers open each night. The few petals are soft and silky and bright yellow in color. The young, tender shoots of this plant are edible.

GINSING FAMILY

DEVIL'S CLUB
Echinopanax horridum (Smith) Dene. & Planch.

Greenish. Stems, shrubby; erect; armed with prickles; leafy at summit; three to twelve feet tall. Leaves, very large; rank-scented; long-petioled; palmately five to many lobed; serrate; the principal veins armed with prickly thorns. Inflorescence, dense; a terminal paniculate umbel. Flowers, greenish; perfect or polygamous. Calyx, teeth; obsolete. Petals, five. Stamens, five; alternating with the petals. Styles, two; filiform. Fruit, a scarlet berry; laterally compressed. Habitat, moist woods.

A most peculiar shrub, with slender, flexible stems closely armored along their entire length with sharp, stiff prickles. The leaves, which are handsomely lobed and maple-like, form a flat tuft at the summit of the stems. The larger leaf veins are also closely armed with prickles, both on the upper and lower sides. The stems of this exceedingly disagreeable plant form a serious obstacle when encountered while threading a tangled thicket, for the wounds made by them are very painful. Such painfully difficult thickets appealed even to the imagination of the Indians. Many of their favorite folk-tales record how the fleeing hero, when in distress, throws behind him some prickly object, which, by his magic, becomes changed into an impassable tangle of devil's club in which the pursuing enemy becomes entangled and sadly torn. Next to the hellebore this was undoubtedly the Coast Indians' most valued medicine. A bit of its bark tied to the hemlock-root halibut hook was believed to insure a large catch of that highly valued fish. Amulets of the wood worn by the shamans enabled them to accomplish prodigies in the overcoming of supernatural beings. Houses or booths constructed entirely of devil's club were sometimes prepared for a shaman of recognized power, that he might escape every form of ceremonial pollution and prepare himself for some important work.

A decoction of the bark is a violent emetic, and to vomit was, by the natives, considered the quickest means of obtaining strength and purity. This medicine, therefore, together with hot sea water was administered to all the members of war parties, as well as to hunters about to start on any difficult expedition.

The flowers appear in a pyramidal cluster at the summit of the plant. They are greenish white, and unattractive, but the fruit that follows is a brilliant scarlet berry, and very showy.

CALIFORNIA SPIKENARD
Aralia californica Wats.

White. Root, large; thick; aromatic. Stems, herbaceous; branched; six to ten feet tall. Leaves, very large; alternate; bipinnate. Leaflets, cordate-ovate; serrate; four to eight inches long. Inflorescence, a racemed umbel. Umbels, almost globular. Flowers, small; white. Petals and stamens, five. Fruit, a fleshy, purple berry. Habitat, deep moist canyons in low mountains. Blooming period, June-July.

The great luxuriant plants of the California spikenard will be found growing in moist, rich canyons where the direct rays of the sun seldom reach. Its leaves are immense, and loosely spreading, and the single leaflets are much larger than the entire leaves of most plants. Unlike its near relative, the devil's club, this plant bears no spiny armor, but the whole plant is smooth and delightful to the touch. This is a southern form, not found north of the Columbia River.

COW PARSNIP   *Heracleum lanatum*

PARSLEY FAMILY

PURPLE SANICLE
Sanicula bipinnatifida Dougl.

Maroon. Stems, stout; six to eighteen inches tall. Leaves, long petioled; mostly basal; pinnately parted; the divisions incised, lobed or toothed. Inflorescence, a loose, long-rayed, unequal umbel. Rays, three to five. Involucre bracts, small leaflets. Umbellets, close; head-like. Flowers, minute; purplish or maroon. Petals, five. Stamens, five; exserted. Habitat, dry soil in open places. Blooming period, April to June.

The flowers of the purple sanicle are not beautiful, but the plant has a certain decorative quality that raises it above a mere weed. Purple seems hardly the proper name to apply to it. To my eye the color of the bloom is rather a deep shade of maroon. Very common in dry soil everywhere.

COW PARSNIP
Heracleum lanatum Michx.

White. Root, perennial. Stems, stout; hollow; rank-scented; four to eight feet tall. Leaves, petioled; mostly basal; ternately compound; large and coarse. Leaflets, round-cordate; irregularly toothed. Petioles, hollow; much dilated. Inflorescence, a large; flat; many-rayed umbel. Bracts of involucre, deciduous. Bracts of involucle, numerous. Flowers, white. Petals, five; obovate. Stamens, five. Stylopodium, conical. Fruit, broad; ovate; much flattened dorsally. Habitat, low rich lands. Blooming period, May-June, extending to August at high altitudes.

To those who wish to vary the monotony of their spring diet by an occasional taste of wildlings I recommended the common cow parsnip. The stout flower scapes are the part that are ordinarily used, although the leaf stalks are also edible. The scapes should be gathered when they are nearly full grown, but before the blossoms have opened. On fine plants they will then have reached a diameter of an inch or more, yet still be fresh and tender. Peel the stems just as you would rhubarb. After peeling, cut them into short sections, and cook by boiling, pouring off the first water. A long cooking is necessary, and they should not be considered done until the little cylindrical pieces

KOUSE

are tender, and begin to fall apart. Add milk, butter, salt and pepper, and serve as you would creamed carrots.

If you are fond of salads, try cutting the raw stalks into very thin slices, together with a few wild onions, and the roots of the spring beauty; serve with dressing, or add a small portion of the above to a lettuce salad to add a piquaint flavor.

All of the tribes from Alaska to California used the fresh stems of the cow parsnip; besides which, according to Chestnut, some of them burned the basal portion of the stalk, and used the ashes as a substitute for salt.

Because of its common name of cow parsnip or wild parsnip, many people have supposed this plant to be poisonous. This is far from the truth; cattle are exceptionally fond of it, so much so that it will never be found in pastures where cattle range because by close grazing they soon eradicate it.

The cow parsnip is the giant of its family, for it grows to a height of six or eight feet, with immense, broad leaves, proportionate in size. The broad umbels are often from a foot to eighteen inches in diameter. The generic name, *Heracleum,* from Hercules, expresses the gigantic proportions of the plant.

KOUSE. BISCUIT-ROOT
Cogswellia utriculata (Nutt.) Jones

Yellow. Root, fleshy; spongy; simple or branched; edible. Stems, short; rarely up to ten inches, often almost acaulescent; slender; smooth. Leaves, compound; ternately dissected into very narrow, linear lobes. Petioles, dilated. Inflorescence, a spreading, unequal umbel. Involucre, conspicuous. Flowers, yellow; small. Petals and stamens, five each. Fruit, elliptical; strongly flattened dorsally. Habitat, open hillsides and dry prairies. Blooming period, April to June.

The writings of nearly all the early explorers contain frequent reference to a plant called kouse or couse—occasionally spelled cows—or biscuit-root, or, among the French, *racine blanch.* These names are applied to a number of species of the genus *Cogswellia* of which the above is our West Coast representative. It is a delicate little plant with finely cut leaves, and umbels of minute yellow blossoms. It grows on dry prairies or hillsides throughout Western Oregon and Washington. The root, which is the part used for food, varies in form

IPO

Carum oreganum

from slender spindle-shaped to contorted, or nearly spherical. They are not large, often no thicker than a common pencil, and it must have required an immense amount of labor to secure the great quantities which the Indians stored for their winter's use. The outer skin is dark, and peels off easily, and the interior is soft, spongy, and white, and easily masticated. Eaten raw they are rather pleasant, having a slightly carroty taste. Boiled, they are rather insipid, but when fried in butter they are quite palatable. The Indian manner of preparing the roots seems to have been to pound them in stone mortars, form them into large flat cakes, and sun-dry them. In the journals of Lewis and Clark the statement is made, "The noise of the women pounding the cows root reminded me of a nail factory."

YAMPAH. YEAR-PAH
Carum gairdneri (Hook. & Arm.) Gray

IPO
Carum oreganum Wats.

White. Roots, fusiform; clustered; fleshy; edible. Stems, erect; simple or branching above; slender. Leaves, few; small; pinnate to bipinnate. Leaflets, linear or lanceolate. Umbels, hemispheric; eight to fourteen rayed. Involucre and involucles, of linear bracts. Petals and stamens, five each. Stylopodium, conical. Fruit, of *C. gairdneri,* orbicular; small; of *C. oreganum,* oblong; larger. Habitat, prairies and swales from low elevations to three or four thousand feet altitude in mountains. Blooming period, May to September.

Frequently the comment of the early explorers on the plant life which they observed is more enlightening than anything that we can write. This is especially true of those plants, the roots of which were used by the Indians for food. The explorers themselves were often forced to eke out an existence from such roots, and have much to say about them. Thus, from the journals of Lewis and Clark, I have chosen the following paragraph:

"Sacajawea gathered a quantity of roots of a species of fennel which we found very agreeable food, the flavor of this root is not unlike anise seed — —. These are called by the Shoshones Year-pah. These roots are very palatable either fresh, roasted, boiled or dried, and are generally between the size of a quill and a man's finger, and about the length of the latter. —— —— The rind is white and thin, the body or consistence of the root is white, mealy, and easily reduced by pounding to a substance resembling flour, which thickens with boiling water like flour, and is agreeably flavored."

Captain Fremont also looked upon these plants with great favor, and appreciation: "At this place I first became acquainted with the yampah which I found our Snake woman digging in the low-timbered bottom of the creek. Among the Indians of the Rocky Mountains, and more particularly among the Shoshones or Snake Indians, in whose territory it is very abundant, this is considered the best among the roots used for food, which they take pleasure in offering to strangers." And again: "For supper we had yampah, the most agreeably flavored of the roots."

I have often gathered these roots and eaten them, and at present am growing them in my garden. When baked they burst open, exposing the dry mealy interior, and are very appetizing. They are also extremely good when fried in butter. Squirrels are fond of these roots, and in the Cascade Mountains gather large amounts of them for their winter stores.

The Klamath name of ipo, epa, or apo, (variously spelled), for *C. oreganum,* is an adaptation from more southern tribes, and is possibly a corruption of the Spanish word, *apio,* celery.

The yampah is common throughout Western Washington, and both species are found in Oregon. Few people, I find, know these plants, which is unfortunate, considering their interesting history. Their white blossoms are often confused with those of the wild carrot, but the leaves are quite different, and the cluster of palatable tubers growing at the base make identification easy.

WATER HEMLOCK
Cicuta douglasii (DC.) Coult. & Rose

White. Rootstock, stout; tuberous. Stem, smooth; branched; upright; twenty to thirty inches tall. Leaves, twice pinnate. Leaflets, ovate-lanceolate; serrate. Inflorescence, an umbel; long peduncled. Involucre and involucles, none. Flowers, white or purplish. Petals and stamens, five each. Stylopodium, conical. Fruit, orbicular. Habitat, wet ditches and swamps. Blooming period, May to July.

The water hemlock or cowbane is an exceedingly poisonous plant, and a menace to stock, especially to cattle, wherever it grows. It is said that a piece of the root as large as a walnut is sufficient to kill a cow. As the first shoots of springtime, when tender herbage is scarce, are fully as baneful, it is no wonder that hungry cows and sheep often fall a victim to this plant. The Klamath Indians of Oregon recognize the venomous character of the roots, and, to poison their arrows, prepare a mixture of the juice of water hemlock, rattlesnake poison, and decaying deer's liver.

Swampy areas, stream borders, and drainage ditches about wet fields are its natural habitat. The stems grow from one to three feet in height, and the ornamentally cut, bright green leaves, and umbels of white flowers are quite attractive.

DOGWOOD FAMILY

PACIFIC DOGWOOD
Cornus nuttallii Audubon

White. Stem, a tree; twenty to sixty feet tall. Bark, smooth; gray. Leaves, alternate; obovate; simple; petioled. Inflorescence, a compact, head-like cyme, surrounded by a conspicuous involucre of white, petal-like bracts. Bracts, four to six; broad; one to three inches across. Calyx, persistent in fruit. Petals, four; small; greenish. Stamens, four. Fruit, a cluster of fleshy red drupes. Habitat, open woods. Blooming period, April-May, also in autumn.

The Pacific dogwood is the finest of our native flowering trees. At every season of the year it is attractive. Its mottled gray bark, and glossy deeply veined leaves make it very ornamental, and when, in early spring, it clothes itself in a garment of magnificent, pure white blossoms, or, in autumn, changes the green of its leaves to brilliant red, it becomes a truly striking tree. Moreover, it has a habit of bearing a second crop of blossoms in the fall, and its scarlet and orange berries round out its season of beauty. Even in winter, it has a curious charm, for then each twig is tipped with a rounded green button —buds prepared for the next season's blooming.

The flowers of the dogwood are of curious construction, for what appears to the casual eye as a single blossom is really a cluster of minute flowers surrounded by white bracts. The whole sometimes measures as much as six inches across.

The trees prefer the moist soil of canyons and stream banks. The

PACIFIC DOGWOOD   *Cornus nuttallii*

wood is fine grained, white, and compact, and is often used as a substitute for box-wood in the manufacture of bobbins, shuttles, mallet heads and other articles requiring hard usage. The bark is bitter and tonic, and has been used successfully in the place of quinine. Townsend, on his journey to Oregon in 1833, reports marked success in curing Indian children of malaria through its use. A similar use was made of the Eastern dogwood by the Confederates during the Civil War.

BUNCHBERRY
Cornus canadensis L.

White. Stem, simple; slender; erect; four to eight inches tall. Leaves, four to six; whorled near the summit of the stem; obovate; pointed at both ends. Pedicels, one to four inches long. Inflorescence, a close, head-like cyme of minute flowers, encircled by four petal-like bracts. Bracts, white; ovate. Petals, four. Stamens, four. Fruit, a drupe; fleshy; red; edible. Habitat, mountain woods. Blooming period, May to August according to altitude.

Imagine, if you can, a dogwood tree reduced in size until it become a slender herb, four to eight inches tall, its abundant foliage replaced by a whorl of from four to seven leaves, and above all a single terminal blossom. The result would be a fairly accurate picture of the bunchberry. It is true that the leaves of this little plant are pointed, and proportionately more narrow, and that the blossoms, which are about an inch across, have only four white bracts, where its larger relative has from four to seven, but in every other way the resemblance is most striking. Like its larger relative, too, it has the habit of producing two crops of bloom, one in spring and the second in late summer. The flowers are followed by compact clusters of brilliant red berries that give the plant its common name. These berries, though somewhat insipid, are edible, and are still an article of diet among the coast Indians of British Columbia. The whites of Northern New England also use them as an ingredient in plum duff, and call them pudding-berries.

The bunchberry is a woodland and mountain plant, appearing at its best in open woods in the Cascades, at an elevation of from one to three thousand feet:

"Where cornel flowers are grouped, in crowds, on strips of turf and moss."

WESTERN DOGWOOD
Cornus occidentalis (T. & G.) Coville

White. Stem, a shrub or small tree; branched; erect; six to twenty feet tall. Bark, of young twigs; red; of older stems, grayish. Leaves, ovate; acute; smooth above; white pubescent beneath; plaited and veined. Inflorescence, a loose cyme; not involucrate. Flowers, white. Calyx teeth, minute. Petals and stamens, four each. Fruits, a drupe; white. Stone, two seeded. Habitat, shores of ponds and along streams. Blooming period, May, producing a second crop of bloom in late summer.

Differing from our other two dogwoods, the berries of this species are white when ripe. The greenish-white blossoms are borne in a loose cyme, and do not have the large white bracts that make the blossoms of our other species so noticeable. The leaves are very deeply veined, green above and whitish pubescent beneath. This is a shrub or small tree found growing along streams and on low land. Like the other dogwoods it often bears two crops of flowers each season.

PYROLA FAMILY

CONE PLANT
Newberrya congesta (Gray) Torr.

White or tawny. Stems, clustered; stout; simple; white or brownish; four to eight inches tall. Leaves, scale-like; imbricated; thin; oval to oblong; entirely without chlorphyl. Inflorescence, a short, closely crowded raceme. Flowers, tubular urn-shaped; four to five lobed. Calyx, of from two to four bract-like sepals. Stamens, eight or ten. Filaments, hairy above the middle. Habitat, deep woods in the mountains. Blooming period, June to August.

The dense forests of the Pacific Coast, with their plentiful moisture, and abundant decaying vegetable matter are particularly suited to the production of saprophytic or scavenger plants. The following group comprises several of these curious forms, among which are strange and interesting plants, but none more curious than the present species.

The cone plant, when it pushes its head through the forest floor, looks more like a fungus than a flowering plant. Indeed, it looks very like a massive head of cauliflower, or one of the large clumps of

WESTERN DOGWOOD

coral fungus which grow in similar locations. The short stems are crowded into a closely packed mass. The whole solid growth is from three to seven inches tall, and from four inches to nearly a foot across. The entire plant is white or tawny, without green foliage. The flowers, which are closely packed at the top of the plant, are also waxy white, clammy, and without scent. Examined closely we find that they are urn shaped, and not entirely lacking in beauty.

STICK CANDY
Allotropa virgata T. & G.

Red and white. Stems, erect; simple; white and scarlet; ten to twenty inches tall. Leaves, scale-like; lanceolate. Inflorescence, a raceme. Flowers, erect; urn-shaped. Sepals, five; small. Petals, none. Stamens, ten. Stigma, capitate; five-lobed. Capsule, globose. Habitat, deep mountain woods. Blooming period, June to August.

One of the most showy of the saprophytes found growing in our deep forests is the striped *Allotropa,* or, as it is often called, stick candy, barber's pole, or devil's wand. These names alone would proclaim it a floral curiosity, and the plant when seen does not disappoint our expectations. It has no green leaves, but its brilliant coloring makes it very noticeable. The whole stem is splashed and striped with scarlet, on pure white, and when the loose scales are removed it resembles nothing so much as a brightly striped stick of candy. At a recent Scout Camp, where I introduced the boys to this plant, they at once realized its possibilities, and few of the adult leaders but fell to the lure of the brilliant, palatable-looking sticks, and literally "bit," to the great delight of the boys.

Although the flowers have no petals, and the sepals are small, they are brightly colored like the stems, and are very attractive. The ten blunt, short stamens stand in a regular circle about the globular ovary and capitate pistil, and suggest a dainty, miniature crown of ruby and white enamel. This plant has a very limited range, being mostly confined to the region covered by this book.

PINE DROPS
Pterospora andromedea Nutt.

Red. Stem, erect; simple; wand-like; glandular; red or purplish;

INDIAN PIPE   *Monotropa uniflora*

one to three feet tall. Leaves, reduced; scale-like; lanceolate; without chloryphl. Inflorescence, a long, many-flowered raceme. Flowers, white or reddish; nodding. Corolla, globular, with five recurved lobes. Calyx, five-parted; persistent. Stamens, ten. Habitat, deep woods in mountains. Blooming period, summer.

This is the tallest of our saprophytes, sometimes reaching a height of three feet. The stems are upright, straight and slender, with numerous scattered scales near the base. The flowers are in long loose racemes, white or pinkish, with a drooping, urn-shaped corolla. The whole plant is disagreeably sticky-viscid.

INDIAN PIPE
Monotropa uniflora L.

White. Stems, clustered; white; waxy; four to ten inches tall. Leaves, reduced to white scales. Flowers, terminal; nodding; solitary. Calyx, white; of two to four irregular sepals. Petals, five or six; oblong. Stamens, twice as many as the petals. Style, stout; short. Stigma, funnel-form. Capsule, ovoid; erect. Habitat, moist deep woods. Blooming period, June-July.

A drooping flower molded from pure white wax, best describes the common Indian pipe. As is clearly shown by its white, almost leafless form, it is dependent upon the predigested remains of other plants for its nutriment. This is the most plentiful and best known of a large group of saprophytic plants that are so peculiarly abundant in the moist woods of the Coast. This species is of wide distribution, growing in forests throughout the breadth of our country, as well as in Japan, but it is nowhere more plentiful than in our own woods, where abundant decaying vegetation makes an environment suitable to its needs. Each stem bears a single drooping blossom, with five petals, ten stamens, and a single stout pistil. They grow in clusters of from three to twelve stems, and to a height of from four to ten inches.

The name, Indian pipe, is only one of its titles, and refers to the drooping pipe-like form. Other names inspired by the color and texture of the stems are ghost flower, corpse plant, and ice plant.

PIPSISSEWA

Chimaphila umbellata

MANY-FLOWERED INDIAN PIPE
Hypopitys hypopitys (L.) Small

Tawny. Stems, tawny or reddish; clustered; six to twelve inches tall. Leaves, bract-like; ovate-lanceolate; lacking chloryphl. Inflorescence, a short raceme. Flowers, three to ten; nodding. Sepals and petals, five each in the terminal flowers; three to four in the lateral ones; all longer than the sepals; saccate at base. Stamens, six to ten. Filaments, filiform. Stigma, funnel-form. Fruit, erect. Habitat, coniferous woods. Blooming period, June to August.

In general appearance and habits this species is much like the preceeding, but the stems never grow in such dense clusters, and the flowers are borne in close, one-sided racemes, and are slightly fragrant. The plants are tawny, cream-colored or reddish. Its range is in North America, Europe, and Asia, and reaches around the world.

PIPSISSEWA. PRINCE'S PINE
Chimaphila umbellata (L.) Nutt.

Pink. Stems, erect; clustered; shrubby; five to ten inches tall. Leaves, evergreen; leathery; whorled; short petioled; oblanceolate; toothed. Inflorescence, a terminal corymb. Scape, erect; leafless. Flowers, numerous; nodding, pink or white. Calyx, five-parted. Petals, five; concave; waxy; thick. Stamens, ten. Filaments, curved; dilated; hairy. Anthers, two-horned. Styles, very short; stout. Stigma, peltate. Habitat, open woods. Blooming period, June-August.

A plant of the evergreen woods, and itself an evergreen, with shiny, leathery, sharply serrate leaves borne in whorls about the stem. The flowers are about one-half an inch in diameter, and are borne in terminal clusters, three to ten blossoms to each stem. They are pink, waxy, and fragrant. Formerly this plant had a considerable reputation as a medicine, both among the whites and Indians, but it is now little valued.

The collecting and picturing of wild flowers is not all sheer pleasure, and the memories connected with this species are especially vivid. The plants were gathered far back near the summit of the Cascades, and sealed, together with wet moss, inside a large baking powder can. Then, carefully carrying them in my hand, for two long days we bumped over the roughest of mountain roads, seated flat on the springless bottom of a farm wagon. It was August, and the sun was hot. Those sixty miles were the longest in all my memory; yet the flowers survived in good shape as the accompanying picture testifies.

MENZIES' PIPSISSEWA. PRINCE'S PINE
Chimaphila menziesii (R. Br.) Spreng.

Pink or white. Stems, erect; three to six inches tall. Leaves, few; ovate; acute at both ends; often veined with white. Scape, few-flowered. Flowers, pale pink or white. Otherwise as for *C. Umbellata.*

A smaller plant than the last, with fewer leaves, and less symmetrical in form. The veins of the leaves in this species are often bordered and variegated with white. The flowers are white or pale pink, and borne in small clusters.

SINGLE BEAUTY
Moneses uniflora (L.) Gray

White. Stems, short; simple; erect or decumbent. Leaves, two to four pairs; whorled; petioled; ovate to orbicular; serrate; obtuse. Flowers, solitary; nodding; on a slender scape. Calyx, four to five parted; persistent in fruit. Petals, five; distinct; spreading orbicular; white or pink. Stamens, ten. Anthers, two-beaked. Style, straight; exserted. Stigma, peltate; five-lobed. Habitat, coniferous woods in the mountains; more abundant northward.

In form and habit this plant resembles the pipsissewa, but the leaves lie closer to the ground, and are ovate or roundish, and the scape bears but a single white or pinkish bloom. The name, "moneses" meaning "delight" is very suitable for this pretty flower. It grows in moist deep woods, often at a considerable altitude in the mountains.

ONE-SIDED WINTERGREEN
Pyrola secunda L.

Green. Rootstocks, slender; branched. Stems, slender; simple; erect; three to eight inches tall. Leaves, evergreen; whorled; near the base of the stem; thin, ovate; short petioled. Inflorescence, a slender one-sided raceme. Petals, five; green. Stamens, ten. Pistils, straight; not declined. Stigma, large; five-lobed. Habitat, coniferous woods in the mountains. Blooming period, June-July.

The wintergreens are an interesting group of plants, in that the genus seems poised upon the verge of parasitism, and the various species show every grade of vegetation from the chlorphyl bearing plants, to those entirely lacking in that essential aid to assimilation. The present species is probably self dependent, since even the flowers, as well as the stems and leaves are green. It is a comparatively small plant, reaching an extreme height of eight inches. The leaves are mostly clustered at the base of the stem, and are oval with toothed margins. The single flower scape bears its blossoms in a one-sided or secund raceme. This is an easy mark of identification and gives the plant its specific name.

GREEN-FLOWERED WINTERGREEN
Pyrola chlorantha Sw.

Greenish. Scape, erect; six to twelve inches tall. Leaves, all basal; evergreen; dull; leathery; orbicular; petioled; the blades shorter than the petioles; one half to one inch broad. Inflorescence, a simple raceme. Flowers, three to ten. Calyx lobes, very short. Petals, five; greenish. Stamens, ten. Styles, curved downward. Habitat, coniferous woods.

The green leaves of this species are roundish in form, thick, and small. The simple scape is naked, or bears but a single small bract. The flowers are nodding, and greenish white.

The pyrolas are the true wintergreens, but must not be confused with the false wintergreen from which the well known flavoring of that name is obtained. The latter is *Gaultheria procumbens,* more properly called checker-berry, and is a plant of Eastern America.

PEAR-LEAVED WINTERGREEN
Pyrola bracteata Hook.

Pink or reddish. Scape, stout; erect; eight to fourteen inches tall; scaly-bracted. Leaves, evergreen; leathery; all basal; oval to ovate. Inflorescence, a many-flowered raceme. Calyx, five-lobed; the lobes acute; lanceolate. Petals, five; thick; waxy; pink or red. Stamens, declined. Styles, exserted; curved downward. Habitat, open coniferous woods. Blooming period, June-July.

There is something both dainty and alluring about this flower. To

LEAFLESS WINTERGREEN   *Pyrola aphylla*

me it seems to express the very spirit of the mountain woods—pure, shy, illusive, yet radiant with a fearless beauty, as though for ages it had breathed the crystal mountain air unsmirched by any contact with the outer world. This is the largest and handsomest of our pyrolas. The stout, many-flowered scape often exceed a foot in height. The flowers are of firm, waxy texture, and extremely beautiful. They vary in color from pale pink to nearly red, and are about half an inch across. The leaves are leathery in texture, bright glossy green, and form a rosette at the base of the plant.

VARIABLE WINTERGREEN
Pyrola picta Smith

Pink. Scapes, erect; six to twelve inches tall. Leaves, evergreen; leathery; all basal; green, veined and bordered with white; purple beneath. Flowers, white or pink. Otherwise as for *P. bracteata*.

In this pyrola the beginning of a parasitic life is clearly shown by the variegated leaves, green with white veinings, and a striking white margin. It is a pleasingly pretty plant, not as tall or fine as the preceding species, for it seldom exceeds ten inches in height, but nevertheless a beautiful flower.

LEAFLESS WINTERGREEN
Pyrola aphylla Smith

Pink or reddish. Scapes, closely clustered; reddish; erect; simple; seven to fourteen inches tall. Leaves, reduced to a few reddish, lanceolate bracts. Inflorescence, a raceme. Flowers, nodding. Calyx, five-lobed; sepals, short; ovate; acute. Petals, five; concave; thick. Stamens, ten; turned upward and clustered under the upper, arching petal. Style, exserted; declined. Habitat, deep coniferous woods. Blooming season, June-July.

The process of degeneration seems nearly complete in this form of pyrola, for the plant has no green foliage, and in fact, no leaves at all except a few pinkish bracts on the scape. It draws all its nourishment from the freshly decayed vegetable matter in which it roots. It is, therefore, confined to deep, moist woods where decomposing vegetation is abundant. The flower stems grow in rather close clusters— from five to many in a place. The stems, flowers, and bracts are all a

EVERGREEN HUCKLEBERRY

pale red or pink color. The flowers are not without beauty, much resembling in form and color those of *P. bracteata*.

Pyrola aphylla paucifolia Howell, is a rare variety of the above species. It bears a few small green leaves.

HEATHER FAMILY

EVERGREEN HUCKLEBERRY
Vaccinium ovatum Pursh

Pink. Stems, shrubby; branched; leafy; three to four feet tall. Leaves, alternate; evergreen; shiny; ovate to oblong-lanceolate; acute; serrate. Flowers, in short axillary raceme near the summit of the branches; pinkish. Calyx, persistent. Corolla, urn-shaped; five-lobed. Stamens, ten. Filaments, hairy. Habitat, open woods, especially near the coast. Blooming period, May-June.

This shrub, with its evergreen foliage, is beautiful at all seasons, but when it is covered with its pinkish, waxy, bell-shaped flowers, or bending beneath a load of blue-black fruit it is exceptionally pleasing. This is our only evergreen huckleberry, and that, together with its reddish branches, and hairy filaments, is a distinguishing feature of this species. The Indians gathered immense quantities of the fruit for food.

RED HUCKLEBERRY
Vaccinium parvifolium Smith

White. Stems, shrubby; branching; three to eight feet tall. Bark, green. Leaves, alternate; oblong or oval; rounded at both ends; pale; small. Flowers, axillary; solitary. Calyx lobes, four or five; persistent. Corolla, globular-urn-shaped; four or five lobed. Stamens, twice as many as the lobes of the corolla. Fruit, bright red; acid. Habitat, woods in low mountains. Fruit ripens, July-August.

"Now since it was known to be bad luck the red huckleberries were not usually eaten. Whenever they were eaten, the reason of that person would probably disappear, and he would attempt to go (wander) into the woods. Therefore they were not eaten because it was known that she (Asin, the monster girl of the woods) was the one that created the red huckleberries—. She was held in fear very much because she always carried off people."—Alsea Myth.

And so the poor natives who went through life, often freezing and half starved; who looked upon rancid fish-oil, black with soot, as a luxury, and ate things unendurable and unspeakable to a civilized mind or stomach, were deprived of this palatable fruit through fear and superstition.

What delightful visions of mountain days the name red huckleberry brings to the western mind; tall bushes with delicate, lace-like leaves, bending beneath their load of blushing, almost transparent fruit; a camp beside a cool, rushing stream; trout browning and sputtering in the pan; and, cooking over the camp-fire a light, fluffy dumpling prepared by mixing into well-sweetened batter all the ripe, red huckleberries that it will hold.

Red huckleberries are very plentiful in all the lower mountains of Oregon and Washington. The plants often exceed eight feet in height.

BLACK HUCKLEBERRY

Vaccinium macrophyllum (Hook.) Piper

Yellowish. Stem, shrubby; smooth; three to six feet tall. Leaves, alternate; oval; acute; serrate. Flowers, axillary; solitary. Calyx, five-lobed; persistent. Corolla, globose; yellowish. Stamens, ten. Fruit, black; without bloom. Habitat, in mountains. Fruiting season, July-September.

To the Indians, the ripening of this abundant and valuable berry marked the season of a tribal migration from the sultry lowlands to the cool, high mountains, and great encampments of Indians still gather annually at the favorite patches. Immense stores of this fruit were gathered and prepared for winter use, a delicious food, but rather marred by the native manner of preparing it, since smoke-drying was formerly the prevailing method. Large amounts were consumed while still fresh, however, and at that time it is said by the Klamaths: *"Bunuapka tchakele iwam"*; literally—"They will drink the red blood of huckleberries."

This shrub reaches a height of six feet; the fruit ripens from July to September according to the altitude at which it grows.

SMALL CRANBERRY
Oxycoccus oxycoccus intermedius (Gray) Piper

Pink. Stems, shrubby; slender; trailing. Leaves, alternate; ovate to oblong; dark; shiny. Flowers, axillary; pink. Corolla, four-cleft; the lobes spreading. Stamens, eight to ten. Anthers, conniving in a cone-shaped point about the style. Fruit, acid; dark red. Habitat, in swamps.

The fruit of our little native cranberry is sometimes gathered for market, but in size, at least, it is far inferior to the commercial species. Among the Indians, especially the more northern tribes where few sweet fruits were obtainable, it was highly prized. No doubt its very acidity was refreshing to their grease-soaked stomachs.

The Haida Indians of Queen Charlotte Island have an interesting myth in which this berry figures. In it we are told of a heroic trip in a carved cedar canoe, adorned along its edges with life-like figures of wild geese. These carved geese had the power of propelling the canoe forward through the water, and this they did as long as they were fed with cranberries; but as soon as their necessary food was withheld the canoe became as inanimate and powerless as any common boat.

This is a delicate trailing vine, an inhabitant of cold bogs. The leaves are small—from one-sixth to one-third of an inch in length—dark green above, but lighter beneath. The flowers are rose-color, deeply four-cleft, the divisions turned abruptly backward. The berries are about half the size of the commercial forms.

SALAL
Gaultheria shallon Pursh

White. Stems, shrubby; branching; erect or declining; two to seven feet tall. Leaves, alternate; evergreen; ovate to oblong; broad; acute; serrulate. Inflorescence, terminal or axillary; a one-sided, slender raceme. Corolla, ovoid-urn-shaped; narrowed at summit; five-toothed. Stamens, ten. Filaments, dilated at base. Fruit, a black berry; edible. Habitat, fir forests. Blooming period, May-June.

Just one hundred years ago today, as I write this,—on April 9th, 1825, to be exact—David Douglas, the Scotch botanist, landed at Baker's Bay, on the Columbia River. The first plant which he saw as he set foot on Oregon soil was the salal, of which he had heard

SALAL

through the works of a previous explorer, Archibald Menzies. "So pleased was I," he exclaims, "that I could scarcely see anything else." Thereafter, through all his journeyings in the West, the salal was one of Douglas' favorites, and he held great hopes of introducing it into England and making of it a cultivated fruit. On his homeward journey, after traveling entirely across the American continent, and enduring great hardships, his one regret was that he had not brought with him growing plants of salal. "Why," he says, "did I not bring Gaultheria alive—across the continent—2900 miles It could be done." Douglas' hopes of making a commercial fruit of the salal were never fulfilled; nevertheless he was correct in thinking it a fine shrub, and in England it has been considerably planted for ornamental purposes. It was, before the coming of the white man, one of the most valued of our native fruits, and was gathered in large quantities by the Pacific tribes. From it they made a sort of syrup, or dried and stored it in the form of thick cakes. The fresh berries, made into pies, are very good, and are used by mountain dwellers.

Every one who travels through the Pacific Coast forests knows this beautiful evergreen shrub. Along the sea coast it thrives in especial abundance. There it attains its largest size, often reaching a height of seven or eight feet. Farther inland, it is somewhat smaller, and in the interior it becomes quite dwarfed. The flowers are urn-shaped, borne in one-sided racemes, and are white or pink. The fruit is dark purple or nearly black.

MADRONA

Arbutus menziesii Pursh

White. Stem, a tree; thirty to sixty feet tall. Bark, smooth; red; exfoliating in summer. Leaves, alternate; evergreen; thick; oval to oblong; entire in mature trees, serrate on young shoots. Inflorescence, a panicle. Flowers, white; sweet-scented. Corolla, urn-shaped. Stamens, ten; included. Anthers, flattened and bearing a pair of reflexed awns. Fruit, red; ridged or granular. Habitat, dry hillsides. Blooming period, April-May.

What a delight the madrona tree is to the birds throughout the year. In spring, when the creamy, urn-shaped flowers appear, they are veritable honey-pots, and the hummingbirds flock to the trees by the score, together with numberless bees and moths, to sip the abun-

MADRONA   *Arbutus menziesii*

dant sweetness. During the season of 1919, I slept beneath the sheltering branches of a wide-spreading madrona, and every morning at the first break of dawn, I was awakened by the humming and twittering of the rufus and caliope hummingbirds, which arrived in swarms and contended noisily among themselves for the coveted nectar. A little later in the morning, would come flocks of brilliant purple finches to feed greedily on the corollas of the fresh blossoms, showing their appreciation by stopping to warble loudly between mouthfuls. In autumn, the blooms give place to great bunches of bright red berries, and then the band-tailed pigeons descend upon the trees in great flocks and gorge themselves with the fruit. Still later, when snow falls, the remaining berries are eagerly sought for, and eaten by the robins and varied thrushes who flock into the valleys from Canada, and from the high mountains.

The fruit was used to a considerable extent as food by the Indians. It is dry and insipid raw; neither have I been able to find any way of improving it by cooking, although the smell of the stewed berries is pleasant, reminding one of a rich, highly-flavored apple.

The name madrona is of Spanish origin, and is also given to the closely related strawberry-tree of Southern Spain.

A peculiarity of this tree is its habit of shedding its outer bark in late summer, so that the boughs are always smooth and scurfless. After shedding, the limbs are at first dull greenish-gray, but the new bark soon turns to a bright cinnamon red, and so remains throughout the year. The leaves are broad, oval, and evergreen, with a shining upper surface. Contrasted with the red of the bark they are most attractive. In our latitude, the trees sometimes attain a great size, with trunks three feet or more in diameter, and a height of from fifty to ninety feet. Farther south they decrease in size, becoming in Southern California merely a dwarfish shrub.

BEARBERRY. KINNIKINNICK
Arctostaphylos uva-ursi (L.) Spreng.

Pink. Stems, shrubby; branched; prostrate and trailing. Bark, reddish. Leaves, alternate; evergreen; leathery; spatulate; obtuse; an inch or less long. Inflorescence, a short, few-flowered raceme. Corolla, ovoid; constricted in throat. Stamens, eight or ten. Filaments, dilated and hairy at base. Anthers, bearing two reflexed awns. Fruit, a smooth red berry; dry and flavorless. Habitat, dry woods.

MANZANITA   *Arctostaphylos columbiana*

Kinnikinnick is an Eastern Indian word signifying, a mixture, and was applied to any smoking preparation, containing such various ingredients as native tobacco, hemlock gum, sumac bark, spice-bush bark, red dogwood bark, dried leaves of the poke plant, and those of the present species. The name kinnikinnick was finally applied to certain plants used, rather than to the prepared mixture. The *engages* of the Fur Companies brought the name to the Pacific Coast, where it became the common appellation of this plant.

The coast Indian name for it seems to have been *sacacomis,* upon which word the French constructed a pun, calling it *sac-a-commis,* from the words *sac,* a bag, and *commis,* a clerk, since the clerks of the Hudson Bay Company were very fond of smoking it, and habitually carried a pouch full of the dried leaves.

The plant itself is a small trailing shrub, with reddish bark, and leathery, evergreen leaves. The fruit is a bright red berry, and although very dry and tasteless was a recognized article of diet among the Indians wherever found. Bears are also very fond of them.

MANZANITA
Arctostaphylos columbiana Piper

White. Stems, shrubby; crooked; branched; three to nine feet tall. Leaves, alternate; evergreen; oblong to ovate; tomentose. Inflorescence, a short raceme. Corolla, urn-shaped. Stamens, ten. Filaments, dilated and hairy at base. Fruit, a dry red-cheeked berry. Habitat, dry soil and rocky hills. Blooming period, early spring.

The very crooked branches of the manzanita are a noticeable feature of its growth. It is an evergreen shrub, from three to ten feet tall, and bears an abundance of red-cheeked berries. These, though rather dry and tasteless, are edible. They make an excellent jelly, and in California, the Indians used them both raw and cooked, as well as producing from them by processes of their own a remarkably fine cider. The bears are also fond of the fruit.

No one who has travelled through Southern Oregon has failed to remark the great tangled stretches of red-stalked, contorted manzanita. Farther north, and in Washington, it is still common, but is usually restricted to the more mountainous regions. The flowers are urn-shaped, and much resemble those of the madrona.

LABRADOR TEA   *Ledum groenlandicum*

LABRADOR TEA
Ledum groenlandicum Oeder

White. Stem, shrubby; erect; one to four feet tall. Leaves, alternate; oblong; obtuse; the margins revolute; evergreen; dark above; rusty-woolly beneath; resinous-dotted. Inflorescence, a terminal corymb. Flowers, white. Calyx, small; persistent; five-lobed. Petals, five; spreading. Stamens, five or ten; exserted. Habitat, in spagnum bogs. Blooming period, June to August, according to altitude.

The Labrador tea is a beautiful and interesting shrub of wet, cold bogs. It grows to a height of from one to three feet. The flowers are white, in a terminal corymb, and very pretty. The leaves are evergreen; they were used for making tea by the Eastern Indians, and later this use was adopted by the white settlers. During the Revolutionary War, when England's taxed tea was taboo, it was much used.

Columbian Labrador Tea. *Ledum columbianum* Piper. Is a very similar species, but lacks entirely the rusty-woolliness of the lower leaf surface, being smooth and glaucous. Found near the mouth of the Columbia River, at Newport, Oregon, and probably at other points along the coast.

RED HEATHER
Phyllodoce empetriformis (Smith) D. Don.

Red. Stems, shrubby; branched; five to fifteen inches tall. Leaves, evergreen; numerous; linear; the margins revolute. Inflorescence, an umbel; terminating the branches. Corolla, campanulate; five-toothed. Stamens, ten; included. Habitat, at high elevations in the mountains. Blooming period, July-August.

We have no true heathers in this country, but their place is taken by a number of heath-like plants of great beauty—high alpine flowers that stir and inspire us by their matchless charm. You must have strong limbs, and a sound heart and lungs to know them, for they dwell in the barren spaces above timber line in our loftier mountains. "Heather bells"! They ring an enticing and almost irresistible call to the high places where the air is pure, and the silence awes but never oppresses. Here, beneath the serene, brooding majesty of towering, snow-capped peaks our callow struggles may end, taut nerves relax, and the heart and mind may be renewed.

RHODODENDRON

The red heather is a shrub, seldom exceeding twenty inches in height. The leaves are evergreen, narrowly linear, and needlelike, and closely clothe the branches, as do the needles of a coniferous tree. The flowers are bell-shaped, and dark rose-red.

Cream-Colored Heather. *Phyllodoce glanduliflora* (Hook.) Coville. This is a high mountain species, found at an altitude of from seven to eight thousand feet. The inflorescence is glandular, and the flowers are globular, and pale cream-colored.

WHITE HEATHER
Cassiope mertensiana (Bong.) G. Don.

White. Stems, shrubby; rigid; branched; eight to twelve inches tall. Leaves, evergreen; small; imbricated and scale-like, covering the branches. Flowers, solitary; white; nodding on slender naked peduncles. Sepals, four or five; ovate. Corolla, campanulate; four or five lobed. Stamens, eight or ten; included. Anthers, short; attached at their summits. Style, thickened at base. Habitat, in high mountains.

The short, thick leaves of the white mountain heather grow in four ranks, and closely clothe the entire stem like overlapping scales. The plant is erect, from seven to fifteen inches tall. Like the read heather, it grows at, or above timber line, often in large patches. The waxy, bell-shaped flowers are white or pinkish.

RHODODENDRON, ROSE-BAY
Rhododendron californicum Hook.

Rose-colored. Stem, shrubby, or almost tree-like; six to eighteen feet tall; branching; erect or spreading. Leaves, alternate; evergreen; leathery; oblong; entire. Inflorescence, terminal; umbellate. Flowers, showy. Calyx, small; five-lobed. Corolla, slightly irregular; funnelform; five-lobed. Stamens, ten; declined; slightly longer than the corolla. Habitat, open woods; in mountains or along the sea coast. Blooming period, May to July, according to altitude.

Our Western rhododendron has been chosen by the people of Washington for their state flower—a worthy flower for a worthy state. No more beautiful blossom has ever been produced by nature, or by the art of man. We would expect such rich perfection to be the product of a tropical clime—to require a shelter under glass—to be coaxed to bloom with artificial heat—but instead it braves the gales of a tempestuous coast, or, like a hardy mountaineer, clings to our rugged, snow-buried heights, and puts forth its blossoms, not in rare, secluded spots, or only occasionally, but in banks and masses. From British Columbia to California, our coast line takes on a rosy blush in spring from the abundance of its blossoms. The annual pilgrimage from our cities to the coast or mountains to view its flowers is so great that the railroads are at times forced to put on special trains for the accommodation of those who wish to go—a spring fete organized and promoted by nature herself. The beauty of a single spray of rhododendron makes you catch your breath in delight; what then of acres, even miles, of them, spread out in a blushing panorama of perfect loveliness.

This shrub grows to a height of from five to eighteen feet, and often forms dense, impenetrable thickets. The long, slender branches run out horizontally from the stem for a great distance, and then turn up at the tips. Being very tough and elastic they spring back when pushed aside, and trip and impede the unwary. The oblong, evergreen leaves form rosettes at the tips of the branches in the midst of which the soft, rosy flowers are set and exhibited to perfection. The flowers are about two inches across, with handsome ruffled and fluted petals, and are marked in the throat with golden-yellow.

Rhododendrons are well worthy of cultivation, but they have heretofore been considered difficult to establish. This difficulty need no longer hinder us if we keep in mind the fact that an acid soil is essential to their health. To secure this, it is only necessary to soak the ground at the time of planting, and once or twice a year thereafter, with a weak solution of aluminum sulphate. About a teaspoonful to each plant, worked into the soil, or dissolved in water and applied to the surface, is sufficient to insure good results.

The popular belief that honey from rhododendron blossoms is poisonous, seems to have no foundation in fact.

WHITE RHODODENDRON
Rhododendron albiflorum Hook.

White. Stems, shrubby; erect; branched; three to six feet tall. Leaves, alternate; membranous; oblong; undulate. Inflorescence, small lateral clusters. Flowers, nodding. Calyx, five-parted. Corolla, five-lobed. Stamens, ten. Filaments, bearded at the base. Style, peltate; five-lobed. Habitat, in high mountains near the limit of trees.

High up in the mountains, throughout our territory, grows this beautiful, white-flowered species of rhododendron. It is a slender, upright shrub, with very thin, deciduous leaves, and campanulate blossoms. The leaves of this plant are reputed to be poisonous to livestock.

SWAMP LAUREL
Kalmia polifolia Wang.

Rose-purple. Stems, shrubby; ten to twenty inches tall. Leaves, opposite; oblong; shiny above; glaucous beneath; the margins revolute. Inflorescence, a corymb. Calyx, five-parted. Corolla, saucer-shaped; five-lobed. Stamens, ten; curved. Anthers, caught in ten pouches in the corolla; released and straightening when shaken. Stigma, depressed. Habitat, spagnum bogs.

In spagnum bogs, with the Labrador tea and native cranberry, will be found this delicate little shrub. The leaves are evergreen, with inturned margins, shiny above, but white beneath. The flowers are of very interesting construction. They are saucer-shaped and five-lobed. Below the margin of the corolla are ten shallow pockets, in which are caught the anthers of the ten somewhat curved stamens. An insect lighting upon the floral cup jars the stamens from their retaining pouches, and, like a spring, they snap quickly forward, powdering the intruder with pollen. The flowers are rose-purple and showy. This plant has an unsavory reputation, being poisonous to livestock, especially to sheep.

PRIMROSE FAMILY

HENDERSON'S BIRD BILLS. SHOOTING STARS
Dodecatheon hendersonii Gray

Rose-purple. Root, fibrous. scape; erect; strict; smooth; four to fourteen inches. Leaves, basal; whorled; oblong to orbicular; narrowing to a short petiole. Inflorescence, an umbel. Flowers, drooping. Calyx, green; five-cleft. Corolla, dark purple with a yellow base. Petals, five; reflexed; lanceolate. Stamens, five; dark purple. Filaments, united, forming a beak-like point about the style. Capsule,

SHOOTING STAR   *Dodecatheon hendersonii*

erect; oblong; circumscissile. Habitat, dry prairies and hillsides. Blooming period, March-April.

This plant is only one of many named after my very good friend, Professor Louis F. Henderson, who is one of the few really pioneer botanists remaining, and who, in spite of his almost eighty years, is still doing active work in field and herbarium. With him I have spent many happy and profitable hours.

The plant itself is too well known to need particular description. Every child knows its pretty flowery umbels with reflexed purple petals, and the sharp beak-like cluster of stamens and pistils, looking like a particularly vicious shuttlecock, that give to the plant its common name of bird bills.

WHITE SHOOTING STARS
Dodecatheon dentatum Hook.

White. Root, perennial. Leaves, all basal; petioled; ovate; dentate; thin; glabrous; light green. Inflorescence, an umbel. Scape, erect; slender; naked; seven to ten inches tall. Flowers, white; nodding. Calyx lobes, five; ovate; reflexed. Stamens, five. Filaments, free; not united. Capsule, cylindric; opening at the tip. Habitat, moist cliffs and banks. Blooming period, April to July according to altitude.

This beautiful flower has a surprising environment for one of its genus. Instead of growing on dry warm hillsides as might be expected, it chooses a place on shaded, moist cliffs, often wet by the spray of waterfalls; its companions, the graceful maiden hair fern, the fragile mist maidens, and the rock loving saxifrages. Ordinarily it belongs in the mountains at a considerable height, but in the Gorge of the Columbia, that wonderful gathering place of the flowers, it may be seen along stream banks at very low levels. Its pure white flowers grow in a nodding umbel, and are formed in true shooting star fashion, so that in naming it you can not be easily mistaken.

Large Shooting Star. *Dodecatheon jeffreyi* Van Houtte. This species has very long, narrow leaves, and is one of our largest species. The flowers are purple. It is quite common in moist meadows in the mountains. The capsules of this species open by a lid.

STAR FLOWER

Trientalis latifolia

STAR FLOWER
Trientalis latifolia Hook.

White. Root, tuberous. Stem, erect; simple; slender; four to eight inches tall. Leaves, four to seven; whorled near the summit of the stem; oval to lanceolate; acute. Flowers, one to four; solitary on hair-like pedicels, above the leaves. Calyx-lobes, linear. Corolla, rotate; six-parted; star-like. Stamens, six. Style, one; filiform. Habitat, in open woods. Blooming period, April-May.

Neatness and symmetry are a marked characteristic of this little wildling that pleases us with its pink tinted star-like flowers in early May. The four to seven broad oval leaves grow in a graceful whorl about the summit of the simple stems, and are dark green and glossy. The plant springs from a plump firm tuber, set rather deeply in the ground.

Trientalis arctica Fisch. The plant of this species is smaller than the above, but the flowers are larger. The leaves are small, and scattered along the stem, but becoming larger and showing a tendency to whorl near the summit. In shape they are obovate, and seldom exceed an inch in length. Found commonly in spagnum bogs.

SEA MILKWORT. BLACK SALWORT
Glaux maritima L.

Pink. Stem, round; smooth; leafy; fleshy; erect; six to twelve inches tall. Leaves, opposite; entire; sessile; oval to oblong. Flowers, small; axillary; solitary. Calyx, campanulate; five-cleft; petal-like. Petals, none. Stamens, five; alternate with the lobes of the calyx. Habitat, sea shores.

A fleshy little seaside plant of the primrose family, having round stems, and sessile, opposite leaves, in the axils of which are borne the small, pinkish-white flowers. These flowers have no petals, but the sepals are showy and petal-like. The roots were dug and eaten by some of the coast tribes. They seem to contain a narcotic principal, for it is said that the Indians ate them only in the evening, since after eating they at once became very sleepy.

DOUGLASIA
Douglasia laevigata Gray

Red. Root, perennial. Stems, tufted; depressed; somewhat woody. Leaves, in a basal rosette; oblong-lanceolate; obtuse; entire or slightly toothed at summit; nearly glabrous. Inflorescence, solitary, or umbellate; one to five flowered. Calyx, campanulate; five-lobed. Corolla, tube somewhat inflated above, and bearing five arched appendages beneath the sinuses. Stamens, included; distinct. Style, filiform. Ovary, top-shaped. Habitat, mountains.

This rare and small but interesting flower will not commonly be found by the amateur botanist, although it is rather abundant in some parts of the Olympic Mountains, and in the Gorge of the Columbia, especially eastward.

GENTIAN FAMILY

BLUE GENTIAN
Gentian calycosa Griseb.

Blue. Stems, tufted; erect; simple; leafy; six to twelve inches tall. Leaves, opposite; ovate. Inflorescence, terminal; usually solitary. Flowers, erect; accompanied by an involucre of leafy bracts. Corolla, cylindrical; five-lobed; the lobes mostly erect; sinuses appendaged. Stamens, five; included. Style, very short. Stigmas, two. Habitat, high mountains, at from five to seven thousand feet elevation.

The blue gentian grows in closely tufted groups of from five to twenty stiff, straight stems. Each stem bears a number of pairs of sessile, ovate leaves, the upper ones forming an involucre for the one or two upright, bell-shaped flowers. These flowers are an inch or more in length, of a fine blue color, marked and dotted with flecks of green. Each flower has five erect lobes, and between the lobes are two small, tooth-like appendages. A late autumn flower, rather common in the mountains in moist situations.

BUCKBEAN FAMILY

BUCK-BEAN
Menyanthes trifoliata L.

White. Rootstocks, thick; spreading. Stems, stout; six to ten inches tall. Leaves, chiefly radical; long petioled; clasping at base; trifoliate. Leaflets, oblong or ovate; sessile. Inflorescence, a ten to twenty flowered raceme; on a long naked scape. Flowers, white and rose. Calyx, five-parted. Corolla, funnelform; spreading; five-cleft; bearded within. Stamens, five. Styles, long; slender. Seeds, few; large. Habitat, in bogs.

The name buck-bean is supposed to be a corruption of the word bog-bean, and it is in swamps and bogs that these flowers will be found. While in no sense a bean, their trifoliate leaves suggest a legume, and may account for that part of the name. Its range in our own country extends from the Atlantic to the Pacific in northern latitudes. It is also a native of Europe and Asia. In point of beauty, the buck-bean has been acclaimed by an English writer as "Britain's most beautiful flower." While this may be an exaggeration, it is undoubtedly a charming blossom. The flowers grow in showy clusters, and are white, tinted with red, and bearded within. The juice of the stems is very bitter, and an extract of the plant under the name of menyanthin is a recognized remedy for bowel trouble and dyspepsia. The plants have also been used as a substitute for hope, "one ounce of the dry leaves," according to Samuel Henry's Herbal, published in 1814, "being equal to a half a pound of hops in brewing."

MILKWEED FAMILY

MILKWEED. SILKWEED
Asclepias speciosa Torr

Purplish. Rootstocks, stout. Stems, stout; erect; simple; two to four feet tall. Juice, abundant; milky. Leaves, opposite; oval or oblong; short petioled; thick; tomentose. Inflorescence, umbellate; terminal or axillary. Flowers, perfect; symmetrical. Calyx, five-parted. Sepals, lanceolate; reflexed. Corolla, five-parted; lobes oblong; reflexed. Stamens, five on the corolla, and opposite its lobes; accompanied by a crown-like, nectar-bearing organ. Pollen masses, attached in pairs by a slender, connecting filament. Pods, ovate; acute; large. Seeds, many; brown; scale-like; accompanied by abundant silky hairs. Habitat, rich low fields. Blooming period, June-July.

The large, almost globular umbels of the common milkweed are very sweet-scented and heavy with nectar. Flies, bees, butterflies and

MILKWEED

Asclepias speciosa

moths all delight in this sweetness, but the plant has decreed that only those of considerable strength—able to carry a heavy load of pollen—shall partake of her sweets and live. Death awaits the unwary weakling who attempts to violate this decree. How does this take place? To reach the nectar, the insect must stand upon the deeply cleft flower crown. In reaching within for the stored sweets, the tongue or foot of the insect will slip into a narrow cleft, and be held firmly. Each cleft is spanned by tenacious threads, terminated at the end by pollen masses, and when the intruding member is withdrawn, with it comes an entangling thread and the two attached pollen sacks. If, however, the insect is small and weak, the tightening cleft holds it in helpless dangling imprisonment until it perishes. The common honey bee is able to gather milkweed honey and depart in safety, and this is a valuable honey plant; nevertheless, the bees from successive visits sometimes become so heavily loaded with the clinging pollen sacks as to fall to the ground and so perish. So sweet are the honey-ladened blooms that the Indians secured a primitive sugar from the dew collected upon them. They also ate the tender, young shoots, as we do asparagus, and many people have learned from them to value this palatable dish. Fishing lines and other cordage were manufactured from the stems and bark. The silky plumes from the ripened seed were used for padding and pillows.

No description of the milkweed would be complete without some mention of its ever present companions, the Monarch butterflies, (*Anosia plexippus*). They hover over every milkweed patch, sipping the honey and laying their eggs upon its foliage. From these eggs are hatched very ugly green and yellow caterpillars that feed upon the leaves. Their complete life history is most fascinating, but too long to be fully described here. A curious thing, however, about the feeding of these caterpillars is that no milk flows where they eat, yet it is impossible to make the least cut or tear in the leaves by any other means without a copious flow following.

DOGBANE FAMILY

INDIAN HEMP
Apocynum cannabinum L.

Greenish. Stems, glabrous; erect; branching; one to six feet tall. Leaves, opposite; oval or oblong; mucronate. Inflorescence, a cyme;

SPREADING DOGBANE   *Apocynum androsaemifolium*

terminal or axillary. Calyx, five-parted. Corolla, greenish; campanulate; five-cleft; the lobes erect; a scale opposite the base of each lobe. Stamens, five; alternate with lobes of the corolla. Follicles, a pair; slender; tapering; two to three inches long. Habitat, low fields.

The Indian hemp or dogbane is not at all handsome or attractive. It grows to a height of from one to six feet, and prefers rich moist soil. It has milky juice, and is rank and weedy, with small, greenish flowers. The name dogbane comes from an ancient superstition which held that dogs feared the plant.

Our chief interest in the dogbane comes from the fact that throughout all the Northern States it was used by the Indians as a fibre plant. From it they spun their lines and cords, and wove fishnets. They also used the thread for filling in the construction of some of their smaller baskets. David Douglas, who visited this coast in 1826, speaks thus of its use: "The seine is resorted to as a means of taking salmon in the still parts of the stream, with great success. The rope of the net is made of a species of willow or of cedar, and the cord of *Apocynum*—a gigantic species peculiar to this country, whose fibre affords a great quantity of flax. The flax is collected from the withered stems in autumn."

SPREADING DOGBANE
Apocynum androsaemifolium L.

Pink. Stems, reddish; erect; branched; six to eighteen inches tall. Leaves, opposite; ovate; dark green above; mucronate. Flowers, cymose; pink; fragrant. Calyx, five-parted. Corolla, campanulate; five-cleft; the lobes strongly reflexed. Stamens, five; opposite the lobes of the corolla. Pods, a pair; two to four inches long; reddish. Habitat, dry open places. Blooming period, May to July.

The spreading dogbane much surpasses its taller relative in beauty, for the flowers are larger, and of an attractive shade of pink, at their best almost covering the plant. This is an extremely variable form. When found on dry hillsides, it is usually low and branching, but at other times it grows erect and unbranched, more nearly like the tall Indian hemp. Both species secrete an abundant milky juice when broken. This milk when hardened, is very similar to the caoutchouc of commerce. Like the preceding, it yields a hemp-like fibre that is strong and durable. Both plants have recognized medical value.

WILD MORNING GLORY   *Convolvulus nyctagineus*

MORNING GLORY FAMILY

WILD MORNING GLORY
Convolvulus nyctagineus Greene

White. Rootstocks, white; spreading. Stems, slender; weak; usually trailing over the ground; sometimes climbing; four to ten inches long. Leaves, petioled; ovate or semicircular; truncate at base. Flowers, axillary. Calyx, enclosed by two ovate, acute bracts. Corolla, funnelform; entire or obscurely lobed; about two inches long; convoluted in bud. Stamens, five; style, filiform. Stigma, two lobed. Habitat, open fields. Blooming period, May-June.

The beauty of this flower is sufficient to make us forget that it is a troublesome weed—provided of course, that it is not our fields in which it grows. Unlike most of its genus, this species seldom climbs to any considerable height, but merely trails along the ground or is supported on low weeds. The pure white flowers open in early morning, but are not quickly wilted, often remaining fresh throughout the day. The sepals are enclosed by two blunt, oval bracts.

Pink Morning Glory. *Convolvulus sepium* L. The floral bracts of this species are acute, and the flowers are usually handsomely striped with pink. The plants climb to a height of from two to six feet.

Beach Morning Glory. *Convolvulus soldanella* L. This small morning glory has trailing stems from six inches to a foot in length, thick, kidney-shaped leaves, and small purplish flowers. It is found on sea beaches.

PHLOX FAMILY

MOUNTAIN PHLOX
Phlox diffusa Hook.

White or purplish. Stems, densely tufted; diffuse; prostrate; three to nine inches long. Leaves, clustered; sessile; linear; sharp-pointed. Flowers, solitary; sessile. Calyx, woolly; five-cleft. Corolla, salverform; five-lobed; the tube long and narrow. Stamens, five; included. Habitat, in mountains at high altitudes.

A prickly, moss-like plant, often forming large patches or mats in the mountains above timber line. The flowers are long-tubed, and salverform, of a white or pale lavender color.

PINK MORNING GLORY   *Convolvulus sepium*

BLUE GILIA
Gilia capitata Hook.

Blue. Stems, slender; erect; smooth; one to three feet tall. Leaves, alternate; petioled; pinnately divided; the divisions again cut and divided into narrow segments. Inflorescence, a dense, globose cluster. Peduncle, slender; naked. Flowers, small; numerous. Calyx, smooth; five-lobed. Corolla, five-lobed; the tube about as long as the lanceolate lobes. Stamens, five. Style, three-lobed. Habitat, open fields. Blooming period, June to September.

The blue gilia can not well be mistaken for any other plant, for no other bears such neat blue flower-balls as this. It is an annual, common in dry fields, or as a weed in cultivated ground, but there is nothing disagreeably weedy about the gilia, for its leaves are finely divided and lace-like, and the globular flower clusters are a pleasing shade of blue, and borne on long, slender stems. This little flower is now becoming quite well known as a garden annual, and it well deserves a place on any flower-lover's list. Handsome as it is in its native state, there is no doubt but that by careful selection and breeding it can be made even more desirable.

Gilia, pronounced *Helia,* is from the name of an early Spanish botanist, Philip Gil. It is pleasing to know that these flowers, and not alone that ugly lizard, the gila monster, bears his name.

TINY GILIA
Gilia bicolor (Nutt.) Piper

Pink. Stems, simple; erect; pubescent; one to four inches tall. Leaves, opposite; palmately divided; segments filiform. Flowers, terminal; pink; mostly solitary. Corolla, tubular-salverform; the tube very long. Stamens, five. Stigma, three-lobed. Habitat, dry fields and hillsides. Blooming period. May-June.

No doubt this flower is a stray from the garden of some fairy, so tiny and fragile is its form. The entire plant seldom exceeds three inches in height. The leaves are cut and slashed into minute, thread-like divisions, giving the whole plant a delicate mossy aspect. At the summit there is usually a single pink flower, truly remarkable for the length of its slender tube—often four or five times as long as the breadth of the cup. The long tube is yellow, and the lobes pink. Very common on dry hillside pastures.

BLUE GILIA   *Gilia capitata*

[284]

SALMON-COLORED COLLOMIA   *Collomia grandiflora*

Navavarretia intertexta

SALMON-COLORED COLLOMIA
Collomia grandiflora Dougl.

Salmon-colored. Stems, slender; erect; mostly simple; six to twenty inches tall. Leaves, alternate; sessile; entire; lanceolate. Inflorescence, terminal; a dense capitate cluster. Calyx, ob-conic; five-lobed; the lobes obtuse; viscid. Corolla, salverform; salmon-colored. Stamens, five; included. Habitat, dry meadows. Blooming period, June.

The light salmon-colored blossoms of the collomia are borne in close head-like clusters at the summit of simple, upright stems. The calyx, as well as the bracts surrounding it, are coated with a sticky secretion. Each flower consists of a slender, narrow tube, widening at the summit into five equal, ovate, spreading divisions. The stamens are surmounted by conspicuous blue anthers, which, against the salmon-colored corollas are quite noticeable. This plant has been introduced into Europe, and is there a popular garden flower.

Navarretia intertexta (Benth.) Hook.

White or bluish. Stem, erect; branching above; leafy; four to eight inches tall. Leaves, alternate; pinnately cleft and divided into many narrow, linear lobes; somewhat spiny. Inflorescence, a crowded bracted head; terminal or axillary. Calyx, cleft into linear, spiny divisions. Corolla, tubular-salverform; small. Stamens, five; exserted. Habitat, poorly drained open land. Blooming period, June.

These small, gilia-like flowers will be found blooming in dried, poorly drained soil from British Columbia to California. The foliage is once or twice pinnately divided into numerous rather spiny lobes. The plants are erect, and at times much branched. The white or pale blue flowers are borne at the summit of the branches in close, head-like clusters, and are surrounded by many narrow, pointed bracts. The stamens in this species are long and prominent, extending well beyond the tube of the corolla.

Skunk Weed, *Navarretia squarrosa* (Esch.) Hook & Arn. A similar, somewhat larger species, with viscid, evil-smelling foliage. The bracts of the flower head are extended in the form of sharp, rigid spines. The stamens are short, and do not protrude beyond the tube of the corolla.

VARI-COLORED JACOB'S LADDER

ELEGANT JACOB'S LADDER
Polemonium elegans Greene

Blue. Stems, viscid; pubescent; slender; two to six inches tall. Leaves, alternate; pinnate. Leaflets, small; numerous; crowded; obovate. Inflorescence, a cyme. Calyx, campanulate; deeply five-cleft. Corolla, blue with a yellow throat; the lobes equalling the tube. Stamens, five. Habitat, in mountains at high elevations.

A densely tufted plant with stems only a few inches tall. The leaflets are numerous and crowded, and the flowers, borne in compact cymes are blue or violet with a yellow throat. The stem is viscid and strong smelling.

Blue Jacob's Ladder, *Polemonium humile* R. & S., also has viscid stems and an unpleasant odor. The plant grows from six to twelve inches tall. The flowers are blue, in loose cymes. An abundant mountain flower.

VARI-COLORED JACOB'S LADDER
Polemonium carneum Gray

Flesh-colored and yellow. Stems, decumbent or ascending; eight to twenty inches long. Leaves, pinnate; smooth; pale green. Leaflets, seven to nineteen; ovate. Inflorescence, a few-flowered cyme. Calyx, campanulate; the lanceolate lobes longer than the tube. Corolla, broadly funnelform. Stamens, five. Filaments, slender; dilated and villiose at base. Habitat, in moist soil in the mountains. Blooming period, throughout the summer.

This is a very lovely plant. The flowers are widely funnel-shaped, and when they first appear they are a light salmon-yellow, soon changing to pink or flesh-colored. These soft tinted blooms, set amidst their light green, frond-like foliage, give an effect seldom equaled. The stems spread over the ground, or are at times somewhat erect. The odd-pinnate leaves are composed of many narrow to ovate leaflets. A mountain flower, found from Central California to west-central Washington. I have observed it in especial abundance about the ranger station of the Santiam Forest at Fish Lake. This is at an altitude of about three thousand feet. The plant is of very easy culture, and should be introduced into the gardens of the country.

MIST MAIDENS
Romanzoffia sitchensis Bong

White. Roots, perennial. Stems, slender; spreading or ascending; scape-like; four to ten inches tall. Leaves, chiefly radical; long petioled; reniform or orbicular; cordate; crenately lobed. Inflorescence, a loose terminal raceme. Calyx, five-parted; glabrous; the lobes subulate. Corolla, funnelform; five-lobed; the lobes orbicular. Stamens, five; alternate with the lobes of the corolla; unequal. Style, filiform; long. Habitat, moist cliffs at high altitudes. Blooming period, from April to late summer, according to altitude.

Both in habit and appearance these little plants resemble some of our cliff-growing species of saxifrages. They love moist rocks in cool shady canyons, where their pure white blossoms nestle among the mosses, kept ever wet by the spray from waterfalls. Here, too, grow their natural companions, the maiden-hair fern and the white mountain shooting-stars. High peaks and clear glacial streams are their delight, also, for they are most often found growing at an altitude of six thousand feet or more. In a few favorable places, such as about waterfalls in the Gorge of the Columbia, they may be found at low levels, and easily accessible.

MOUNTAIN PHACELIA
Phacelia sericea (Graham) Gray

Purple. Root, perennial. Stem, leafy; straight; slender; erect; a foot or less in height. Leaves, silky-downy; alternate; pinnately divided; the lobes again pinnately cut. Inflorescence, an oblong, raceme-like cyme. Calyx, five-parted; the lobes linear. Corolla, broadly campanulate; appendaged in throat; one-third to one-half inch across. Stamens, five; long-exserted; inserted on the base of the corolla and alternate with its lobes. Style, two-cleft. Habitat, at high altitudes in the mountains.

This is a beautiful alpine species, a lovely treat for the eyes of those who strive for the heights. Like so many members of the waterleaf family, this flower pleases with its soft, silky foliage, which, with the long protruding stamens, give to the whole plant a fuzzy, feathery aspect.

WATERLEAF
Hydrophyllum tenuipes Heller

Lavender or pale violet. Stems, soft; hairy; eight to twelve inches tall. Leaves, palmately cleft; thin; soft; hairy; long petioled. Inflorescence, a dense; one-sided; cymose cluster. Calyx, five-parted; margins hairy. Corolla, campanulate; five-cleft; thin; a grooved appendage attached to the base of each segment. Stamens, five; exserted. Filaments, slender; bearded near the middle. Style, filiform; exserted. Habitat, moist woods. Blooming period. May.

Popular description of this species of waterleaf are rare, if not entirely wanting, yet it is by no means scarce, and has undoubtedly a high order of beauty. A true shade lover, it will be found at its best beneath scattered trees, and in rich alluvial land. The leaves are soft in texture, soft-hairy, lightest beneath, and palmately cleft into a number of coarse segments. The flowers are borne in compact cymose clusters, in fine specimens nearly globular in form. They are soft, delicate lavender in color. The flowers are set off by protruding stamens and pistils, and the whole plant has a soft, fuzzy appearance.

Hydrophyllum albifrons Heller, is a very common coarse species, much resembling the above but with unattractive whitish or pale green flowers.

NEMOPHILA. BABY-EYES
Nemophila menziesii H. & A.

White. Stems, short; diffuse; one to two inches long. Leaves, opposite; oblong; five to seven pinnately lobed. Inflorescence, solitary. Peduncles, slender; erect. Flowers, large; white. Calyx, five-parted; with reflexed lobes on each sinus. Corolla, saucer-shaped. Petals, five; appendaged at base; white, marked and blotched with dark blue or black. Stamens, five. Habitat, moist open fields. Blooming period, March-April.

The naturalist Nuttall, on his trip to Arkansas in 1819, discovered a new genus of plants which he named *Nemophila,* or "grove lovers." Our representative of this genus is a plant of open, moist fields rather than of groves, but it lacks none of the qualities of grace and beauty that so pleased Nuttall on his wilderness trip.

NEMOPHILA

They are among the most delicate and charming of our flowers, an epitome of modesty and purity. Compared with the size of the plants, the flowers are very large, often one to one and a half inches across. They are raised on slender peduncles well above the foliage, so that in a breeze they nod and flutter like white butterflies. In color they are bluish white, conspicuously blotched and spotted near the centre with dark blue. This is one of our earliest flowers, usually appearing in early March, but in mild seasons they may appear much earlier. The plants cling close to the ground and are never conspicuous, so that when they burst into bloom, whitening whole fields, we are often astonished at their presence.

BORAGE FAMILY

HOUND'S TONGUE
Cynoglossum grande Dougl.

Blue. Root, stout; large; woody. Stem, erect; stout; one to three feet tall. Basal leaves, large; long petioled; ovate-oblong; subcordate; acute. Stem lower, smaller; ovate to lanceolate; contracted at base; all soft villose. Inflorescence, terminal; panicled. Calyx, five parted. Sepals, ovate. Corolla, salverform; the limb five-lobed; the tube short; crested in throat. Stamens, five, included. Habitat, open woods. Blooming period, March to May.

All the freshness and beauty of springtime seem expressed in the clear blue flowers of the hound's tongue. Like innocent blue eyes, they gaze up at us from the margins of wayside thickets with an air of truthfulness that has earned for them one of their common names, that of "blue-eyed babies." The flowers are of true forget-me-not blue, and of all our plants none more than these impersonates the constancy implied in that name. When the buds first appear they are tinged with red or purple, but when fully opened they are clear light blue. Each petal bears at the base two white, bead-like crests—ten to the flower—which form a highly decorative margin at the summit of the short tube. Although at maturity the leaves are rank and coarse, at the time of blossoming they are still soft and delicate enough to be a fitting background for this lovely flower. The name *Cynoglossum* means hound's tongue, and both the botanical and common names refer to the shape of the leaf.

HOUND'S TONGUE   *Cynoglossum grande*

This is one of our early spring flowers, often appearing as early as the first of March.

TALL LUNGWORT. MOUNTAIN BLUEBELLS
Mertensia subcordata Greene

Blue. Stems, erect; branched; ten inches to three feet tall. Leaves, alternate; petioled; papillose; broad; ovate; acute; cordate at base. Inflorescence, drooping panicles at the ends of the branches. Flowers, blue; on slender pedicels. Calyx, five-cleft; the lobes lanceolate, pubescent on back. Corolla, tubular-funnelform; appendaged in throat; five-lobed. Stamens, five; included. Style, filiform. Habitat, moist low woods. Blooming period, April-May.

The blossoms of the tall *Mertensia* droop like graceful pendant jewels from the ends of the branches. In bud they are a soft pink color, but as they open they change to a clear, pure turquoise, a lovely and exceptional shade. This changing in color from bud to blossom seems typical of the family, and is shared likewise by the closely allied hound's tongue, and one or two species of *Myosotis*. Look for these flowers in rich moist woods and along stream borders. While not related to the true bluebells, the name mountain bluebell, commonly given to these plants, is suitable and descriptive.

GLAUCOUS LUNGWORT
Mertensia laevigata Piper

Blue. Stems, erect; leafy; little branched; glaucous; twenty to thirty inches tall. Leaves, glabrate; glaucous; ovate; short petioled. Otherwise much as for *M. subcordata*. Habitat, in mountains up to six thousand feet altitude. Blooming period, June to August.

An erect mountain species, easily known by its smooth leaves that are covered with a whitish bloom. It is found in the Cascades, from comparatively low levels to an altitude of five or six thousand feet.

Besides the two preceding species there are in Oregon and Washington nearly a dozen kinds of *Mertensia,* but as their identification is difficult, and their specific differences not well established, no further description has been given. All are very similar in general appearance, so that the amateur can not fail to recognize them as belonging to this genus.

MOUNTAIN BLUEBELL
Mertensia subcordata

FIDDLE-NECK
Amsinckia intermedia Fisch. & Meyer

Yellow. Stems, erect; leafy; heavily covered with whitish, bristly hairs; one to three feet tall. Leaves, alternate; lanceolate or linear. Inflorescence, a terminal, one-sided scorpioid raceme. Sepals, lanceolate. Corolla, salverform; five-lobed. Lobes, rounded; appendaged in throat. Habitat, dry open ground. Blooming period, May-June.

Most species of the borage family are characterized by having scorpioid, indeterminate racemes, by which is meant that their flower stems are curled over in bud like the tail of a scorpion, and beginning to open from below, slowly uncoil as the blossoms progress upward. This characteristic is so marked in the present species as to give the plant its common name of fiddle-head, from the resemblance of the coiled buds to the scroll of a violin. These are upright, rank, coarse, bristly-hairy plants, sometimes becoming troublesome weeds in cultivated ground. The flowers are dark yellow or orange in color, each with a slender tube, surmounted by five spreading lobes. It is said that in the Southwest this is considered a valuable range plant, and is there know nas *saccato gordo,* or fat grass.

Amsinckia lycopsoides Lehm., a very similar species, but with spreading, decumbent stems, and a less bristly, ovate calyx.

NIEVITAS
Cryptanthe ambigua Greene

White. Stems, slender; canescent; five to ten inches tall. Leaves, alternate; linear; entire. Inflorescence, a terminal raceme. Flowers, small; white. Corolla, salverform; crested in throat. Crest, five; yellow. Calyx, five-parted; the lobes twice as long as the seeds. Stamens, five. Ovary, five-lobed. Habitat, dry prairies and rocky hillsides.

This tiny "white forget-me-not" though rare here may be found growing in dry spots throughout our territory. It is a small slender plant that alone attracts little attention, but when it becomes abundant it whitens whole fields, and by its numbers makes up for its small size and modest mien. The name "nievita," from *nieve*—snow—is of Spanish-California origin, and refers to this sprinkling of the fields with flowery snow.

FIDDLE-NECK   *Amsinckia intermedia*

Cryptanthe ambigua

NIEVITAS

SCOULER'S ALLOCARYA

Allocarya scouleri

SCOULER'S ALLOCARYA
Allocarya scouleri (Hook. & Arn.) Greene

White. Stems, erect; slender; branched from base; ten to twenty inches tall. Leaves, sessile; linear; the lower ones opposite. Inflorescence, a terminal scorpioid raceme. Flowers, white; fragrant. Calyx, five-parted; erect; rusty-pubescent. Corolla, salverform; five-lobed; yellow appendaged in throat. Stamens, five; included. Fruit, four ovoid nutlets. Habitat, low wet fields and ditches. Blooming period, May-June.

There are about eighty species of *Allocarya,* all Western American plants, but since the division of the species is very technical, based principally on the form and coating of the seeds, and often of a microscopic character, it is useless for the novice to attempt to separate them. One of the commonest forms here is the present one, named after Dr. Scouler, a physician of the Hudson Bay Company, and a friend and companion of David Douglas. It is very plentiful in moist, undrained lands throughout our territory, being especially abundant in the so-called "white lands" of the Willamette Valley, where it whitens whole fields with its blossoms. No distinctive common name has been given to this species, but it shares with the closely allied *Plagiobothrys,* the title of white forget-me-not. One distinctive feature common to most of our species is a yellow-appendaged throat, quite distinct from the plain, white blossoms of the popcorn flower.

POPCORN FLOWER
Plagiobothrys nothofulvus Gray

White. Stems, erect; simple or branched from the base; scantily leaved; hirsute. Leaves, radical, oblong to lanceolate; numerous; whorled at the base of the stem; cauline, lanceolate to linear. Inflorescence, a scorpioid terminal raceme. Calyx, cleft for about half its length; circumscissile; the upper half deciduous. Corolla, white; short funnelform; appendaged in throat. Stamens, five; included. Nutlets, four; ovoid. Habitat, dry prairies. Blooming period, May.

The white popcorn flower, or forget-me-not, grows in great abundance on dry open prairies from Oregon southward. The stems, from six to twenty inches tall, rise from a whorl of whitish, hairy leaves, and are rather stout. They terminate in a raceme of small

BLUE-CURLS   *Trichostema lanceolatum*

[302]

white flowers. The plants usually fork near the base, and the stronger of the two branches again forks a little higher up, thus giving the appearance of a three-pronged plant. The stem leaves are alternate, but where the stems fork the two branches are usually nearly equal, and spread at an equal angle, so that in appearance it is more like the branching of an opposite leaved plant. The upper forkings usually have a solitary flower in their axils. The terminal racemes are scorpioid in bud. An interesting habit of this plant is the shedding of its calyx lobes as the fruit matures. These lobes divide from the base of the calyx in an even, regular line, leaving the saucer-shaped tube still attached below the four nutlets. The base of the leaves and stems secrete a bright red or purple stain, quite permanent and lasting. Boys are very fond of painting their faces with this stain, and the Coast Indians used it for the same purpose, making it a part of their "regalia" on festive occasions.

Slender Popcorn Flower, *Plagiobothrys tenellus* (Nutt.) Gray. This is a similar, smaller species found from Vancouver Island to California. The nutlets of this form are widened abruptly, somewhat cruciform; and the slender stems seldom exceed seven inches in height.

MINT FAMILY

BLUE-CURLS
Trichostema lanceolatum Benth.

Blue. Stem, round; simple or branched from the base; leafy; pubescent; six to eighteen inches tall. Leaves, opposite; short petioled; entire; longer than the internodes. Inflorescence, clustered in the axils of the upper leaves. Calyx, campanulate, the lobes ovate; acute; longer than the tube. Corolla, almost equally five-lobed; the tube slender; narrow. Stamens, four. Filaments, long-exserted; slender; curved. Ovary, deeply four-lobed. Habitat, dry fields and gravelly places. Blooming period, July-August.

David Douglas discovered this species on the banks of the Santiam River, in 1825, and speaks of it as "a delightful plant." Some of us may think that he was over enthusiastic in his praises, for the leaves, stems, and blossoms are all permeated with a penetrating, almost overpowering scent. Because of this strong scent, it has variously been called camphor weed, turpentine weed, and vinegar weed. Inter-

WILD MINT   *Mentha canadensis*

esting the plant undoubtedly is, but delightful is scarcely the word by which to describe it. Though a trifle rank and weedy in growth, it still deserves a place among the flowers, for its attractive blue blossoms are interesting in form, and beautiful in color. The very long, curved, blue stamens extend far beyond the two-lipped corolla, and give to the plant its commonly accepted name of blue-curls. The buds, leaves, and stems are plentifully covered with long, fine, whitish hairs. The most interesting fact about this plant was its use by the Indians as a means of obtaining fish. During the summer months, when the streams were reduced to a succession of pools, connected by a mere trickle, the fish were all forced to seek the deep places. On finding such a place where fish were plentiful, the men constructed willow wiers at each end to prevent their escaping. During this time, the women collected large quantities of blue-curls which they bruised and pounded between rocks, and threw into the water. When all was ready, the youths and children sprang into the pool among the floating plants, and beat and churned them about in the water, at the same time stirring up all the mud possible. The fish, stupefied by the scent of the plants, and stifled by the muddy water, soon floated to the surface and were easily secured.

Wherever it grows in abundance the blue-curls is considered a valuable honey plant, but the honey from it is said to crystalize very quickly, sometimes even before the bees have capped the comb which contains it.

Trichostema oblongum Benth., is a less showy species, having smaller flowers, and a strong, but not unpleasant scent.

WILD MINT
Mentha canadensis L.

Light purple. Stems, erect; simple or branched from the base; square; six to twenty-four inches tall. Leaves, aromatic; short petioled; narrowly ovate to lanceolate; tapering at both ends; serrate. Inflorescence, whorled; axillary. Calyx, campanulate; the teeth short. Corolla, five-lobed; slightly two-lipped. Stamens, four. Styles, two-cleft. Ovary, four-parted. Habitat, low rich soil. Blooming period, July-August.

The wild mint is our only native species, for although the spearmint and peppermint are both abundant here, they are not native,

YERBA BUENA

Micromeria chamissonis

but naturalized plants. This one may be easily recognized by its habit of bearing its flowers in whorls in the axils of the leaves, while the European species bear theirs in terminal spikes. In flavor it most resembles the peppermint, and the oil extracted from it is a very satisfactory substitute for the peppermint of commerce. The plants are common in low alluvial soil, and on stream banks. As early as 1817 we read that the adventurers of the Columbia Basin were accustomed to resort to such places to secure a supply of the leaves for tea. A prairie near the mouth of the Willamette River bore, in the early days, the name of *La Prairie du Thea,* because of the abundance of wild mint at that place.

YERBA BUENA
Micromeria chamissonis (Benth.) Greene

White. Stems, slender; weak; trailing; one to three feet long. Leaves, opposite; short petioled; ovate; crenate; green above, purple beneath. Flowers, small; axillary; solitary; white. Calyx, tubular; five-toothed; nearly equal. Corolla, bilabiate; upper lip erect; two-cleft; lower lip spreading three-lobed. Stamens, four; included; posterior pair shortest. Habitat, dry open woods. Blooming period. May to July.

This is the *yerba buena* of the Spanish Californians, and the Oregon tea of the more northern coast settlements. It is a slender trailing vine, with small white flowers, borne singly in the axils of the opposite, evergreen, aromatic-scented leaves. It grows abundantly throughout Oregon, Washington, and British Columbia, and will be found in dry brushy tracts and open woods, where its weak trailing stems creep over the ground. Of itself it is a dainty, pleasing plant, and when we study its history we find it linked in a most interesting manner with that of the Pacific Coast. In earliest times the Spanish priests of California recognized its virtues, and conferred upon it the name of *yerba buena,* or good herb. Among the Coast Indians the plant was steeped as a beverage, and also used for medicinal purposes. Besides this, they considered it essential, when watching for deer at springs or salt-licks, to annoint their bodies and weapons with the crushed leaves to prevent the game from detecting the human odor; "When they took this precaution they generally had good success." From the Indians, the Hudson Bay *voyageurs* and

SKULLCAP   *Scutellaria antirrhinoides*

trappers learned its use, and later the emigrants found it a delightfully refreshing beverage. In numerous places it is recorded how
delighted the settlers were when they could procure brown sugar
"to use in their Oregon tea."

This "Little vine with small white flowers," as Fremont described it, gave name to the "miserable village" that grew up on San
Francisco Bay. That "miserable village" boasted a good anchorage
for ships, however, and because of that fact it soon outstripped the
original Spanish Mission and Precedio there. Later, in 1847, the
combined settlement was renamed San Francisco, but within the
memory of many of us there were old men still living who frequently
spoke of California's metropolis as "Yerba Buena."

Interesting as is the past history of this plant, its future may be
of greater value, for from recent medical investigations, it seems
likely that it can be made of remarkable benefit in the treatment of
certain serious organic disorders.

SKULLCAP
Scutellaria antirrhinoides Benth.

Blue. Stems, square; branched; seven to ten inches tall. Leaves,
opposite; short petioled; oblong to lanceolate; entire. Flowers, solitary; axillary. Pedicels, curved, so that the flowers stand side by side.
Calyx, campanulate; bilabiate; gibbous above. Corolla, tubular; dilated in throat; two-lipped; the upper lip arched, nearly entire; the
lower lip spreading, three-lobed, vilious. Stamens, four; included.
Habitat, dry hillsides. Blooming period, June-July.

The dark blue flowers of the skullcap are borne singly in the axils
of the opposite leaves, but, by a characteristic twist of each flower
stalk, they are made to appear quaintly side by side, instead of opposite each other as we might expect. The flowers are long-tubed and
two-lipped, and in bud are closely sealed within an extremely curious
two-lipped calyx. This plant is said to have been discovered at Vancouver, Washington, by David Douglas, but it is not now known
north of the Columbia River.

Small Flowered Skullcap. *Scutellaria lateriflora* L. This is a tall,
leafy species, its rather weak stems sometimes reaching a height of
three feet. The flowers are light blue, small, and borne in axillary,

HEDGE NETTLE   *Stachys bullata*

one-sided racemes. The calyx is peculiar and quite noticeable after the flowers have fallen, having a curious projection on the upper side, and a covering lid, that completely hides the four seeds.

HEAL-ALL
Prunella vulgaris L.

Purple. Stems, square; simple; erect to ascending; three inches to three feet tall. Leaves, opposite; petioled; thin; ovate to oblong-lanceolate; entire. Inflorescence, a terminal spike; dense; obtuse; stout; bracted. Bracts, broad; ovate or orbicular. Calyx, tubular-campanulate; many-nerved; two-lipped; upper lip broad, flat, three-toothed; lower lip two-cleft. Corolla, purple, blue, pink or white; bilabiate; upper lip entire, arched; lower lip three-lobed, spreading, the central lobe fringed. Stamens, four; all fertile; two longer. Habitat, dry open soil. Blooming period, June to August.

The common prunella, heal-all, or carpenter weed, is a native of North America, Europe, and Asia. Its long heads of dark purple flowers are a common sight by every roadside. Under ordinary conditions it is a slender plant, from a few to fifteen inches tall, but I have found rank specimens that measured three and one half feet in length, and on closely clipped lawns, it sometimes develops into a creeping, almost stemless form. On the Pacific Coast pink flowered specimens are not uncommon, and pure white blossoms may sometimes be found. In Europe this plant formerly had considerable repute as a remedy for quinsy, and for sores and bruises. The Indians also used it, crushing the plants and mixing them with grease as an ointment. Among modern physicians it is considered of little value.

HEDGE NETTLE
Stachys ciliata Dougl.

Red. Stems, square; stout; erect; simple; harsh-hispid on the angles; three to six feet tall. Leaves, opposite; petioled; dark green; thin; wrinked; ovate to oblong; sub-cordate; crenately dentate. Inflorescence, terminal; in an interrupted, bracted spike. Calyx, campanulate; five-toothed; the teeth equal. Corolla, tubular; bilabiate; upper lip erect, concave, nearly entire; lower lip three-cleft, the central lobe broad. Stamens, four; beneath the arched upper lip; the posterior pair shortest. Habitat, wet low lands. Blooming period, June.

BLACK NIGHTSHADE

The hedge nettle is a coarse, rank herb of the mint family, having, however, very evil smelling foliage, quite different from the pleasing scent of the true mints. This is our tallest species, often reaching a height of six feet. The flowers are dark red, with a long tube, and two arching lips, the lower one considerably the longer. Because of its coarse growth, this plant has a weedy aspect, but the flowers are bright enough to attract considerable attention. This plant is found in low wet land, usually in shade, and its range extends throughout our territory.

HEDGE NETTLE
Stachys bullata Benth.

Pink. Stems, twelve to twenty inches tall. Leaves, ovate to oblong; subcordate; obtuse or acute; light green. Flowers, pink, dotted and blotched with white. Corolla tube, little longer than the calyx. Otherwise as for *S. ciliata.*

A more sun-loving plant than the previous, this species will be found in wet swales and ditches in open fields. The leaves are light green and much wrinkled. The whole plant is soft hairy, and seldom reaches a height of over thirty inches. The flowers are light pink in color.

All species of hedge nettle have a considerable reputation as a healing application for cuts and bruises. Woundwort is the name of the common European species, and is also often applied to our North American plants.

NIGHTSHADE FAMILY

BLACK NIGHTSHADE
Solanum nigrum L.

White. Stem, green; glabrous; branched; erect; one to two feet tall. Leaves, alternate; petioled; ovate; entire or sinuate; smooth. Inflorescence, lateral; solitary or in small umbels. Calyx, five-parted. Corolla, rotate; five-parted. Petals, ovate. Stamens, five; alternate with the petals; exserted. Anthers, connivant into a cone. Style, exserted. Fruit, a black berry. Habitat, fields and stream banks. Blooming period, June to August.

My mother was my first botany teacher. When I was a small child she used to amuse me by telling me that when she was a girl they called tomatoes "love apples," growing them in their flower gardens for ornament, and that they considered the fruit a deadly poison. She also showed me the black nightshade, a close relative of the tomato, and warned me that here was the truly poisonous member of the family, whose berries I must never eat.

After my mother had carefully taught me that nightshade would certainly kill me, my wife began our married life by feeding me upon nightshade pies. Certainly these were not "pies like mother used to make." Naturally, after a number of years' experience with these pies I have lost my suspicion of the fruit, and as my mother learned to value the "love apples" of her childhood, I now grow and value the so-called deadly nightshade.

This berry is cultivated and used as food extensively throughout the Dakotas, and in other sections adjacent to the one hundredth meridian, and is there variously known as "blueberry" and "stubbleberry." The Californian Indians also knew and used the fruit.

Not only are the berries good to eat, but the leaves and stems are wholesome as well, being cooked like spinach. According to the U. S. Dispensary, "the leaves are said to be consumed in large quantities in the Isles of France and Borboun, as it is in the Hawaiian Islands."

It is unfortunate that this innocent and attractive little plant should have such an evil reputation thrust upon it. The mistake comes, evidently, from confusing two plants. It is true that there is a deadly nightshade, but it does not grow in this country. It is a native of Europe—*Belledona atropa*—from which the powerful drug atropine is made.

The black nightshade has a wide range, growing in Europe as well as throughout the northern United States. By many it is supposed to be a foreign introduction to the Pacific States, but this idea is incorrect, since Dr. John Scouler collected it at Baker's Bay, on the Columbia River as early as 1825.

NATIVE TOBACCO
Nicotiana quadrivalvis Pursh

White. Stems, stout; viscid; branching from the base; one or two feet tall. Leaves, large; alternate; oblong below to lanceolate at the summit of the stem; acute. Flowers, a terminal panicle; few-flowered; slender pedicled. Calyx, tubular-campanulate; five-cleft; persistent; the lobes shorter than the tube. Corolla, funnelform; plaited; five-lobed; about one inch long. Stamens, five. Stigma, capitate. Habitat, along streams.

This rank weed is interesting as being the only plant cultivated by the North Coast Indians, and this culture was, indeed, of a very primitive form. It consisted merely in scattering the seeds in the ashes of a burned over tract, and then allowing the plants to grow with little further care. Smoking, with the Indians, was largely a matter of ceremony and religion, and not, as a rule, simply for self indulgence. Among the sea-shore tribes, the lime from burned shells was added to the tobacco leaves to temper their drastic qualities.

FIGWORT FAMILY

PURPLE BEARD-TONGUE
Pentstemon diffusus Dougl.

Purple. Stem, herbaceous; smooth; slender; diffuse; branched from a woody base; the branches strict; height, ten to eighteen inches. Leaves, opposite; ovate to lanceolate; serrate; the upper ones sessile. Inflorescence, an interrupted, bracted panicle. Calyx, five-parted. Corolla, tubular-funnelform; two-lipped; the lips widely spreading; upper one two-lobed; lower one three-lobed. Stamens, five; included; one sterile; the filaments hairy above. Style, long; filiform. Stigma, entire. Habitat, on stream banks. Blooming period, May-June.

The pentstemons are a charming group of flowering plants, mostly restricted to Western America, and largely high altitudes in the mountains. The present species, however, grows at comparatively low levels, and will be found along the borders of mountain streams from British Columbia to Southern Oregon, west of the Cascades. It is thus restricted almost exclusively to the territory treated in this book, and is one of our characteristic flowers.

Pentstemon comes from two Greek words meaning five, and stamen, which fittingly describes the flowers which have five stamens, but the fifth stamen, although long and often prominently bearded, is imperfect and sterile, having no pollen-bearing anther.

PURPLE BEARD-TONGUE   *Pentstemon diffusus*

MENZIES' BEARD-TONGUE
Pentstemon menziesii Hook.

Blue or pink. Stems, shrubby; diffuse; branched; erect or prostrate; four to eight inches tall. Leaves, evergreen; thick; leathery; opposite; ovate; dentate. Inflorescence, panicled. Calyx, five-parted; sepals, lanceolate; acute. Corolla, tubular-funnelform; an inch or more long; flattened vertically; bilabiate; upper lip two-lobed; lower lip three-cleft. Stamens, five; one sterile. Sterile filament, densely bearded. Habitat, rocky ground in mountains at tree limit. Blooming period, July-August.

On high bleak mountain peaks, where the deeper clefts are filled with never melting snow, and the prevailing silence is broken only by the chatter of the Clark's Crow, or the whistle of the cony, is the home of this beautiful beard-tongue. Often barely ten weeks of summer intervene from snow to snow, yet, in this apparently unfavorable location, the plants not only survive from year to year, but actually thrive, bringing forth with each season an abundance of showy bloom. Transplanted to a lower level, in fertile soil and a salubrious climate, they refuse to grow, soon withering and drooping as though homesick for their alpine heights. The shrubby pentstemon bears shiny, evergreen leaves, leathery in texture, and makes a refreshing sight against the encircling rocks, literally covering itself with large tubular bloom, each flower an inch or more in length, and varying from purplish blue to a soft clear pink.

SMALL PURPLE BEARD-TONGUE
Pentstemon procerus Dougl.

Blue. Stem, smooth; slender; erect; eight to twenty inches tall. Leaves, opposite; lanceolate; entire; the upper ones sessile. Inflorescence, axillary or terminal; whorled. Calyx, five-parted. Sepals, glabrous; scarious-margined; dentate or erose. Corolla, small; about half an inch long; tubular; the tube slender; bilabiate; lips widely spreading; the throat hairy. Stamens, five; one sterile. Sterile filament, bearded. Habitat, high mountain meadows. Blooming period, July-August.

The flowers of this pentstemon are small but numerous, forming closely crowded whorls in the upper leaf axils, or at the summit of

FIGWORT   *Scrophularia californica*

the stem. A mountain flower, varying greatly in size with the altitude at which it grows, the high alpine form attaining only a few inches in height.

Yellow Beard-Tongue, *Pentstemon confertus,* Dougl. Very similar to the preceding except in the color of the flowers, which, in this species, are yellow or cream-colored.

CRIMSON BEARD-TONGUE
Pentstemon rupicola (Piper) Howell

Crimson. Stems, shrubby; branched; dense; four to eight inches tall. Leaves, opposite; glaucous; leathery; petioled; ovate; dentate. Inflorescence, a raceme; glandular. Calyx, five-parted. Corolla, tubular; bearded in throat; an inch or more long; two-lipped; upper lip two-lobed; lower lip three-cleft. Stamens, five; the fifth one sterile, long and bearded. Anthers, woolly. Habitat, rocky cliffs. Blooming period, April to August according to altitude.

This wonderful pentstemon makes brilliant patches of beauty on barren cliffs in the mountains. Normally it ranges to high altitudes, up to seven or eight thousand feet, but in the Gorge of the Columbia it descends almost to the level of the river. There it may be seen in all its beauty without the effort of a wearisome climb to the heights. There, also, it blooms in early spring, while its mountain sisters may not open their blossoms until the hot sun of late summer has thawed the alpine snowbanks and uncovered the mat-like plants.

Richardson's Beard-Tongue. *Pentstemon richardsonii* Dougl., will be found growing with the crimson beard-tongue in the Gorge of the Columbia, but blooms later in the season. The stem is shrubby and erect, branching from the base. The leaves are rather thin, ovate to lanceolate, pinnately parted or merely toothed. The red or crimson flowers are not quite an inch in length. Its range is in the mountains of Oregon and Washington.

FIGWORT
Scrophularia californica Cham.

Purplish brown. Stems, stout; erect; two to five feet tall. Leaves, opposite; oblong; serrate; acuminate; upper pairs triangular. Inflorescence, a panicle; loose; tapering. Calyx, five-cleft nearly to the

BLUE LIPS   *Collinsia grandiflora*

[320]

base. Corolla, brown or purplish; irregular; the tube ovoid to globular; the limb two-lipped, five-lobed; lower lip short, reflexed; two upper ones long, and naked in bud. Stamens, five; one sterile and represented by a scale on the upper side of the corolla tube. Style, filiform. Stigma, capitate. Habitat, moist meadows. Blooming period, from June in the valleys, to August at high elevations.

The rank angled stems of the figwort grow to a height of from two to six feet. The leaves are opposite, ovate, acutely pointed and coarsely toothed. The blossoms which are small and inconspicuous are borne in terminal panicles, or in the axils of the upper leaves. In color they are dull red, or reddish purple, or brown, and, although not showy, are curious and interesting in form. In California, where they are considered of value by apiarists, they are known as the California bee plant.

BLUE LIPS
Collinsia grandiflora Dougl.

Blue. Stems, clustered; smooth; slender; six to twelve inches tall. Leaves, opposite; the lower ones petioled, orbicular to ovate; the upper ones often whorled, spatulate to lanceolate. Flowers, solitary or whorled in the axils of the upper leaves. Calyx, campanulate; deeply five-cleft; the lobes lanceolate. Corolla, bilabiate; the tube saccate above, declined; the upper limb erect, two-cleft; lower limb three-lobed, the lateral lobes spreading, the central one folded into a narrow keel and enclosing the style and stamens. Stamens, five; declined; one sterile and represented by a scale at the base of the corolla. Habitat, dry open soil. Blooming period, April-May.

This flower was one of those introduced into English gardens, one hundred years ago, by the great botanist, David Douglas. In this country it is seldom cultivated, although, even in its wild habitat, the plant has a quality that suggests cultivated gardens and formal borders. In favorable locations, I have found it forming such symmetrical groups, and orderly edgings that it was hard to believe that it had not been trained and tended by human hands. One such place, in particular, was a deserted rock quarry where it had taken complete possession, and the jutting, thinly-soiled escarpments rose, terrace on terrace, a perfect garden of thickly sown, purple bloom.

The name blue lips it shares with other species of *Collinsia,* as also that of innocence. A more distinctive name, found in use among

GROUSE FLOWER

Synthyris rotundifolia

the students at the Oregon State College is, "sunbonnet babies," a name, which, because of the peculiar shape of the flowers, seems quite appropriate.

TURTLE-HEAD
Chelone nemorosa Dougl.

Purple. Stems, erect; leafy; simple; one to four feet tall. Leaves, opposite; ovate to lanceolate; serrate; short petioled. Inflorescence, a terminal spike. Calyx, five-parted; pubescent; bracted. Corolla, tubular; bilabiate; upper lip, concave, two-cleft; lower lip three-lobed, spreading; woolly in throat. Stamens, five, one sterile and smaller. Habitat, along streams in the mountains.

The erect, leafy stems of the turtle-head show a marked preference for wet stream banks. The name turtle-head refers to the rather grotesque, head-like form of the flowers.

GROUSE FLOWER
Synthyris rotundifolia Gray

Blue. Scapes, simple; leafless; four to six inches tall; about equaling the leaves. Leaves, all basal; petioled; orbicular; crenately lobed; pubescent; green above, reddish beneath. Inflorescence, a few-flowered terminal raceme. Calyx, four-parted; the lobes ovate, acute. Corolla, short campanulate; four-lobed; lobes slightly unequal. Stamens, two; exserted. Habitat, in open woods. Blooming period, January to May.

In the middle of winter, in open fir woods or along sheltered stream banks, where they are almost covered by hazel or alder leaves, you may find little plants whose roundish leaves are usually green above, but red beneath. When February comes, or even in January, if the season is favorable, though the rain still falls drearily, and the days are damp and chilly, we may know that spring is on the way, for the plants put forth their modest bloom, our first real spring flower. It is the *Synthyris*. Children sometimes call them blue-bells; some people call them spring queen, though there is nothing queenly in their low growth and modest, retiring habit. They are also called dolly-flowers, and mowich, the latter being an Indian word for deer, but I prefer still another name—that of grouse-flower. The name is particularly fitting, for just when the "blue," or sooty grouse are

SPEEDWELL

filling the woods with their "hooting," these flowers are at their best. There is something especially fitting, it seems to me, in thus connecting this first retiring blossom with this, the most illusive of all our bird calls.

"Oo-O-Oo-Oo-O-" comes the call of the grouse, first from one direction and then from another. It can hardly be called a sound, more a vibration of the air, to be felt rather than heard. Only a trained, keen eye can locate the author, a big, plump, gray bird high in the firs, sitting motionless and almost invisible against the gray boles. The giant gray bird knows, and his shy, silent mate knows, and the modest grouse-flower knows, and from the courting birds, and the shy blue flower, *we* may know that spring has come to the land of the trailing mist.

The first precocious grouse-flowers blossom upon sunny banks, and sheltered southern slopes. It is by preference, however, a plant of moist, cool shade, and in such places the later flowers will be found.

Synthyris reniformis Benth., differs from the above by having stouter, taller flower stems, and thickish, smooth leaves. It is found in the Gorge of the Columbia, on the shaded, Oregon side, but not on the sunny, Washington shore.

SPEEDWELL. AMERICAN BROOKLIME
Veronica americana Schwein.

Blue. Stems, smooth; succulent; decumbent or ascending; rooting at the nodes; ten to thirty inches tall. Leaves, opposite; short-petioled; oblong-ovate to lanceolate; serrate; truncate at base. Inflorescence, a raceme; loose; slender; axillary. Pedicels, slender; one half inch or more long. Calyx, four-parted. Sepals, oblong. Corolla, four-cleft; rotate; blue veined with purple; soon falling. Stamens, two: diverging. Habitat, wet places. Blooming period, May-June.

The pretty little speedwells are often called forget-me-nots, nor is this name entirely unsuitbale, for in tradition, a gift of blue flowers presented at parting was supposed to bring good-luck, and whether the message that accompanied them was God-speed, speedwell, or, as in forget-me-not, a plea for remembrance, was immaterial.

These plants are old in tradition, and were considered of great medicinal value in medieval Europe. All speedwells may be easily known by their spreading, four-parted corolla, and two stamens, a

YELLOW MONKEY-FLOWER   *Mimulus langsdorfii*

combination not commonly found in other plants. The range of this species extends entirely across North America. Horace Kephart recommends it as a salad plant; "equal to water-cress, and very delicious."

MARSH SPEEDWELL
Veronica scutellata L.

Light blue or purplish. Stems, glabrous; slender; erect or ascending; rooting at the lower nodes; five to ten inches tall. Leaves, sessile; linear or lanceolate; acute; entire or toothed; reddish. Inflorescence, slender; axillary racemes. Flowers, scattered; on slender pedicels. Calyx, four-parted. Stamens, two. Habitat, along the borders of ponds, or in shallow ditches and sloughs. Blooming period, May-June.

The marsh speedwell, as its name indicates, will be found in wet situations. It is a small, slender plant, with narrow sessile leaves and light purple flowers. The foliage is a pale reddish green, which gives the whole plant an unthrifty, sickly look, as though its marshal habitat did not agree with it.

YELLOW MONKEY-FLOWER
Mimulus langsdorfii Donn.

Yellow. Root, perennial. Stems, angled; erect; leafy; light green; six to twenty-four inches. Leaves, opposite; the lower petioled; the upper sessile, reduced; all palmately veined; ovate; obtuse or acute; dentate. Inflorescence, axillary, or whorled, or in short bracted racemes. Calyx, tubular-campanulate; five-angled; persistent; the upper lobes longer; the lower lobes ascending and closing the throat; inflated in fruit. Corolla, yellow; tubular-funnelform; bilabiate; the tube flattened horizontally; much longer than the calyx; lips spreading, the upper one lobed, the lower one three cleft; bearded in throat. Stamens, four. Stigma, two-lobed; sensitive. Habitat, moist open places. Blooming period, May to July.

The yellow monkey-flower, with its attractively scalloped leaves and long-tubed, monkey-faced blossoms would be a most satisfactory plant were it not for its provoking habit of wilting and dropping its flowers almost as soon as picked. In spite of their common abundance,

RED MONKEY-FLOWER

Mimulus lewisii

and my familiarity with them, they impress me at every new view with their delicate and exotic beauty. In color the flowers are a rich canary yellow, marked in the throat with crimson dots, and finely bearded. The whole flower is strongly flattened from above, and the two-lobed stigma protrudes upward into the narrowly compressed throat, so that no insect may enter without brushing against it, and depositing upon it any pollen that it may be carrying. These curious two-lobed stigmas are characteristic of all species of *Mimulus*. They are remarkably sensitive, and at the slightest touch the lobes close together. This action may be observed in any fresh flower by lightly touching the stigma with a pin or straw.

The favorite haunts of the yellow monkey-flower are along moist ditches or the borders of ponds.

Annual Yellow Monkey-Flower. *Mimulus nasutus* Greene. Very similar to the above, but the plants are annuals.

RED MONKEY-FLOWER
Mimulus lewisii Pursh

Rose red. Root, perennial. Stems, clustered; pubescent; rather viscid; slender; erect. Leaves, opposite; ovate to oblong; acute; dentate. Inflorescence, axillary; erect; slender pediceled. Calyx, prismatic; five-lobed; the lobes triangular; acute. Corolla, tubular; bilabiate; the tube longer than the calyx, the lips spreading. Stamens, four; included. Stigma, two-lobed; sensitive. Habitat, along mountain streams. Blooming period, July-August.

You will find the red monkey-flower bordering mountain streams, its brilliant flowers and bright foliage mirrored in the quiet pools, or nodding in the breezes on tiny islands or low peninsulas among the splashing ripples. Here it makes a picture entrancing and unforgettable, its companions the leaping trout and the erratic water ousel— illusive mountain spirits like itself.

The flowers appear in pairs on slender pedicels in the axils of the leaves. The whole plant is hairy and somewhat sticky.

DITCH MONKEY-FLOWER
Mimulus subuniflorus Hook. & Arn.

Rose purple. Stems, short; branching; pubescent; two to six inches tall. Leaves, opposite, or basal ones whorled; entire. Inflorescence, axillary. Calyx, irregular; five-angled; five-lobed; the upper lobes longest; tube much longer than the lobes. Corolla, tubular-funnel-form; bilabiate; the tube slender, tapering, becoming very broad in throat; the lips wide spreading. Stamens, four; in two unequal pairs; united by their anthers. Style, filiform. Stigma, two-lobed; sensitive. Habitat, wet ditches and pond borders. Blooming period, May-June.

For so small a plant, the flowers of this species are of truly remarkable size. A plant only an inch or two in height may bear a flower three-fourths of an inch across, and a plant four inches in height may have from four to ten of these showy blossoms at the summit. Because of this prominence of bloom over foliage they are unique, for a wheel-track or a dead-furrow in a wet field may be completely filled with flowers. Nothing short of a conservatory or a tropical clime could reveal a richer, more delicate blending of colors. In color they are rose purple, or pinkish, blotched within with the richest shades of violet and purple, and with a showy yellow beard. This is a rare plant with us, but is more abundant eastward and southward.

MUSK PLANT
Mimulus moschatus Dougl.

Yellow. Root, perennial. Stems, clustered; weak; spreading; declined; villous; viscid; sometimes musk-scented; five to twelve inches tall. Leaves, opposite; petioled; ovate; denticulate. Flowers, solitary; axillary. Calyx, persistent; five-angled; five-lobed; the lobes nearly equal; the tube twice as long as the lobes. Corolla, tubular-bilabiate; the tube little longer than the calyx; the lips spreading, the upper one two-lobed; the lower three-lobed. Stamens, four; included. Stigma, two-lobed. Habitat, moist soil and stream banks. Blooming period, May to August.

Do not expect to identify this plant by smell alone, for though some plants have a musky odor, this is by no means true of all specimens. David Douglas sent seed of this species to England, and the plants grown from them were of the decidedly musky type. From the plants so grown, the flower received its name, but in its native habitat, I find that musky plants are the exception rather than the rule. In later years the English gardeners have been concerned by the loss of scent in their cultivated plants, and are striving to regain it.

Recently, at the request of a correspondent, I gathered seed from the strongest scented plants available, but these, when grown in England, also reverted to the scentless type. Perhaps some unknown factor of soil or environment is the real determining cause. Personally, I do not consider them desirable as a garden flower, for the whole plant is clammy, and often drips slime in a most disagreeable manner.

LOUSEWORT. ELEPHANT'S TRUNK
Pedicularis racemosa Dougl.

White, pinkish or pale yellow. Stems, slender; ascending; leafy; glabrous; simple or branched; one to two feet tall. Leaves, all cauline; petioled; lanceolate; doubly crenate; reddish. Inflorescence, a short leafy raceme. Calyx, deeply cleft before; toothed behind. Corolla, two-lipped; the upper lip compressed and curved into a tapering, arched beak, or galea; lower lip three-lobed. Stamens, four; didynamous; enclosed in the arched galea. Habitat, dry soil in mountains. Blooming period, June-August.

The name lousewort comes from a belief of the ancients that if their flocks fed among these plants they would become infested with lice. In like manner, today, in the South, the wild carrot and goldenrod bear the unsavory name of chigger-weed. Elephant's trunk refers to the peculiar and uncommon shape of the flowers. They are white or pinkish in color, and with a galea, or upper lip extended in a tapering point that curves downward and backward in a trunk-like form. The flowers appear in terminal, leafy racemes at the summit of the plant. The leaves and stems of this species are brightly tinged with red or purple. The leaves are simple, wavy-margined, and tapering, a characteristic point, since all our other louseworts have pinnate leaves. An abundant plant in low alpine regions, seeming to prefer dry, sunny slopes.

Contorted Lousewort, *Pedicularis contorta* Benth., also sometimes called elephant's trunk. It has pale yellow flowers with slender, curved beaks. The leaves are pinnately divided. A plant of high mountains.

Butterfly-Tongue. *Pedicularis surrecta* Benth. In this flower the beak is extremely long, slender, and up-curled like a butterfly's tongue. The flowers are small and reddish-purple in color. Found in wet places in the mountains.

INDIAN PAINT-BRUSH. PAINTED CUP
Castilleja angustifolia (Nutt.) G. Don.

Red. Root, perennial. Stems, clustered; erect; simple; leafy; six to twelve inches tall. Leaves, alternate; pubescent; the lower one linear and entire; the upper ones broader, and three to five-lobed; those of the inflorescence bright red. Inflorescence, a terminal bracted spike. Bracts, red or scarlet; broader and more deeply cleft than the leaves. Calyx, tubular; flattened. Corolla, tubular; irregular; galea, or upper lip about as long as the tube; lower lip three-lobed, short. Stamens, four; didynamous; enclosed in the arched galea. Habitat, dry gravelly ground. Blooming period, April to August according to altitude.

One of the tribal Gods, or super-beings of the Chinook Indians was Bluejay. In a characteristic tale of that tribe the story of his death is told. "Once when Bluejay was about to go upon a journey he was given five buckets full of water with which to quench five burning prairies through which he would have to pass. Coming, as he journeyed, to a meadow where red, flame-like flowers grew—the weather being exceedingly hot—he was deceived into thinking that this was the fire of which he had been warned, and in an attempt to quench the blazing flowers, poured out and wasted a great deal of the water. Later, coming to the real fires, he had not enough left, and in attempting to pass he perished." There is little doubt in my mind that the flowers which deceived Bluejay were the common, scarlet-tipped paint-brushes. When, as often occurs in some of our mountain meadows, it forms extensive waving fields, the keen imagination of the natives could not but mark its resemblance to running flame, and so about the plant they built this cunning tale.

The beauty of the paint-brush is not in its flowers, which are hidden, but in its gayly colored floral bracts. Each bract is tipped with crimson, as though it had been dipped in a pot of brilliant paint.

Castilleja miniata Dougl., is a larger species than the above—from ten to thirty inches tall—and may be distinguished from it by its smooth stem, and entire leaves and bracts. It is found both at sea level and in the mountains.

Castilleja oreopola Greenmann, is a white or crimson bracted mountain species.

Castilleja camporum (Greenmann) Howell. The foliage of this species is soft-hairy. The bracts are yellow in color; lobed; the middle lobe widest, and rounded. The bracts are folded closely over the small blossoms, not loose and spreading as in other species. Found in moist places; rare.

WHITE OWL'S CLOVER
Orthocarpus hispidus Benth.

White. Root, annual. Stems, simple; slender; erect; hispid; six to fourteen inches tall. Leaves, lanceolate to linear; attenuate; three-lobed; the lobes linear. Inflorescence, a compact; bracted; terminal raceme. Bracts, similar to the leaves but smaller. Calyx, tubular; four-cleft. Corolla, tubular; two-lipped; the upper lip or galea compressed laterally, slender, little longer than the lower lip; lower lip inflated, tri-saccate. Stamens, four; in two pairs; ascending beneath the galea. Style, filiform. Stigma, entire. Habitat, wet fields. Blooming period, May-June.

Just why these plants have received their curious name is not known, but it is probable that the peculiar, two-lipped corolla is supposed to suggest the face of an owl. Our northern species are rather inconspicuous, but some of the Californian species are very showy. The characteristics of the genus are well marked, but the species are at times difficult to determine. This, the common white owl's clover of the Willamette Valley, will be found along wet ditches and about moist field borders. The individual flowers are short lived, so that, although many blossoms may be borne in a season, very few of them are open at any one time.

Orthocarpus attenuatus Gray, is also a white-flowered species common in dry soil from California to British Columbia. It differs from the above by having the lobes of the lower lip much longer. The foliage is slender and long-tapering, and the divisions of the flower bracts are often tipped with white. A small and inconspicuous plant.

PINK OWL'S CLOVER
Orthocarpus bracteosus Benth.

Pink. Stem, erect; simple; leafy; four to twelve inches tall. Leaves, alternate; pubescent; all deeply three-cleft into linear or

PINK OWL'S CLOVER   *Orthocarpus bracteosus*

lanceolate lobes. Inflorescence, a terminal, bracted spike. Bracts, wider and shorter than the leaves; three-lobed; often purplish or reddish. Calyx, tubular; four-cleft; the teeth as long as the tube. Corolla, pink or purplish; narrow tubular-funnelform; two lipped; the upper lip short, abruptly hooked at summit; the lower lip saccate, slightly three-lobed. Stamens, didynamous; ascending under the curved galea. Habitat, poorly drained prairies. Blooming period, May-June.

By the first of June, in favorable localities, the moist fields and roadsides of the valleys will begin to show patches and spots of soft pink from the blossoms of this pretty owl's clover. Only the slender pink *Valerianella* can equal it in imparting a pink blush to the vernal landscape. The bracts which surround the flowers of this species are three-lobed, broader than the leaves, and often tinged with red or purplish.

Orthocarpus purpurascens Benth., is another pink or purple flowered species. The leaves of this form are divided into many linear divisions. The flowers are borne in a dense, short spike at the summit of the plant, and are surrounded by three to five-cleft purple bracts. A Spanish-Californian name for this flower is said to be "escobitas," or "little brooms." The range of this species extends from Washington to California.

BLADDERWORT FAMILY

BUTTERWORT
Pinguicula vulgaris L.

Violet. Leaves, elliptic; entire; greasy to the touch. Flowers, solitary. Calyx, three-cleft. Corolla, hairy in throat; spurred; two-lipped; lower lip longer. Habitat, moist banks in the mountains.

This little plant is insectivorous, for it catches live prey by means of a grease-like mucilage which is spread over the surface of its clammy leaves. Whether or not the name of butterwort is derived from this greasy secretion, is uncertain. Possibly, another quality of the leaves is responsible for the title, for the leafy secretion also has the power to coagulate milk, just as rennet does. The Laplanders of Northern Europe are said to use it in this manner. Reindeer milk is poured over the fresh leaves and set aside for a time. It then becomes thick, and is used as food.

SWEET-SCENTED BEDSTRAW   *Galium triflorum*

ANNUAL BEDSTRAW
Galium aparine L.

White. Stems, angled; with long internodes; weak, trailing or climbing by means of hooked bristles on the angles; one to five feet tall. Leaves, in whorls of six to eight; linear to oblanceolate; the margins and veins retrorsely hispid. Inflorescence, axillary, on slender pedicels; few-flowered. Flowers, minute. Calyx, ovate; limb wanting. Corolla, rotate; usually four-lobed. Stamens, as many as the lobes of the corolla. Styles, two. Fruit, dry; globular; two-lobed; hispid. Habitat, along streams in open woods.

The bedstraws are common little herbs, with weak, four-angled, trailing or reclining stems, clinging to other plants and shrubbery, and often climbing by means of hooked hairs or bristles on the angles of the stems and leaf-veins. The leaves are whorled, and in this species there are six to eight leaves to each whorl. The flowers are white, minute, and appear singly in the axils of the leaves. The fruit is a tiny globular burr, covered with hooked bristles.

Three-Petaled Bedstraw, *Galium trifidum pacigcum* Wiegand. This is an extremely slender, delicate bedstraw, having its whorled leaves in fours, smooth fruit, and three lobes to the tiny blossoms in place of the usual four.

SWEET-SCENTED BEDSTRAW
Galium triflorum Michx.

White. Roots, perennial. Stems, angled; slender; weak; climbing by hooked bristles on the angles; three feet tall. Leaves, one-nerved; lanceolate; in whorls of six. Inflorescence, pediceled; cymose; axillary. Flowers, minute; in groups of threes. Calyx, tube ovate; limb wanting. Corolla, rotate; mostly four-cleft. Stamens, as many as the lobes of the corolla; short. Styles, two. Fruit, globular; two-lobed; armed with hooked hairs. Habitat, open woods.

Sometimes while handling freshly cut hay, especially along field borders, your nostrils will be pleasantly greeted by a sweet vanilla-like fragrance from among the wilting grass. A careful search may reveal the stems of this slender little bedstraw as the source of the perfume. A common name sometimes given to it is "lady's bouquet";

NORTHERN WILD LICORICE   *Galium kamtschaticum*

similarly, among the Ponca Indians, we are told, it is known as *"wau-inu-maka,"* meaning "woman's perfume." According to Mr. M. R. Gilmore, the Indian women wore a handful of the stems tucked under their girdle for the sake of the scent.

The range of this species extends across North America. It is a very common plant with us, growing in open woods in great abundance. The flowers, as its specific name indicates, are usually borne in threes. Its stem is very slender, and supports itself by climbing over brush, or sprawls on the ground if no support is available.

NORTHERN WILD LICORICE
Galium kamtschaticum Steller

Cream-colored. Root, perennial. Stem, square; smooth; erect; six to fifteen inches tall. Leaves, in whorls of fours; ovate or orbicular; three-nerved. Inflorescence, a terminal cyme. Flowers, small; cream-colored. Corolla, four-parted; rotate. Fruit, globular; hispid. Habitat, in mountain woods. Blooming period, May-June.

This fine large bedstraw has smooth, straight, erect stems, not trailing or declining as in most species, but strong enough to stand by their own strength. The soft leaves, too, which are in fours, are broad and large, often an inch or more across, a variation from the usual narrow leaves of this genus. The name wild licorice, as applied to various species of bedstraw, comes from the fact that they have sweetish-tasting roots.

HONEYSUCKLE FAMILY

BLUE-BERRIED ELDER
Sambucus glauca Nutt.

White. Stems, woody; erect; branched; brittle; six to forty feet tall. Branches, pithy. Leaves, opposite; pinnate; rank-scented. Leaflets, five to nine lanceolate to oblong; serrate. Inflorescence, a cyme; large; flat-topped. Flowers, small; white. Calyx, minute. Corolla, five-lobed; spreading. Fruit, black with a blue bloom. Habitat, open woods. Blooming period, June.

The rank, pungent smell of the elder blossoms bring back far-off memories of childhood, when elder-blow tea was considered essential

Sambucus glauca

BLUE-BERRIED ELDER

for breaking up a cold and bringing on a profuse sweat. The whole plant is a natural medicine chest, for the inner bark is a powerful emetic, the blossoms cooked in oil make a cooling ointment, and the fruit made into a conserve, or rob is relished by children, easy to administer, and acts as a mild aperient and diuretic. Besides its medicinal use, the fruit is good for pies, and elder-berry wine and jelly have long been renowned.

Every country boy knows the use of the pithy, young elder shoots in the manufacture of pop-guns and squirt-guns, those twin delights of youth, though less popular with older persons. Eastern boys, too, know how to shape them into spiles to catch the oozing sap of the tapped "sugar tree," and conduct it outward into the piggin. They also make excellent whistles, and the botanical name *Sambucus,* refers to a flute-like instrument once made from elder stalks.

Ordinarily the blue-berried elder is a shrub or small tree, reaching a height of from six to fifteen feet, but at times it forms really large trees. One well shaped specimen in central Linn County, Oregon, has a trunk measuring over two feet in diameter, and even larger trees may occasionally be found.

RED-BERRIED ELDER
Sambucus callicarpa Greene

White. Stems, shrubby; erect; six to twenty feet tall. Leaflets, five to seven; narrowly oblong; acute; serrate. Inflorescence, a pyramidal thrysus. Fruit, scarlet. Habitat, rocky hillsides. Blooming period, April. Otherwise as for the preceding species.

One of the most beautiful colors in nature, and very striking in their leafy setting, is that of the ripe fruit of the red-berried elder. The berries are like brilliant coral beads upon a background of clear jade, and if viewed from below, and the whole outlined against a dazzling turquoise sky, the picture is indeed complete. The berries are reputed to be poisonous, but this is questionable.

VIBURNUM
Viburnum ellipticum Hook.

White. Stems, shrubby; clustered; three to eight feet tall. Leaves, opposite; petioled; oval to oblong; dentate; thick. Inflorescence, a

Linnaea borealis longiflora

TWIN-FLOWER

dense, flat-topped cyme. Corolla, white or cream-colored; thick in texture; five-lobed; broadly campanulate or rotate. Stamens, five; exserted. Fruit, black; one-seeded. Habitat, rocky stream banks. Blooming period, May.

A typical stream-side shrub, the stiff, brittle stems forming close thickets in rich bottom lands from the Columbia River, southward. The leaves are thick and firm in substance, deeply veined, and very dark green. The creamy, thick-petalled flowers appear in May, and are borne in flat-topped cymes.

TWIN-FLOWER
Linnaea borealis longiflora Torr.

Pink. Stems, slender; weak; trailing; ten to thirty inches long. Leaves, opposite; evergreen; shiny; ovate; slightly toothed. Flowers, in pairs at the summit of slender upright branches. Pedicels, bracted; nodding. Calyx, five-cleft; the teeth lanceolate. Corolla, tubular-funnelform; five-lobed; pink. Stamens, four; in two pairs; one pair shorter. Style, exserted. Habitat, in woods; common at high altitudes. Blooming period, May to August, according to altitude.

The twin-flower often carpets large areas both at low levels and in the mountains, and wherever found it is a beautiful plant. The leaves are evergreen, and evergreen vines are a rare form of plant life on our coast. The drooping flowers are borne in pairs at the summit of slender, forked pedicels, and in their uniformly symmetrical arrangement have a completed look, as though the plant were confident that by no alteration could they be improved upon. The corolla is funnelform, and hairy within the throat. The flowers are very fragrant.

HIGH-BUSH CRANBERRY
Viburnum opulus americanum (Mill.) Ait.

White. Stem, shrubby; two to ten feet tall. Branches, erect. Bark, gray. Leaves, opposite; orbicular; three-lobed; the lobes triangular, acute, dentate. Petioles, bearing reddish glands. Buds, scaly. Inflorescence, a cyme. Flowers, of two forms; the central flowers small, perfect; marginal flowers large, showy, sterile. Corolla, spreading; five-lobed in perfect flowers; flat and three to five-lobed in sterile ones. Stamens, five; exserted. Fruit, red; juicy. Habitat, along mountain streams.

SNOWBERRY   *Symphoricarpos albus*

The fruit of this viburnum is bright red in color, and when cooked, makes an almost perfect substitute for cranberry sauce. In the early days it was a great favorite among the Northern Pioneers from the Atlantic to the Pacific, but since the true cranberry has been so extensively cultivated, this old-time fruit has largely fallen into disuse. I distinctly remember that, up to my twelfth year, I was acquainted with no other form of cranberry, and if childhood memories can be trusted, the flavor is fully equal to the commercial fruit, though its preparation, because of the large seeds, is no doubt more tedious.

The flowers of the high-bush cranberry are white or greenish, and the small, central ones, alone, are fertile. A circle of large, showy blossoms compose the margin of the cyme, and this margin is composed entirely of sterile, unfruitful bloom. The common snowball bush is a form of the above, having all its blossoms sterile.

SQUASH BERRY
Viburnum pauciflorum Pylaie

White. Stems, shrubby; straggling; three to seven feet tall. Leaves, broadly oval; dentate or lobed. Inflorescence, a small terminal cyme. Flowers, all perfect. Corolla, spreading; five-lobed. Stamens, five. Fruit, a drupe; red. Habitat, along mountain streams.

This species is also sometimes known as high-bush cranberry. The fruit is red and quite acid. It is a rare species with us, but more plentiful northward. Among the Indians of British Columbia the fruit is an important article of diet. Each family or clan claimed and defended for its own use certain favorite berry-picking ground. A box of viburnum berries was considered equal in value to two pairs of blankets. The great feast of viburnum berries was formerly ranked second in importance only to the extravagant and wasteful "feast of oil."

SNOWBERRY
Symphoricarpos albus (L.) Blake

Pink. Stem, shrubby; slender; erect; one to five feet tall. Leaves, opposite; short petioled; pubescent beneath; extremely variable. Inflorescence, clustered or in racemes; terminal or axillary. Calyx, short; four or five toothed; persistent. Corolla, campanulate; four or five-lobed; the lobes spreading. Stamens, included; as many as the

PINK HONEYSUCKLE   *Lonicera hispidula*

lobes of the corolla. Fruit, an inflated white berry. Habitat, dry open places. Blooming period, May-June.

"Thomas Jefferson, President of the United States, to Madame La Comtesse de Tesse: December 8, 1813.

"Lewis' journey across our continent to the Pacific has added a number of new plants to our former stock. Some of them curious, some ornamental, some useful, and some may by culture be made acceptable to our tables. I have growing, which I destine for you, a very handsome little shrub of the size of a currant bush. Its beauty consists in a great production of berries the size of currants, and literally as white as snow, which remain on the bush through the winter, after the leaves have fallen, and make it an object as singular as it is beautiful. We call it the snow-berry bush, no botanical name having yet been given it."

Madame de Tesse was an aunt of Madam Lafayette. We may hope that she received her plants safely, and found great pleasure in their snow-white berries.

In spring, when the fresh, tender foliage of the snow-berry begins to appear, the effect is very pleasing, looking as though the entire thicket were illuminated with a misty green light. At this time, also, when wet with rain, they give off a soft, sweet fragrance. There are few plants that show greater variation in foliage on different plants, and at different stages of growth. Old, slow growing plants have very small, entire leaves, while young, vigorous shoots put out astonishingly large ones, much lobed and divided, or with serrate margins. The flowers are pink. The white berries hang upon the bushes until late in winter, for birds, and other woodland foragers do not seem to relish them. The berries are extremely bitter, but are said to have been eaten by some Indian tribes. The stems are slender and pithy, and were used for pipe stems. Mr. Chestnut gives the Pomo Indian name for this plant as "sa-ka-hi," literally, "wood for tobacco."

Trailing Snowberry. *Symphoricarpos mollis* Nutt. Very like the above, save that the stems are weak, and trail over the ground in vine-like manner. They are slender, and covered with a fine pubescence.

PINK HONEYSUCKLE
Lonicera hispidula Dougl.

Pink. Stems, woody; slender; twining; trailing over the ground or

ORANGE HONEYSUCKLE   *Lonicera ciliosa*

climbing on other brush; six to twelve feet long. Leaves, opposite; ovate; the upper ones connate. Inflorescence, terminal; interrupted. Flowers, whorled. Calyx, minute. Corolla, tubular; gibbous at base; two-lipped; the lip strongly recurved; pink outside; yellow within. Stamens, five; long exserted. Anthers, versatile. Fruit, a berry. Habitat, dry hillsides. Blooming season, June-July.

The weak, trailing stems of the pink honeysuckle scramble over low brush and stumps, or creep over the ground on dry hillsides. They are found from British Columbia to Oregon. The flowers are tubular, pale pink, with whitish or yellowish, strongly reflexed lobes. They are born in whorls of from three to seven blossoms in an interrupted raceme, terminally, or in the axils of the upper, connate, oval pairs of leaves. Many of the blossoms are abortive, and fall without ever having opened.

ORANGE HONEYSUCKLE
Lonicera ciliosa (Pursh.) Poir

Orange. Stems, shrubby; twining; climbing over brush and trees to a height of from five to twenty feet. Leaves, opposite; ovate or oval; glaucous beneath; short petioled; those of the inflorescence connate; perfoliate; oval or orbicular; concave. Inflorescence, terminal; whorled. Flowers, sessile. Calyx, minute; five-toothed. Corolla, narrow tubular; gibbous at base; bilabiate; the limb short. Stamens, five; little exserted. Style, filiform. Fruit, a cluster of red berries. Habitat, woodland borders. Blooming period, May-June.

The trumpet-shaped blossoms of the orange honeysuckle are a brilliant splash of color along our woodland borders in May. The shrubby trailing stems draped across the limbs of trees, or over logs and brush are tipped at the ends with flame-colored flowers, and it needs only a darting, jeweled hummingbird, poised on wing beneath the drooping honey ladened tubes, to complete a picture true to nature. The two clasping leaves, just below the flower clusters, are united into a saucer-shaped disk, which is typical of this plant. The other leaves are short petioled, bluntly oval, and light green. These vines bear dark red berries, sweetish and edible. They were formerly much sought by the Indians. So closely does this vine clasp the trees to which it clings, that its stems often become embedded in the wood. and the supporting plant dies.

TWIN-BERRY   *Lonicera involucrata*

TWIN-BERRY
Lonicera involucrata Banks

Yellow. Stems, shrubby; erect; three to nine feet tall. Leaves, opposite; ovate to lanceolate; acute. Flowers, pedicled; axillary; in pairs; involucrate. Involucre, reddish. Corolla, viscid; tubular; swelled at base, contracted at throat; the limb short; five-lobed. Stamens, five. Style, filiform; exserted. Fruit, borne in pairs; black. Habitat, in mountains and along the sea shore. Blooming period, May to July.

This species of honeysuckle is a shrub—not twining—and grows erect to a height of from three to six feet. The leaves are opposite, two to five inches long, and from their axils spring slender pedicels, each pedicel bearing a pair of tubular yellow flowers. These flowers are about three-fourths of an inch in length, and each pair is cupped at their base in a peculiar leafy involucre consisting of four broad green bracts. These bracts persist throughout the season, and as the fruit matures they turn red, in fine contrast to the two plump, purplish-black berries.

VALERIAN FAMILY

SEA BLUSH
Valerianella congesta Lindl.

Pink. Stem, simple or branched above; angled; erect; four to twelve inches tall. Leaves, opposite; sessile; oval; entire. Inflorescence, a congested, capitate cyme. Calyx, limb obsolete. Corolla, pink; funnelform; spurred; the limb two-lipped, five-cleft. Stamens, three. Fruit, winged. Habitat, open hillsides and dry fields. Blooming period, early May.

On the sides of some dry buttes there are patches of waste land, not even fit for good pasture, where each season the pink sea blush blooms in such abundance that the whole landscape is rosy with the color—acre on acre of soft shell-pink of the finest, rarest hue. Perhaps it is from such patches as this that the species receives its name of sea blush. *Valerianella* is simply the diminutive form of valerian, and congesta refers to the crowded form of the flower heads. The whole plant is smooth and rather succulent. A white flowered form is occasionally found.

Valerianella samolifolia (D. C.) Gray. This similar form has more slender, branching stems, and its flowers are pale blue.

SEA BLUSH   *Valerianella congesta*

[352]

MOUNTAIN VALERIAN
Valeriana sitchensis Bong.

White or pink. Rootstock, stout; rank-scented; perennial. Stems, smooth; erect; branched; one to four feet tall. Leaves, basal leaves petioled; simple or trifoliate; cauline leaves pinnately parted. Leaflets, thin; three to seven; sessile; sinuate; the terminal one the largest. Inflorescence, a cyme. Calyx, in-curled and hidden in flower; pappus-like in fruit. Corolla, funnelform; five-lobed; the tube gibbous at base. Stamens, three. Pistil, simple; long exserted. Stigma, three-lobed. Habitat, in mountain meadows, often at high altitudes. Blooming period, April to August, according to altitude.

The tall wild valerian forms magnificent fields at, or near timber line in the mountains. This is one of the showy plants in high meadows from Oregon, northward to Alaska. The low-land gardener, coming upon a field of valerian, may well feel that here, in strange surroundings, he has found an old friend, so much does the wild plant resemble the well known cultivated form, commonly grown under the name of "garden heliotrope." The flowers appear at the summit of the plant in compact cymes, white or shaded with pink, and rendered softly pleasing by the long protruding pistils. They are very sweet-scented, but there is a strong medicinal smell to the crushed leaves and root that is far from pleasant. This is the smell of the drug valerian, found both in the wild and cultivated plants, and of medicinal value.

Valerian sitchensis scouleri (Rydb.) Piper, is a variety of the above, found along stream banks at low levels. The leaflets of this form are mostly entire, or merely wavy in outline.

GOURD FAMILY

WILD CUCUMBER
Micrampelis oregana (T. & G.) Greene

White. Root, perennial; woody; very large. Stem, elongated; climbing by tendrils; eight to thirty feet long. Leaves, alternate; palmately five to seven-lobed; lobes triangular. Inflorescence, monoecious; of two kinds. Flowers, staminate, in racemes; pistillate, solitary. Corolla, six-parted. Petals, lanceolate; spreading. Stamens, five; united. Fruit, globose; spiny; two-celled. Habitat, low rich soil. Blooming period, April-May.

MOUNTAIN VALERIAN

The wild cucumber is a stout, ample vine, with coarsely angled stems, and bright green, handsome foliage. It trails over brush and fences or upon the ground. The leaves are broad, palmately lobed, and netted-veined, the veins showing prominently on the back of the leaf. The flowers are white, and of two sorts, the staminate ones borne in slender racemes, and the pistillate ones solitary in the axils of the leaves. The prickly, green, cucumber-like fruit is usually about two and one-half inches in length, and consists of a very juicy flesh, in which the seeds are embedded, surrounded by a fibrous, lace-like envelope. The seeds are large and flat, and are filled with a firm meat. They are eaten by squirrels, but are probably poisonous to human beings. Certain Indians are said to have used the seeds of similar species as a means of committing suicide. The roots of this plant attain a great size, and from them the plant is sometimes given the name of "old man," and "man-in-the-ground."

BELLFLOWER FAMILY

BLUE CALICO FLOWER
Bolelia elegans (Dougl.) Greene

Blue. Stems, glabrous; branched; from the base; upright or declining; six to twelve inches tall. Leaves, sessile; alternate; entire; lanceolate; the upper ones larger, becoming floral bracts. Inflorescence, a leafy raceme. Flowers, sessile. Calyx, adherent to the ovary; five-lobed; the lobes linear, spreading. Corolla, two-lipped. Upper lip, two-lobed; the lobes lanceolate. Lower lip, large; broad; concave; three-lobed; the lobes triangular. Stamens, filaments and anthers united in an arching tube; exserted. Ovary, long; twisted; angled. Habitat, wet ditches and pond borders. Blooming period, May to August.

In June, you may find the blue calico flower coming into bloom in wayside ditches and along the borders of drying ponds. In form the blossoms are decidedly two-lipped. The lower lip is broad and flat, and cut at the margin into three triangular lobes. The upper one is divided into two upright lanceolate divisions. Both are blue, but the lower lip has a conspicuous white blotch in the centre. The whole flower is strangely suggestive of a bizarre figure in light blue cotton print. The flowers are sessile, but they are borne at the summit of a slender twisted ovary, which has the appearance of a pedicel

WILD CUCUMBER

Micrampelis oregana

of considerable length. The calico plant is usually restricted to small areas, but it sometimes makes a much greater showing. I know a large mucky pasture, trampled and pitted by winter grazing, where, in summer, every cow track is filled with these blossoms, giving the whole swale a pale bluish tinge. Across this pasture the wheel tracks of a disused wagon road stretch away in two parallel blue lines of bloom, blending into one in the distance.

There is another little known color phase of this plant, the flowers of which are a peculiar pink shade, very hard to describe. Perhaps "chocolate pink," or pink blended with a shade of brown, best describes it. There are also occasional white-flowered specimens.

SCOULER'S BLUEBELL
Campanula scouleri Hook.

Blue. Stems, smooth; leafy; slender; six to ten inches tall. Leaves, ovate to lanceolate; acute; serrate. Inflorescence, a loose, slender raceme. Flowers, drooping. Calyx, angled; five-lobed; the lobes subulate. Corolla, campanulate five-cleft; the lobes spreading or recurved; longer than the tube. Stamens, five. Filaments dilated at base. Style, rather stout; long exserted. Stigma, three-lobed; lobes spreading or recurved. Habitat, dry open woods. Blooming period, June-July.

The Scouler's bluebell has light blue flowers with recurved perianth lobes, and a very long pistil with a striking, three-cleft stigma that protrudes far beyond the floral bell. There is something strangely suggestive of a lily in these litle flowers, but they are a true bluebell, and by their grace are well worthy of the praise bestowed upon that tribe.

HAREBELL. BLUEBELL OF SCOTLAND
Campanula rotundifolia L.

Blue. Leaves, cauline linear; basal, orbicular to cordate. Flowers, solitary or in racemes; dark blue. Corolla, campanulate; five-lobed; the lobes shorter than the tube, not spreading. Style, included. Habitat, dry prairies and hillsides. Otherwise as for *C. scouleri.*

It seems to me a painful thing that though ninety per cent of our school children can speak glibly of the "Bluebells of Scotland," not one in a thousand knows those same bluebells when they find them

BLUE CALICO FLOWER

Bolelia elegans

growing in our own valleys, and on our own mountain sides. The bluebell is, in truth, an international plant, for it is found not only in Scotland, and in our Northwest, but throughout Northern America from the Atlantic to the Pacific, as well as in Northern Europe and Asia. The lovely deep blue flowers, drooping on their slender hair-like stems, are worthy of all the praise that has been bestowed upon them. They are a flower that is loved and remembered after more showy blooms have been long forgotten, for they are a flower of simple grace—of lovely memories.

VENUS LOOKING-GLASS
Specularia perfoliata (L.) A.DC.

Violet. Stems, angled; leafy; simple; erect; slender; six to twenty inches tall. Leaves, alternate; sessile; clasping round-cordate. Flowers, axillary; sessile; the lower, earlier ones never opening, self-fertilized; the upper ones opening, and with a showy corolla. Calyx, three to five-lobed in the lower flowers; five-lobed in the upper ones; lobes lanceolate. Corolla, five-parted; campanulate to rotate. Stamens, five. Capsule, conical; opening by valves on the side. Habitat, dry fields and hillsides. Blooming period, June.

The clasping leaves of the Venus looking-glass, borne at regular intervals along the length of the stem, look like the successive basins of a graceful fountain. Within each of these basins appear from one to three pretty buds, but the curious feature of this flower is that of these many buds only a few, near the summit, ever open into true bloom. All of the others remain tightly closed and form seed by self-fertilization in a manner similar to the late blossoms of the wild violet. In the Venus looking-glass, these self-contained, or clystega-meous flowers mature first, and begin to ripen their seed at about the same time that the showy, terminal flowers begin to open. Individual plants vary greatly in the number of the showy flowers borne. Small, starved plants, indeed, never develop any, but have only the self-fertilized form, while large, thrifty plants have as many as ten or twelve of the showy blooms.

VENUS LOOKING-GLASS   *Specularia perfoliata*

Scorzonella laciniata (Hook.) Nutt.

Yellow. Root, fleshy; fusiform; with abundant milky juice. Stem, slender; simple; upright. Leaves, mostly basal; lanceolate; laciniately lobed; light green. Heads, campanulate. Tegules, lanceolate; the outer ones calyx-like. Flowers, all strap-shaped. Pappus, brownish; plumose; stiff. Habitat, open fields. Blooming period, June-July.

The interesting buds of the *Scorzonella* are rather deceitful in appearance, for they nod gracefully on their slender stems and suggest those of a stately lily, rather than the dandelion-like flower into which they finally open. The leaves are light green, often spotted with purplish brown, and have finely laciniate margins. The seed heads are globular, very regular in form. The pappus is stiff and slightly tawny. The roots of some species of *Scorzonella* were eaten by the Indians. When raw they are full of milky juice, and are very bitter, but when cooked they resemble salsify.

Scorzonella borealis (Bong.) Greene. This is a more northern species with leaves all basal and entire.

Scorzonella leptosepela Nutt. Another, very similar species, differing from *laciniata,* in part, by having its pappus scales more slender and bristle-like.

GUM PLANT
Grindelia integrifolia DC.

Yellow. Stems, erect; branching ten to thirty inches tall. Leaves, basal leaves petioled; spatulate; cauline leaves sessile; clasping; serrate; broadest at base. Heads, gummy. Tegules, terete; with recurved points. Ray flowers, fifteen to thirty; yellow. Habitat, poorly drained fields. Blooming period, July to October.

When the summer heat is well established, and the fields begin to take on a brownish hue, the gum plants, which up to then have been inconspicuous, begin to attract our attention, for they remain fresh and green. At this time, also, the yellow blossoms begin to appear, and in the heavy, poorly drained parts of the Willamette Valley, where the plants cover thousands of acres, it becomes the most conspicuous vegetation. They continue to bloom until late autumn, when

GUM PLANT   *Grindelia integrifolia*

the frosts, or heavy rains, check their growth. The flower buds, when they first appear, are thickly and heavily covered with a white, sticky gum, so much so that it does not seem possible that they could ever force their way open. This gum is the grindelia of commerce, and to secure it, the buds are collected in large amounts. In medicine, it is used for the relief of asthma, bronchitis, and whooping-cough. Its use is a heritage from the Western Indians who, ages ago, recognized its merits.

Grindelia oregana Gray. A tall, stout species of sea shores. Its stem leaves are smooth, and broadest at the base.

Grindelia nana Nutt. This species has small heads—about a third of an inch tall—hemispheric in form. The tegules are stiff and strongly recurved at the tip.

GOLDENROD
Solidago elongata Nutt.

Yellow. Stems, tufted; upright; smooth; two to three feet tall. Leaves, alternate; thin; lanceolate; acute; serrate. Inflorescence, a pyramidal panicle; dense. Heads, numerous; small. Ray-flowers, small; narrow; yellow. Habitat, moist ground. Blooming period, July-August.

If ever our country adopts a national flower there is great likelihood that the choice will fall upon the goldenrod. A humble, simple plant, it is nevertheless universally loved, and it is said that some of its many species grow in every state of the union. There are more than eighty kinds known in America, so that no locality need lack a type suitable to its soil and climate. The North Pacific Coast can not boast of great fields of goldenrod as can New England and the Central States, nevertheless we have about seven kinds in our territory, of which the present species is perhaps the most common. The bright pyramidal clusters begin to appear in July, and continue until late fall. This kind prefers moist, low situations, where it usually grows in rather dense clusters.

Varnished Goldenrod. *Solidago glutinosa* Nutt. The plants of this species are coated with a sticky gum or resin. They are found in dry, gravelly fields from Vancouver Island, southward.

Several of our species, such as *Solidago algida* Piper, *Solidago belli-*

GOLDENROD   *Solidago elongata*

difolia Greene, and others, are alpine plants, so that both in mountain and valley we may be cheered by:

"The sunshine of the goldenrod."

Some species of goldenrod have had considerable vogue in the past as a source of yellow dye. The flower tops were boiled and used in the same manner as butternut bark, hickory shells, or sumac-bobs. The resulting dye was very permanent.

PINK FLEABANE
Erigeron philadelphicus L.

Pink or white. Stems, erect; branched; leafy; one to four feet tall. Leaves, basal leaves short petioled; oblong; obtuse; toothed; cauline leaves entire; sessile; clasping. Heads, corymbed; many. Ray-flowers, very numerous; extremely narrow; pink or white. Habitat, moist fields. Blooming period, May-June.

The fleabanes and asters are very similar in appearance, but the fleabanes are spring and summer flowers, while the asters properly belong to the late summer and autumn. Besides this the fleabanes, as a rule, have very narrow, much more numerous rays, a characteristic feature which should be carefully noted.

The pink, or Philadelphia fleabane is a common plant both in the East and West. It is a perennial plant, blooming in May and June, and will be found in moist open meadows and along stream banks. The plant is tall and branching, rather hairy, and leafy nearly to the top. The flowers are flat with very numerous fringe-like rays—either pink or white. The pink flowered plants are especially beautiful. The plant has recognized medicinal properties, being used as a diuretic and stomatic.

WHITE FLEABANE
Erigeron ramosus Walt.

White. Stem, slender; erect; leafy. Leaves, small; spatulate to lanceolate; entire or toothed; the upper ones sessile. Heads, in loose corymbs at the summit of the plant. Ray-flowers, white; numerous; very narrow. Habitat, dry open fields. Blooming period, May to July.

The flowers of this species are like the preceding, but are smaller,

LARGE PURPLE FLEABANE   *Erigeron speciosus*

and always white. The plants, however, are annuals, and slender, straight, and little branched except near the top. There are a few much reduced leaves on the stem. A common flower in dry, upland pastures and meadows.

The name fleabane originates in an old belief that the plants when hung in a room would rid if of fleas.

LARGE PURPLE FLEABANE
Erigeron speciosus DC.

Purple. Stems, tufted; erect; simple; leafy to the summit; ten to twenty inches tall. Leaves, acute; entire; the upper ones sessile. Heads, at the summit of the stem; corymbed. Flowers, large; showy; disk-flowers, yellow; numerous. Ray-flowers, purple; very numerous; linear. Habitat, dry fields and hillsides. Blooming period, early summer.

This is the largest and most beautiful of our fleabanes. The handsome purple-rayed flowers are often two inches or more across, and they are borne in profusion on long, stiff stems. They are excellent for cutting, and last a long time. It is strange that this fine native flower is not more generally cultivated in America. In England and Switzerland it is widely and favorably known, being another of the many plants carried to Europe by David Douglas. An interesting incident was told me by a Portland, Oregon, correspondent, herself a native of England. The first season after her arrival on the Pacific Coast, her mother sent her a collection of seeds from London, and among them a package of *Erigeron speciosus.* These seeds arrived just as the native plants were beginning to blossom in the fields, the first intimation she had that her garden favorite was a native of Oregon.

In its wild state this plant blossoms in May and June, but under cultivation its blooming period is extended throughout the summer. I have picked the flowers in my garden as late as the eleventh of December.

BEACH ASTER. SEASIDE DAISY
Erigeron glaucus Ker.

Purple. Stems, viscid; six to ten inches tall. Leaves, basal leaves fleshy; pale green; viscid; spatulate to oblong; entire; cauline leaves much reduced; spatulate. Heads, large; solitary; showy. Ray-flowers,

BEACH ASTER

numerous; light purple; rather broad. Disk-flowers, numerous; yellow. Habitat, along sea shores. Blooming period, April to July.

This is neither an aster or a daisy, but a fleabane, one whose handsome, rather wide-rayed flowers are reminiscent of some single forms of the garden aster. The leaves are mostly basal, rather fleshy, and inclined to be viscid. The flowers appear from April to May and onward, and make a handsome show of color on the bluffs and sandy beaches of our sea shores.

GOLDEN FLEABANE
Erigeron aureus Greene

Yellow. Stems, slender; clothed with grayish hairs; from a woody base; three to six inches tall. Leaves, basal leaves ovate to spatulate, entire; cauline leaves few; small. Heads, solitary. Involucre, woolly. Ray-flowers, twelve to eighteen; bright yellow. Habitat, high mountains.

The flowers of this little alpine fleabane are a bright golden yellow, a most unusual shade for this genus. Only those who climb to the extreme heights may expect to find this plant, for its home is among the high peaks at an altitude of from seven to nine thousand feet. This is a dwarf species, seldom exceeding six inches in height.

Erigeron corymbosus Nutt.

Purple. Stems, slender; tufted from a woody base; six to twelve inches tall. Leaves, linear to spatulate; entire. Heads, solitary or few on the stem. Ray-flowers, light purple; rather wide. Habitat, dry gravelly soil. Blooming period, early summer.

This is a rare species in our region, known to me from only a few stations. The leaves are narrow—linear to spatulate—borne on slender, mostly one-flowered stems. The plants are branched from a woody base, forming close, compact tufts. The flowers are light purple, with rather broad rays. This species prefers dry gravelly uplands.

Besides the kinds already described there are about eleven other species of *Erigeron* found here, most of them, however, are rare. Among them are:—

Howell's Fleabane. *Erigeron howellii* Gray. A very fine plant.

The ray-flowers are pure white and of fine substance, nearly as large as *E. speciosus*. Leaves shiny green; alternate; ovate to lanceolate. Stems eight to twelve inches tall, simple. Tegules loose, awl-shaped, acute, fringe-like. A rare plant found only in the Gorge of the Columbia.

Mountain Daisy. *Erigeron salsuginosus* (Richards) Gray. A beautiful pink flower found at high elevations in the mountains.

Erigeron acris debilis Gray. Another smallish, pink, alpine form.

Erigeron oreganus Gray. Also pink. Found only in the Gorge of the Columbia.

GREAT NORTHERN ASTER
Aster major (Hook.) Porter

Purple. Stems, upright; branching; leafy. Leaves, alternate; sessile; lanceolate to oblong; entire or toothed; thin; narrowed at base. Heads, numerous; in corymbs or panicles. Tegules, green; viscid. Ray-flowers, twenty-five to forty or more; purple. Habitat, along mountain streams. Blooming period, late summer and autumn.

This is a dark purple aster usually found on stream banks, northward, and in the mountains. The stems are tall, leafy, and rough—hairy throughout. The leaves are thin, dark above and paler beneath, and are sessile or somewhat clasping at the base. The flower heads are glandular or viscid.

> "Fringing the stream at every turn
> Swing low the waving fronds of fern;
> From stony cleft, and mossy sod
> Pale asters sprung, and goldenrod."

Our native asters are known in England as Michaelmas daisies, because their blooming season is at the time of the feast of St. Michael.

DOUGLAS' ASTER
Aster douglasii Lindl.

Purple. Stems, erect; smooth; leafy; one to four feet tall. Leaves, alternate; sessile; lanceolate. Heads, numerous in loose terminal panicles. Involucre, hemispheric. Tegules, green-tipped; the lower ones

DOUGLAS' ASTER   *Aster douglasii*

grading into the small leaves of the stem. Ray-flowers, purple. Habitat, moist fields and roadsides. Blooming period, summer and autumn.

This, our commonest purple aster, is another of the plants named after that indefatigable botanist, David Douglas. Autumn would not seem complete without these pleasing star-like flowers with their spreading purple rays. The Douglas' aster is a tall plant, partial to moist, but not wet, roadsides. The flowers often begin to appear in June, becoming more common as the season advances, until in September and October they are in their glory. From then on, they begin to decline, but if the season is mild and open a few stray flowers may be found almost throughout the winter. The leaves of this kind are sessile, broadest in the middle, tapering at both ends. This is the most abundant species of aster found on the North Pacific Coast, and is plentiful throughout the territory covered by this book.

WHITE ASTER. HALL'S ASTER
Aster hallii Gray

White. Stems, smooth; slender; erect; ten to twenty inches tall. Leaves, alternate; lanceolate to linear. Heads, numerous; in racemes. Involucre, campanulate. Tegules, linear; green-tipped. Ray-flowers, white. Habitat, dry open soil. Blooming period, late summer.

The Hall's aster is our most conspicuous white species. It is a slender, erect form, with narrow leaves, bearing its flowers in compact clusters. The central disk is small, but the surrounding white rays, though narrow, are numerous and long. Found from Washington to Oregon in dry soil.

TAR-WEED
Madia sativa Molina

Yellow. Stems, viscid; stout; erect; ten to thirty inches tall. Leaves, alternate; lanceolate to linear; entire; sessile. Inflorescence, a narrow panicle. Heads, clustered. Ray-flowers, six to ten; yellow. Disk-flowers, few. Habitat, dry fields. Blooming period, summer.

The common-tar-weed is such an abundant nuisance in this region that few people recognize its beauty, or realize that it is capable of being put to any use. To the farmer, it is an ever present weedy

WHITE ASTER   *Aster hallii*

[374]

pest, and to the out-door enthusiast, the secretion from its tarry, sticky stems is a menace to clothes and comfort. Most of us see its flowers only in a half-wilted state, for they open at night, and fade with the first warmth of morning. Nevertheless, it is a shapely, interesting plant with softly tinted flowers and ornamental seed vessels. Seek it in the early morning, or on a cloudy day before the blossoms have wilted, and you may acknowledge that it is worthy of a place among the flowers.

The seeds of this species are rich and oily, and were gathered by the Indians for food. Mrs. Hargreaves writes of the Indian's autumn as the time when "the *le-mo-lo sap-o-lil* (wild wheat or tar-weed) had all been gathered and winnowed and the whole countryside could now be baptized with fire." Stephen Powers speaks of these plants as "a species of yellow-blooming, tarry-smelling weed, the seeds as rich as butter." In Chile, where it is also native, as well as in Europe and Asia, where it has been introduced, it was formerly cultivated for its oil which is very palatable, and of a quality equal to the best olive oil. The plants are now seldom cultivated, for the abundance and cheapness of refined cotton seed oil has rendered its culture unprofitable.

Seen under the lens of a microscope the hairs of the involucre are a wonderful study. Each gland-like bristle is tipped with a translucent ball of the viscid secretion, of a clear green color, and very beautiful.

Madia glomerata Hook. This abundant tar-weed scents the air over low valley fields with a peculiar semi-acid smell somewhat resembling that of freshly cut rhubarb. A typical and familiar autumn scent.

Madia racemosa (Nutt.) T. & G. This species has smaller, more scattered heads. Very common, and a more northerly species than the preceding.

WILD COREOPSIS
Madia elegans Don.

Yellow. Stems, erect; branching towards the summit; one to three feet tall. Leaves, mostly basal; lanceolate; entire; viscid; cauline leaves alternate. Inflorescence, corymb-like. Flowers, large; showy; opening only at night or on cloudy days. Ray-flowers, ten to eighteen;

WILD COREOPSIS   *Madia elegans*

three-lobed; bright yellow with a brown base. Habitat, dry fields. Blooming period, summer.

This large handsome species of tar-weed, like its less showy relatives, has a habit of opening its blossoms only at night or on dark days. It is thus often overlooked, even though it is quite common. The flowers are borne at the summit of the plant on slender branches, and are often two inches across. Each petal-like ray is deeply three-lobed, bright yellow at the summit, with a velvety brown base. The whole effect is very pleasing, and much like the garden coreopsis after which it is called. Most of the leaves are borne in a whorl at the base of the plant, and are viscid. Under the lens of a microscope the tiny disk flowers appear wonderful in color and structure. The perianth is fringed and scalloped in a most beautiful manner, and is glistening and soft in texture. This plant is not commonly found north of the Columbia River.

BALSAM ROOT
Balsamorhiza deltoidea Nutt.

Yellow. Root, large; woody; balsam-scented. Stem, upright; ten to eighteen inches tall. Leaves, sagittate to deltoid; cordate at base; three to eight inches long; cauline leaves, two; small; lanceolate; borne near the middle of the stem. Flower heads, solitary or in twos or threes; three to five inches across. Habitat, dry prairies and hillsides. Blooming period, March to May.

"Spring sunflowers," these plants are called by Mr. E. N. Wilson in his book, "The White Indian Boy," and this name describes them very well. The flowers appear in early spring, and are from three to five inches across, and look very like a small sunflower. The ripe seeds are rich and oily, and were a source of rich nutriment for the Giosute Indians among whom Mr. Wilson spent his boyhood, as well as to almost all the tribes of the west. These seeds were prepared in several ways; they were pounded in stone mortars and drunk with water in the form of a thin gruel; used as a thickening for soup; or mixed with marrow or grease into a sort of dough, and so eaten. On the Sandy River, in Oregon, in 1806, Captain Lewis speaks of a sort of native bread made from the seed of balsam root and dried service-berries.

The whole plant grows to a height of from ten to eighteen inches. It is strongly balsam-scented, and the root has medicinal properties.

BALSAM ROOT

COMPASS PLANT. WYETHIA
Wyethia angustifolia (DC.) Nutt.

Yellow. Stems, simple; upright; ten to twenty inches tall. Leaves, radical leaves lanceolate; entire; pointed; seven to fifteen inches long; cauline leaves smaller, sessile. Heads, large; peduncled. Involucre, campanulate. Tegules, broad; green; loose. Ray-flowers, broad; yellow. Habitat, moist open places. Blooming period, April to June.

There is an old belief, apparently with no foundation in truth, that the leaves of the compass plant always point north and south. This belief, beginning no one knows where or how, has been handed down from generation to generation, and is earnestly and solemnly vouched for, and with a vehemence that is hard to explain when even an hour's study at the proper season would reveal its fallacy. That this is deliberate deceit, I do not believe, but rather that an innate love for the mysterious and poetical makes people wish to believe in strange and beautiful tales.

The flowers of the wyethia much resemble those of the balsam root, but the leaves are quite different, so that the plants need never be confused. This plant often covers large tracts in low, moist fields. Both the seeds and the young tender shoots are eaten by the Indians, the former being ground into a meal, and the latter in its fresh, raw state. The root was also used for medicinal purposes.

In the name of this plant we do honor to that adventurous and enterprising traveler and trader, Nathaniel Wyeth, who crossed the continent to Oregon in 1832.

OREGON SUNSHINE
Eriophyllum lanatum (Pursh) Forbes

Yellow. Stems, tufted; rather woody at base; white-woolly; slender. Leaves, alternate; spatulate to obovate; entire or from three to seven-lobed; whitish. Heads, long-stemmed. Involucre, woolly; campanulate. Ray-flowers, spreading; bright yellow. Disk, yellow. Habitat, dry open fields. Blooming period, May to July.

To the student of Western botany, the work accomplished by that enthusiastic Scotch explorer, David Douglas, is a source of constant wonder. Besides the dried specimens that he forwarded to his patron, Dr. Hooker, he collected seeds and live plants in great numbers for

Wyethia angustifolia

COMPASS PLANT

OREGON SUNSHINE

Eriophyllum lanatum

AUTUMN SNEEZE-WEED · *Helenium autumnale grandiflorum*

the London Horticultural Society, and, as a result of this intensive labor, it is a fact that even to this day many of our native flowers are more generally known in England than in their native habitat! Among them, our showy species of *Eriophyllum* has there been highly prized for nearly a century, while here, until recently, it has been almost disregarded. There is now an attempt being made to popularize it under the name of Oregon sunshine. This name seems to me especially appropriate, but it should be recognized as applying in a broad sense to all the old Oregon Country, a great territory now divided into three or more states.

The whole plant is soft, woolly, and both the generic and specific names refer to this fact, as does also one of its common names—that of woolly sunflower. The plants are much too slender and delicate, however, to be called sunflowers. The blossoms are a bright golden yellow, throughout, and are borne singly on flexible upright stems.

AUTUMN SNEEZE-WEED
Helenium autumnale grandiflorum (Nutt.) Gray

Yellow. Stems, leafy; stout; upright; two to four feet tall. Leaves, ovate to lanceolate; dentate or nearly entire; sessile; the blades decurrent. Heads, many; large. Ray-flowers, ten to sixteen; three-lobed; bright yellow. Habitat, stream banks and moist open fields. Blooming period, late summer.

In low land here, the autumn sneeze-weed spreads great masses of golden bloom, and its cultivated form make bright spots in garden borders throughout Europe and America. There are two characteristics which, taken together, are enough to identify this plant. The first is the three-lobed margins of the golden yellow ray-flowers; the second is the peculiar angled form of the stems, caused by the decurrent blades of the leaves, which extend—wing-like—for a considerable distance below their sessile bases. These plants are leafy, with dark green, bitter tasting foliage. The leaves are said to be poisonous to cattle and sheep. The flower heads are borne on slender, naked scapes. When dried and powdered these heads produce a strong snuff, capable of causing the most violent sneezing. This fact accounts for the common name of sneeze-weed. The blossoms and tender green tops made into a tea are a permanent yellow dye, and were used by some Indian tribes in their ornamental basketry.

YARROW   *Achillea millefolium*

ROSILLA. SNEEZE-WEED
Helenium puberulum DC.

Yellow. Stems, upright; branched; two to five feet tall. Leaves, alternate; lanceolate; sessile; decurrent. Heads, solitary; globular. Ray-flowers, very small; reflexed. Habitat, moist open fields. Blooming period, late summer.

The peculiar flowers of this rare sneeze-weed look like little yellow balls, set on the summit of long, bare branches. It is only after a closer look that you notice the tiny, reflexed ray-flowers that form an almost concealed fringe at the base of the head. The plants are slender and upright, and very scantily clothed with narrow leaves. These leaves clasp the stem, and the blades run down their length in a winged form, the same as in the autumn sneeze-weed before mentioned. The flowers have a rather pleasant smell, but are very hot and peppery to the taste, and if inhaled too strongly, especially when dry, are likely to bring on a violent sneezing fit. According to Mr. Chestnut, its Indian name is *"kot-ka-ya-chdo,"* which sounds, indeed, like a sneeze, but is said to refer to a resemblance between the winged stems and the tail of a beaver.

This is a common plant in California, its range extending as far north as Humbolt County. North of that it is known only from the valley of the Callapoia River, in Oregon, where the writer was so fortunate as to discover it in 1921. At that place it is quite abundant, and it seems likely that a careful search will reveal it in other places.

YARROW
Achillea millefolium L.

White. Stems, upright; branched above; one to three feet tall. Leaves, basal leaves lanceolate, long, pinnately divided into filiform segments; stem leaves alternate, small. Heads, small; terminal; in a flat-topped corymb. Ray-flowers, white. Habitat, dry fields. Blooming period, summer.

Our common yarrow is a native of Europe, and also of the Pacific States of America. Many writers take it for granted that it has been introduced here, but there is abundant proof that the first botanist

SWEET COLTSFOOT   *Petasites speciosa*

[386]

found it common when they arrived, and that it grew not only in the valleys, but also in unvisited, isolated mountains.

This plant has a history that reaches back into the remotest ages. Its very name, Achillea, was given it because at the siege of Troy, Achilles, the Greek hero, used it in curing the wounds of his soldiers. From that time forth, it holds a prominent place in folk-tale and legend. Simply to mention all the uses, some foolish, some practical, to which it has been put, would cover several pages. A spray of yarrow picked from a grave at midnight was a potent love charm; it was used for bridal wreaths; the green leaves were used for toothache; plants worn by a timid person would drive away fear; it was used to stop nose-bleed; and so on, indefinitely. In Sweden it has been used instead of hops for making beer. Among the Indians it was used for medicine, besides which, among the Klamaths, a bunch of yarrow was placed inside each drying salmon to promote quick curing.

The blossoms of the yarrow are usually white, but very pretty; clear pink flowers may occasionally be found. The specific name, millefolium, refers to its exceedingly fine cut leaves.

SWEET COLTSFOOT
Petasites speciosa (Nutt.) Piper

Purplish. Stems, upright; one to two feet tall. Leaves, mostly radical; orbicular; very large; deeply seven to nine cleft; smooth above, white woolly beneath. Flowers, appearing before the leaves. Rayflowers, none. Disk, light purple. Habitat, moist ground and stream banks. Blooming period, March.

The immense broad leaves of the sweet coltsfoot are a familiar sight in moist woods and along streams, where they grow in close clusters, or spread over considerable tracts. Few people, however, are acquainted with the pale purplish flowers which appear in early spring before the leaves unfold. These flowers are borne on stout stems, in racemes, and are very sweet scented. In form they suggest those of a soft, spineless thistle. The leaves and young stems of the coltsfoot are said to have been cooked and eaten by the Indians. Mr. Chestnut also records another curious use for this plant. Among those Indians who were kept by their enemies from having access to the sea, the stems and leaves were carefully dried and burned, and the ashes so obtained made an acceptable salt substitute.

CLASPING-LEAVED ARNICA　　　　　*Arnica amplexicaulis*

Our illustration is of a leaf and seed, yet it might easily pass for a flowering plant, so similar in form are the blossoms, consisting solely of numerous fine disk-flowers, to the pappus of the ripening fruit which follows them.

CLASPING-LEAVED ARNICA
Arnica amplexicaulis Nutt.

Yellow. Stems, tufted; six to eighteen inches tall. Leaves, glabrous; rather gummy; opposite; clasping; ovate; acute; toothed. Inflorescence, terminal and axillary. Flowers, long-pediceled; yellow. Pappus, grayish-brown. Habitat, stream borders and moist rocks. Blooming period, June to August.

This bright-flowered plant is a common sight along streams and in the mountains at low altitudes. It loves moisture, and its tufted stems often grow where they are continually wet by the spray blown from waterfalls. The gummy-coated, shiny leaves are margined with small, abrupt teeth, and have a drug-like smell.

Arnica macounii Greene. A similar form, but with narrower or lanceolate leaves.

BROAD-LEAVED ARNICA
Arnica latifolia Bong.

Yellow. Stems, erect; eighteen to thirty inches tall. Leaves, glabrous; opposite; the basal ones cordate, dentate, petioled; cauline, one or two pairs; ovate; sessile. Heads, long-peduncled. Rays, one-third to two-thirds of an inch long. Habitat, moist mountains and stream banks.

The flowers of the broad-leaved arnica are about two inches across. As its specific name indicates, the leaves are rather broad.

Heart-Leaved Arnica. *Arnica cordifolia* Hook. This species has long-petioled, cordate, rather hairy leaves. The heads are borne on slender pedicels, usually one terminal, and two axillary blooms at the summit of each plant. It prefers dry soil.

The European type of the genus *Arnica* supplies a popular homely remedy of the same name, much used in the treatment of cuts and bruises.

PEARLY EVERLASTING   *Anaphalis margaritacea occidentalis*

RAGWORT
Senecio fastigiatus Nutt.

Yellow. Stems, erect; slender; sparingly leafy above; two to five feet tall. Leaves, lanceolate to spatulate; entire; the basal ones petioled; cauline sessile. Inflorescence, a cyme. Ray-flowers, yellow. Habitat, dry prairies. Blooming period, June-July.

The genus *Senecio* contains a great number of species, about sixteen of which grow in the humid west, though some of them are quite rare. The common groundsel, an introduced, troublesome weed in our gardens, is *Senecio vulgaris.* The name *Senecio* is derived from the same source as is the word, senile, and refers to the white pappus or down of the seed heads, which is supposed to resemble the snowy hair of an aged man. The present species is rather common in dry prairies.

Senecio triangularis Hook. One to three feet tall. Stem simple. Has smooth, triangular leaves, acute and evenly dentate, clothing the plant to the summit. Flowers numerous; bright yellow. It grows in wet places in the mountains.

PEARLY EVERLASTING
Anaphalis margaritacea occidentalis Greene

White. Stems, erect; leafy; tufted. Leaves, alternate; sessile; lanceolate; entire; the margins revolute; green above; white-woolly beneath. Heads, small; in terminal corymbs. Involucre, campanulate; sub-globose. Tegules, scarious, pearly-white. Habitat, dry fields and roadsides. Blooming period, June-July.

The pretty little blossoms of the pearly everlasting appear in June. They grow in clustered corymbs at the summit of slender, leafy stems. Although the flowers are small, the plants usually grow in close tufted formation, so that they make a considerable showing, and are well known wherever found. Each individual blossom is a delicate study in soft, pearly shades. The centre is yellow when in bloom, becoming brown with age, and the regular arrangement of the imbricated, parchment-like scales, which, shingle-like, surround each tiny bloom, is very interesting. The whole effect of the arrangement is like that of a half-opened white water-lily. The flowers if picked when mature do not wilt, but dry up and retain their attractive shape indefinitely.

EDIBLE THISTLE   *Cirsium edule*

AMERICAN THISTLE
Cirsium americanum (Gray) Robinson

White or buff. Stems, erect; branching; two to six feet tall. Leaves, lanceolate; pinnate or merely coarsely dentate; green above; white-woolly beneath; armed with weak prickles. Flower-heads, large; at the ends of long slender branches. Tegules, with scarious, dilated tips; cut and slashed. Disk-flowers, white or buff. Habitat, open fields and prairies. Blooming period, June-July.

The scale-like bracts, or tegules, that surround the flower heads of this species of thistle, are its distinguishing mark. Instead of being pointed and armed with rigid spines like other thistles, they are parchment-like, broad, and dilated, and handsomely cut and slashed at their margins. The flowers are buff or whitish, borne singly on long naked pedicels, and the leaves are deeply cut and lobed.

EDIBLE THISTLE
Cirsium edule Nutt.

Purple. Root, a somewhat fleshy tap-root. Stem, erect; little branched; leafy; three to ten feet tall. Leaves, lanceolate; pinnately cut or lobed; pubescent or woolly; armed with weak prickles. Heads, clustered among the upper leaves. Involucre, woolly. Tegules, tapering into weak spiny points. Flowers, light purple. Habitat, moist rich soils in open woods. Blooming period, spring and early summer.

"The root of the thistle, called by the natives *Shan-ne-tah-que*, is from nine to fifteen inches in length, the rind somewhat rough and of a brown color; its consistance when first taken from the earth is white and nearly as crisp as a carrot; when prepared for use by the same process before described for the *pashshequo quamash*, it becomes black, and is more sugary than any fruit or root that I have met with in use among the natives. The sweet is precisely that of sugar." So does Meriweather Lewis describe the edible thistle, of which he ate during the winter spent in Oregon. I have personally tried these roots, though never when cooked by the Indian method. Boiled, they are a fair vegetable, tender and edible, but not especially appetizing, slightly resembling salsify.

This is our tallest thistle. It will be found growing in rich, moist streamside thickets, sometimes reaching a height of ten feet or more.

Somehow I can not admire this plant as I do its openly antagonistic relative, the bull-thistle. Its leaves are too ragged and indeterminate in the front that they present to the world—not armed and frankly vicious as a thistle should be, but softened down and indecisive. They remind me of a would-be bad man without the proper determination for the role to which he aspires—a "tin-horn sport," as it were—or of a weak-spined Christian with no retribution in his Gospel.

GLOSSARY

GLOSSARY

Acaulescent: Stemless.

Acuminate: Taper-pointed.

Adherent: Growing, or sticking together.

Akene: A one seeded fruit, as those of the buttercup or avens.

Anther: The part of the stamen that bears the pollen.

Appendaged: Bearing an appendage, or super-added part.

Attenuate: Long and slender pointed.

Auriculated: Bearing ear-like appendages.

Awn: A bristle-like appendage.

Axil: The angle at the juncture of leaf and stem.

Axillary: Pertaining to the axil.

Basifixed: Attached at the base.

Beaked: Culminating in a narrow tip.

Bilabiate: Two-lipped.

Bloom: A light colored, powdery coating on leaf or fruit.

Bract: A small leaf or scale; the leaflets accompanying an inflorescence.

Bulb: A thickened, scaly stem-base, as that of the lily.

Bulblet: A small bulb, often borne above ground, or on the stem.

Caespitose: Growing in tufts or mats.

Callus: A hard protuberance.

Campanulate: Bell-shaped.

Capitate: Head-like.

Capsule: A dry seed vessel; a pod.

Carpel: A simple pistil, or one division of a compound pistil.

Caudex: The persistent base of a plant having an annual stem.

Cauline: Pertaining to the stem.

Chlorophyll: The green coloring matter of leaves.

Circumscissile: Dividing by a horizontal line.

Claw: The abruptly narrowed stalk-like base of some petals.

Column: The organ that holds the united stamens and pistils in the blossoms of orchids.

Congested: Crowded.

Connate: United; growing together.

Conniving: Growing close together.

Constricted: Contracted; bound together.

Convoluted: Rolled together lengthwise.

Cordate: Heart-shaped.

Coriaceous: Leathery.

Corm: A solid bulb.

Corolla: The inner floral envelope; the part within the calyx.

Corymb: A flat or convex flower cluster in which the marginal flowers first open.

Crenate: Scalloped, or with rounded teeth.

Crenately: In a crenate, or scalloped form.

Cuneate: Wedge-shaped.

Cyme: A flat flower cluster like a corymb, but in which the central flowers first open.

Cymose: Pertaining to, or shaped like a cyme.

Deciduous: Soon falling, or falling at the close of the season, as the calyx of the California poppy, or the leaves of the ash.

Declined: Turned downward or to one side.

Decompound: Several times compound.

Decumbent: Trailing over, or lying upon the ground.

Decurrent: Prolonged on the stem.

Dentate: Toothed.

Diadelphous: United into two groups or brotherhoods.

Didymous: Twins.

Didynamous: Stamens in two pairs of unequal length.

Diffuse: Branched and spreading.

Dioecious: Stamens and pistils borne on different plants.

Disk-flower: The small central flowers of a composite head.

Dissected: Finely cut or divided into many narrow segments.

Divergent: Spreading apart; growing in opposite directions.

Diverging: Growing apart, or in opposite ways.

Divaricate: Widely diverging.

Dorsally: On the back part.

Drupe: A stone fruit, as the cherry.

Entire: Not at all toothed or divided.

Exfoliating: Peeling; separating and coming off in scales.

Exserted: Protruding.

Fascicle: A cluster.

Fascicled: Growing in a cluster.

Fertile: Productive; fruitful; as a fruitful plant, or a stamen that bears pollen.

Fibrous: Formed of fibres.

Filament: The lower part, or stalk of a stamen.

Filiform: Long and slender.

Flaccid: Flabby; lax; drooping.

Foliaceous: Leaf-like.

Follicle: A simple pod.

Fusiform: Spindle-shaped, as the root of the radish.

Galea: The helmet-shaped upper lip of the corolla of some flowers.

Gibbous: Swelling out or protuberant.

Glabrate: Nearly glabrous; becoming glabrous:

Glabrous: Smooth; without hairs.

Gland: An organ that secretes oil or nectar, etc. A gland-like growth.

Glandular: Bearing glands.

Globose: Globe-shaped.

Head: A dense, compact cluster of sessile flowers.

Herbaceous: Not woody; herb-like.

Hirsute: Clothed with stiff hair.

Hispid: Bristly.

Hooded: Curved or arching in the form of a hood.

Imbricated: Overlapping in scale-like manner.

Included: Not projecting; the opposite of exserted.

Inflated: Swelled out; bladdery.

Inflorescence: A flower cluster; the manner of flowering.

Internode: The parts between the nodes or joints of a stem.

Interrupted: Broken; not continuous.

Involucel: A small involucre; the involucre of a part of a floral cluster, as that attending the umbellets of a compound umbel.

Involucrate: Having an involucre.

Involucre: The bracts enclosing or attending a floral cluster.

Keeled: Folded into a keel or sharp longitudinal ridge.

Laciniate: Deeply and narrowly slashed and cut.

Laciniately: In a laciniate manner.

Lanceolate: Lance-shaped.

Lateral: Pertaining to the sides.

Laterally: In a lateral form or manner.

Limb: The blade of a leaf or petal.

Linear: Very narrow and with parallel margins.

Lip: One of the principal divisions of an irregular corolla or calyx.

Lyrate: Lyre-shaped.

Membranaceous: Thin and membrane-like.

Membranous: Same as preceding.

Monadelphous: In one group or brotherhood.

Monoecious: Flowers having pistils or stamens only.

Mucronate: Tipped with a sharp, abrupt point.

Node: The joints of a stem.

Obconic: Conical, but with the broadest part above.

Obcordate: Heart-shaped, but with the broad end at the apex.

Oblanceolate: Lanceolate, but tapering towards the base.

Obovate: Ovate, with the broad end uppermost.

Obsolete: Wanting; not in evidence.

Odd-pinnate: Pinnate, with an odd, or terminal leaflet.

Orbicular: Circular in outline.

Ovary: The part of a flower that bears seed; the lower part, or base of a pistil.

Ovate: Egg-shaped.

Palmate: Divided and spreading, like the hand with spreading fingers.

Panicle: A flower cluster like a raceme, but branched or compound.

Paniculate: In the form of a panicle.

Papilionaceous: Butterfly-shaped; applied to flowers like the pea.

Papillose: Covered with nipple-like protuberances.

Pappus: The hair-like calyx of certain flowers becoming noticeable in seed, as the head of a dandelion.

Parasitic: Growing on other plants.

Pedicel: The stalk of a single flower in a cluster.

Peltate: Shield-shaped; a leaf having the petiole attached near the centre, not at the margin.

Perfect: A flower bearing both stamens and pistils.

Perfoliate: Opposite leaves joined at the base, through which the stem appears to pass.

Perianth: The entire floral envelope; used when the petals and sepals are joined, or are difficult to distinguish.

Persistent: Remaining permanently, or, past its time.

Petal: A leaf or division of the corolla.

Petiole: The stem or stalk of a leaf.

Petioled: Having a petiole.

Pinnate: Like a feather; referring to the opposite leaflets of such plants as the pea, etc., which are evenly distributed along a common petiole.

Pistil: The seed-bearing organ of a flower, composed of ovary, style and stigma.

Plaited: Folded.

Plumose: Feathery; having hairs along the sides like a plume.

Polygamous: Having perfect and imperfect flowers on the same plant, or on different plants.

Polygamo-dioecious: Having perfect and staminate flowers on some plants, and perfect and pistilate flowers on others.

Pome: A fruit formed like an apple or pear.

Prismatic: Angled; prism-like.

Pubescent: Hairy or downy.

Punctate: Dotted.

Raceme: A flower cluster composed of one-flowered pedicels arranged on the sides of a common peduncle.

Radical: A root; of, or pertaining to the root.

Rhizome: A rootstock.

Rootstock: A root-like underground stem.

Saccate: Sac-shaped; inflated or purse-like.

Sagittate: Arrow-shaped.

Scape: A peduncle rising from the ground.

Scarious: Thin and dry; parchment-like.

Scorpioid: Curved at the summit like the tail of a scorpion.

Sepal: A division of the calyx.

Serrate: Saw-like; having regular teeth like a saw.

Serrulate: Finely saw-toothed.

Sessile: Stemless.

Sheathing: Wrapped about, like a sheath.

Sinuate: Wavy-margined.

Sinus: The angle between two projecting parts.

Spadix: A fleshy flower spike.

Spathe: A bract or leafy part enwrapping an inflorescence.

Spatulate: Shaped like a spatula.

Spike: An inflorescence like a raceme, but bearing crowded, sessile flowers.

Spur: A projection or horn-like appendage.

Spurred: Bearing a spur.

Stamen: The pollen-bearing organ of a flower.

Staminiodium: A sterile stamen; an organ resembling a stamen.

Stellate: Star-like; spreading like the rays of a star.

Sterile: Imperfect; incapable of bearing fruit, or, if applied to a stamen, of bearing pollen.

Stigma: The upper part of a pistil; the part that receives the pollen.

Stipules: Appendages, usually leaf-like, at the base of certain leaves.

Stoloniferous: Bearing stolons or runners; multiplying by means of stolons, as the strawberry.

Strap-shaped: Flat and narrow.

Strict: Straight and narrow.

Style: The part of the pistil that supports the stigma.

Stylopodium; An extension at the base of the style, found in the fruit of many umbelliferous plants.

Subulate: Awl-shaped.

Tap-root: A stout, tapering central root.

Tegules: The bracts, resembling sepals, surrounding the heads of composite flowers.

Tendril: A curling, thread-like organ by which some vines climb.

Terete: Long and round.

Terminal: Borne at the summit or end.

Ternate: In threes.

Ternately-compound: Several times compound, the divisions all in threes.

Thyrsus: A compact, pyradimal cluster.

Tomentose: Covered with woolly matted hairs.

Trifoliate: Three-leaved.

Tri-saccate: Three saccate.

Truncate: Cut off short at the summit.

Tuber: A thickened part of a root-stock, as the potato.

Tuberous: Bearing, or having tubers.

Umbel: An inflorescence shaped like an umbrella.

Umbellate: Having, or bearing umbels.

Umbellet: A partial umbel; the lesser divisions of a compound umbel.

Undulate: Wavy-margined.

Versatile: Attached at the center and swinging free.

Viscid: Coated with a sticky or glutinous substance.

Whorl: Arranged in a circle.

Whorled: In a whorl-like form.

INDEX TO LATIN NAMES

(Page numbers of cuts in black figures)

INDEX TO ENGLISH NAMES

(Page numbers of cuts in black figures)

THE AUTHOR

LESLIE LOREN HASKIN was born at La Valle, Wisconsin, on March 9, 1882. His father, Harley T. Haskin, was of Dutch-English descent, and a native of New York; his mother, Emily Rowley, of New England ancestry, was a native of Illinois. Both parents removed to Wisconsin at an early age.

Leslie Haskin was educated in the schools of Wisconsin, and in the fields and hills of the Mississippi Valley and the Pacific Coast, which education is still in active progress. He removed to Oregon in 1907, where he has since resided, being occupied in this state, first, as a farmer. His present home is at Brownsville, Oregon.

In 1919 he took up photography as a profession, working under Mr. J. G. Crawford of Albany, Oregon, pioneer photographer, geologist, and anthropologist. At the close of the same year he was married to Lilian G. Hoy of that place, also a professional photographer of many years' experience.

At an early age Mr. Haskin became interested in botany, his mother being his first teacher. As an amateur photographer he soon began collecting wild flower photographs, first for pleasure only, but later with a more serious purpose. After taking up photography as a profession he continued this work, being actively assisted by his wife. Together they have accumulated a noteworthy collection of botanical negatives, numbering over fifteen hundred separate studies. Throughout these years Mr. Haskin has been reading, observing, and making original investigations and field notes looking towards the publication of this work. His notes on Indian plant lore, as well as on ornithology and American bird folk-lore and mythology, of which he is also a student, number many hundreds of pages. He has also contributed special articles on botany, ornithology and other nature topics, to various publications.